A YEAR OF
ADVENTURES

A GUIDE TO WHAT, WHERE AND WHEN TO DO IT

lonely planet

MELBOURNE | LONDON | OAKLAND

↗ CONTENTS:

IT'S TIME FOR SOME
ADVENTURE!

Lonely Planet's *A Year of Adventures* will inspire you to put a sense of adventure in your next journey. Over 100 exciting journeys are outlined, and we've presented them in a way that guarantees the best experience. Choosing the right time of the year can often turn a great trip into an incredible one. Rainy seasons, peak tourist times, migration patterns ... they're all factors when planning your trip. We've organised the journeys by week and month, so you'll get the best shot of catching a glimpse of tigers in India or ski touring the Haute Route.

The diversity of activities caters to all passions and ability levels. Whether it's a challenging, long-distance bike trek, or the peaceful pursuit of whale watching in Mexico, you'll find inspiration for all times of the year, all around the world. On the last page of each week you'll also find a description of some events that occur around that time of year; links are provided for more information.

Of course, 12 four-week months only adds up to 48 weeks. What happened to the missing weeks? Was it an astronomer playing tricks? Is it a grand conspiracy from your employer, or a subversive government tactic? Whatever the case we're giving the weeks back to you. Every three months, we've added a special section – the 7s we call them – the seven continents, the seven summits, the seven natural wonders, the seven heavenly objects.

Hearing the word 'adventure' makes most of us think of the more extreme challenges; climbing mountains, sailing around the globe, being lost on a deserted island. But when we use the word ourselves, it can refer to a holiday in an exotic place (where lying on a beach reflects the necessary intensity level), a weekend camping trip, a day-walk on a coastal track, and sometimes even a trip to a part of our own city that we've not visited before. Despite this variety, there's a common theme – an adventure takes us away from the everyday. So take some time and do something different – they're the experiences you'll never forget.

January

↙ Go to QUEENSTOWN,
NEW ZEALAND

week

↙ .01

www.yearofadventures.com/january

WHY NOW? GET STARTED ON AN ADVENTURE BEFORE THE SUN'S EVEN RISEN ON THE REST OF THE WORLD

One of New Zealand's proud claims is that it's among the first lands on earth to see the sun rise on the New Year. Get an early adventuring start, then, by beginning the year in the South Island town of Queenstown, where the adrenaline flows as fast as the water in its churning rivers. This self-appointed 'adventure capital of the world' has one of the finest settings ever handed a town, hugging the shores of Lake Wakatipu and looking across to the aptly named Remarkables mountain range. Yet it was neither water nor peaks that spawned Queenstown's reputation for thrills; it was an elastic band.

In 1988 the world's first commercial bungy jump began operating from the Kawarau Suspension Bridge, 23km from Queenstown. For those who fancied it – and there were queues of them – this was the opportunity to plunge 43m towards the Kawarau River without worrying about a landing.

Catch your breath at the top of the Remarkables and then have it taken away again by the view over Lake Wakatipu.

↗ DO: **BOBSLED AT LAKE PLACID**

COUNTRY USA **TYPE OF ACTIVITY** Bobsledding **FITNESS/EXPERTISE LEVEL** Not required. **WHY NOW?** The season usually opens in late December; be certain of a run by visiting in January. **DESCRIPTION** Become a momentary Olympian as you step aboard a bobsled on Mt Van Hoevenberg at Lake Placid, the venue for the 1932 and 1980 Olympic Winter Games, host to the 2009 World Bobsled Championships, and the United States' only dedicated bobsled track. Pressed between a professional driver and brakeman, you'll spend little more than 30 seconds covering the 800m public run, whooshing through the self-explanatory Zig Zag turns and up the finishing curve at such speed you'll think you're on the launch pad at Cape Canaveral rather than in the Adirondacks. If you prefer to be your own pilot, take a seat on the Luge Rocket and scurry through its 16 bends. www.orda.org

When you're travelling at 130km/h with 5 Gs pressing in on you, thank the Swiss for inventing bobsledding.

Years on, bungy remains Queenstown's signature activity but there are more highs in this town than there are peaks in the Southern Alps. For bungy basics, the Kawarau Suspension Bridge continues its stock in trade, but if 43m sounds pedestrian try a jump from the Nevis Highwire, a cable car suspended 134m above the Nevis River, or combine sightseeing with bungy jumping by leaping from the Ledge, 400m above Queenstown.

Even after you've completed the inevitable bungy jump, your adventuring dance card for the week remains full. If you still fancy aeronautics, you can paraglide, skydive, hang glide or parafly on the lake. You can jetboat or raft the foaming Shotover or Kawarau Rivers, or get even more intimate with the

river by clinging to a glorified boogie board as you discover white-water sledging. Ride the 800m-long luge, go canyoning, mountain biking, heli-skiing or heli-biking, or skip town to revel in the awesome beauty of nearby Fiordland and Mt Aspiring National Parks. Here, you'll find some of the world's great walking tracks – the Milford, Routeburn, Kepler, Hollyford and Dusky Tracks – and fiords and lakes that scream to be paddled.

Draw up your New Year's resolutions at www .queenstownadventure.com.

You too can share a magic moment with one of the last 650 mountain gorillas in the world.

↗ DO: GORILLA TRACKING AT BWINDI

COUNTRY Uganda **TYPE OF ACTIVITY** Wildlife watching

FITNESS/EXPERTISE LEVEL Good fitness a benefit.

WHY NOW? It's the middle of the dry season in Uganda's rainforested southwest.

DESCRIPTION It's estimated that there are only about 650 mountain gorillas remaining in the world, and half of these live in Uganda's Bwindi Impenetrable National Park. Seeing them is one of Africa's magic moments.

There are three groups of gorillas habituated to the presence of humans in the so-called Impenetrable Forest, and they move daily. They may be only 15 minutes' walk from the park entrance, or they may be hours of hard walking away, up hillsides and along slippery paths (wear gloves for grasping branches and nettles).

Only 16 tracking permits are issued per day, with each permitted group limited to six people. Most of the permits are snapped up by the big safari companies, so plan ahead. If you're determined to snaffle your own permit, all bookings must be made through the office of the Uganda Wildlife Authority in Kampala (www.uwa.or.ug) – the authority recommends booking two years in advance! Children under 15 years of age are not permitted, and anyone with a cold or other illness is likewise excluded, because such sicknesses could endanger these rare creatures' lives.

Once you finally join a trekking group, the chances of finding the gorillas are excellent, though the time you actually spend with the gorillas is limited to exactly one hour.

An adult male mountain gorilla – a silverback – can grow to more than 160kg, but despite his size he's usually placid and gentle unless he feels threatened. His reaction to danger – and sometimes strangers – is to scream and charge at the intruder. It's important not to lose your nerve. Stay still and look away from him. He may come close but there's little chance he'll actually hurt you.

↗ DO: CYCLE CUBA

COUNTRY Cuba **TYPE OF ACTIVITY** Cycle touring
FITNESS/EXPERTISE LEVEL Moderate fitness required.
WHY NOW? It's Cuba's coolest, driest time of the year.
DESCRIPTION See the land behind the politics as you pedal across the Caribbean's largest island. Fly into the capital, Havana, and stretch out your legs with a ride along the waterfront Malecón (complete with bike lane), where you'll have waves on one side and colonial grandeur on the other. Continue east out of Havana to find the tropical treats of the Varadero beaches. Cross to the island's eastern tip to pit yourself against the 300km-long Sierra Maestra, Cuba's highest range, or to attempt the country's most notorious climb, ascending 1200m over 12km to the enormous La Gran Piedra rock. There's always the descent to look forward to.

↗ DO: PARIS DAKAR RALLY

COUNTRY Varies **TYPE OF ACTIVITY** Motoring rally
FITNESS/EXPERTISE LEVEL Off-road driving and navigation skills required.
WHY NOW? The rally begins on New Year's Day.
DESCRIPTION In 1977 Frenchman Thierry Sabine became lost in the Sahara Desert, where one of his hallucinations was that this would be a grand place for a motoring rally. Two years later, the illusion became reality with the first running of the Paris Dakar Rally. Rarely starting in Paris these days, the Dakar is less a rally than an endurance event, with vehicles and motorcycles trying to survive the brutal conditions of the Sahara and West Africa, covering around 10,000km in 20 days. Although a professional race, around 80% of entrants are amateur, but get in early as places can fill up to six months ahead. Of the 400-plus competitors each year, less than half usually finish. www.dakar.com

↗ DO: CLIMB ADAM'S PEAK

COUNTRY Sri Lanka **TYPE OF ACTIVITY** Hiking
FITNESS/EXPERTISE LEVEL Moderate fitness required.
WHY NOW? Blend into the pilgrims.
DESCRIPTION Adam's Peak (2243m) has fired imaginations for centuries. Sri Lanka's holiest peak has a huge 'footprint' on its summit, which is variously claimed to be the place where Adam first set foot on earth, a sacred footprint left by Buddha as he ascended to paradise, or the indent of St Thomas or Shiva. Little wonder it's become a haunt for pilgrims. The pilgrimage season begins in December and runs until May, during which time a steady stream of people make the climb up the countless steps from the small settlement of Dalhousie. The route is illuminated in season by a string of lights, making it possible to come for the peak's other great attraction, the dawn view across the hill country to the east and the land sloping away to the ocean to the west. The Sri Lankan capital, Colombo, 65km away, is easily visible on a clear day.

Pass up the yank tank and encounter Cuba with all five senses on two wheels.

It's the dustiest way to see West Africa, but those who finish the Paris Dakar Rally join the elite of extreme sports.

Ice Marathon
www.adventure-network.com/display
.asp?navid=1&id=59
Run a marathon, half-marathon or 100km race in Antarctica at 80° south

Siberian Ice Half-Marathon
www.sim.omsknet.ru
Drag your feet through 21km of Siberian snow.

Lorne Pier to Pub
www.lornesurfclub.com.au
A 1.2km open-water swim off Great Ocean Road, Victoria, Australia.

Turquoise Lake 20 Mile Snowshoe Run
www.salidarec.com/ccrc
Plough through 32km of powder in snowshoes around Colorado's Turquoise Lake.

week .01

www.yearofadventures.com/january

Below the water the view is just as spectacular – there's something on the Andaman Coast for every adventuring appetite.

January

↙ GO: **ANDAMAN COAST, THAILAND**

week

↙ .02

www.yearofadventures.com/january

WHY NOW? **VISIT THE ANDAMAN COAST NOW WHEN YOU'LL FIND AN ENTICING MIX OF GOOD WEATHER AND CLEAR WATER**

Soaring peaks of jagged limestone provide a heady backdrop to the emerald-green waters and white-sand beaches of Thailand's Andaman Coast. The region is a feast for the eyes, serving overflowing portions of some of Southeast Asia's most striking scenery, though it's unlikely that you'll be content to just look at it.

Pinched between Malaysia and Myanmar (Burma), Andaman Coast is not long but there's something for every adventuring appetite. For divers, the coast is a watery wonderland, with around 210 hard corals and 108 reef fish recorded here.

Glam, glitzy Phuket is indisputably the hub of diving in Thailand and is one of the world's top dive destinations. It's also a good place to arrange live-aboard boats to the Surin and Similan Islands to the north. The nine Similan Islands are world-renowned, with their huge and smooth granite

Going up, or going down?

↗ DO: BALLOON AT CHÂTEAU D'OEX

COUNTRY Switzerland **TYPE OF ACTIVITY** Ballooning **FITNESS/EXPERTISE LEVEL** Not required. **WHY NOW?** To coincide with International Hot Air Balloon Week. **DESCRIPTION** If hot-air ballooning has a heartland, it's Château d'Oex. Not only did Switzerland's Bertrand Piccard and his British team-mate Brian Jones start the first nonstop around-the-world balloon flight from here in 1999, the town also hosts the annual International Hot Air Balloon Week, one of ballooning's marquee events. In addition, Château d'Oex has daily flights – weather permitting – that will have you skimming across the top of the Alps. Balloons take off from the town, south of Bern, and rise to views that can include the Alps' highest mountain, Mont Blanc; its most shapely peak, the Matterhorn; the Eiger and Lake Geneva. Flights operate year-round, but come now and you'll be peering down on to peaks pasted with snow. www.chateau-doex.ch

With close to 100 balloons in the air, who needs an airbag?

formations plunging into the Andaman Sea and forming seamounts, rock reefs and dive-throughs. At the Surin Islands, you'll find granite islands and coral reefs, and whale sharks and manta rays with which to share the water.

What's good below the water is equally delightful on top. With a sea kayak you have the opportunity to go where other vessels cannot, namely into the semi-submerged caves (hong), that characterise kayaking on the Andaman coast. A good place to explore hong is in Ao Phang-Nga Marine National Park.

For landlubbers, central Krabi is synonymous with rock climbing. Blessed with some amazing scenic karst formations along its coast and even

in the middle of Krabi River, there are endless climbing opportunities, though the industry and most climbers' attentions are on the serrated peninsula of Railay, west of Krabi city. The cliff-backed isthmus is one of the world's leading climbing destinations, providing high-quality limestone with steep, pocketed walls, overhangs and the occasional hanging stalactite. About 700 sport routes have been bolted. Novices usually begin with Muay Thai, a 50m wall with around 20 climbs.

o1 o2
o3 o4

Find your own *Lost World* dreamscape high on the Venezuelan mesas.

↗ DO: TREK TO RORAIMA

COUNTRY Venezuela **TYPE OF ACTIVITY** Trekking

FITNESS/EXPERTISE LEVEL Moderate fitness required.

WHY NOW? Be thankful it's the dry season (December to March); at other times of the year it really rains.

DESCRIPTION Sir Arthur Conan Doyle's *Lost World* was a place frozen in time, a plateau so removed from the world that dinosaurs continued to roam atop it. The inspiration for Sir Arthur's tale were the sandstone mesas *(tepuis)*, of the South American jungles, and particularly the tales of exploration then emanating from the *tepui* Roraima.

Stretching 34 sq km across the borders of Venezuela, Guyana and Brazil, Roraima is the highest of the *tepuis* – its plateau is at about 2700m and its tallest peak at 2810m – but it is also the easiest to ascend. A trek to this massive table mountain provides some of the most memorable experiences a trip to Venezuela can offer. The hike up the steep walls is fascinating, and the top of the plateau is nothing short of otherworldly.

It will take a minimum of five days to do the round trip, and you'll need camping equipment and food. Be prepared for a strenuous trek and some discomfort, including plenty of rain, cold and *jejenes* (a biting gnat).

Gather up guides and porters in the village of Paraitepui and walk for two days to the plateau, where the scenery is a dreamscape evocative of a science-fiction movie: impressive blackened rocks in myriad shapes, gorges, creeks and pink beaches. Few living organisms have adapted to the inhospitable conditions of the barren, rocky plateau. Those that have include curious endemic species such as a little, black frog that crawls instead of jumps, and the *heliamphora*, a carnivorous plant that traps unwary insects in beautiful, bucket-shaped, red flowers filled with rainwater. Plan on staying at least two days on the summit to allow time for exploration.

o1 o2
o3 o4

↗ DO: **KAYAK BASS STRAIT**

COUNTRY Australia **TYPE OF ACTIVITY** Kayaking
FITNESS/EXPERTISE LEVEL High degree of expertise required.
WHY NOW? Paddle in summer in hope of the smoothest crossing.
DESCRIPTION Around 15,000 years ago, Australia's island state of
Tasmania was joined to the mainland by a land bridge across the eastern
end of what is now stormy, shipwreck-sprinkled Bass Strait. Today, the
remains of that bridge form a chain of islands that serve as stepping
stones for a small number of sea kayakers willing to brave the Strait's
notorious currents and swells. Most kayakers leave from Wilsons
Promontory National Park, the southernmost point of the Australian
mainland, and paddle through the Hogan Group to two of the country's
most striking islands: Deal and Flinders. After a final tussle with the tidal
races of Banks Strait, the 300km journey ends in Tasmania's Musselroe
Bay. A trip for the experienced paddler only.

↗ DO: **WHITE-WATER SLEDGE IN ROTORUA**

COUNTRY New Zealand **TYPE OF ACTIVITY** River surfing
FITNESS/EXPERTISE LEVEL Moderate fitness required.
WHY NOW? If you're going to expose yourself to glacial-melt rivers, do it
when New Zealand is at its warmest.
DESCRIPTION Essentially rafting for one, white-water sledging is a
personal fight-or-flow with the rapids of a river, aided only by flippers and
the sledge you push ahead of you. One moment you might have proudly
backed your sledge into a standing wave, surfing it like a master; the next,
you'll be yanked underwater into a damp black hole, wondering where –
and if – you'll get your next breath. The activity isn't unique to Rotorua –
Wanaka and Queenstown also offering sledging trips – but the grade-five
rapids of the Kaituna River do contain white-water sledging's ultimate
moment, plunging over the 7m-high Tutea Falls. Hold on tight.
www.kaitiaki.co.nz

↗ DO: **SKI THE ALBORZ MOUNTAINS**

COUNTRY Iran **TYPE OF ACTIVITY** Skiing
FITNESS/EXPERTISE LEVEL Beginners to powder hounds.
WHY NOW? For mid-winter's best skiing conditions.
DESCRIPTION Iran has several ski resorts in the Alborz Mountains, a range
higher than the European Alps, including four within day-trip distance of
the capital, Tehran. Dizin is the largest of Iran's ski fields, and thanks to its
altitude – its highest run begins at around 3500m, making it one of the
world's highest ski fields – it gets about a six-month season (and converts
to a grass-skiing venue in summer). Another ski field worth a look is
Shemshak, nearer to Tehran and offering the chance for night skiing on
floodlit slopes. Expect easy to moderate runs at Dizin, while Shemshak
is noted for its moguls and more difficult runs. Just be aware that if you
come to ski in the Alborz it's purely about the snow, not the parties.

Say goodbye to the mainland
and hello to a rough ride on
Bass Strait.

White-water sledging? It's kind of
like this, but by yourself and without
a raft ... are you crazy?!

Alpine Classic
www.audax.org.au
Cycle 200km between three of the
highest points in the Australian state of
Victoria, ascending more than 3000m.

Dolomitenlauf
www.dolomitensport-lienz.com
A 60km ski marathon through the
Austrian Dolomites.

Desafio de los Volcanoes
www.desafiovolcanes.com
Seven-day multisport race through the
Andes' Route of the Volcanoes.

Fulda Challenge
www.fulda-challenge.com
Deep-winter, 2500km Arctic Circle
race involving such means as skidoo,
bike, dog-sledding and ice climbing.

week
.02

A sun-parched version of Middle Earth, Pays Dogon is defined by the 150km-long Bandiagara Escarpment.

January

week

↙ .03

www.yearofadventures.com/january

↙ GO: PAYS DOGON, MALI

WHY NOW? NOW IS THE COOLEST TIME OF THE YEAR, THOUGH TEMPERATURES MAY STILL BE ABOVE 30°C

Mali's Dogon Country – the land of the Dogon people – resembles Hobbiton, with villages like scattered rocks, granaries with witch-hat straw roofs, shocked-looking baobab trees and perfect, small fields spread across unlikely, inhospitable terrain. What sets it apart from Middle Earth, and into an adventuring world of its own, is the 150km-long, copper-red, cracked and wrinkled Bandiagara Escarpment that towers through the scene.

The best way to see the Pays Dogon is to trek along this escarpment for anything between two days and three weeks, walking from village to village along ancient tracks, sometimes above the escarpment, sometimes below it, and sometimes zigzagging along it.

Food and accommodation are available in the villages, and guides can be hired in the gateway towns of Bandiagara, Bankass or Sanga. While

⬈ DO: ICE CLIMB VALDEZ

COUNTRY USA **TYPE OF ACTIVITY** Ice climbing **FITNESS/EXPERTISE LEVEL** High level of expertise required. **WHY NOW?** Get the best of the winter ice. **DESCRIPTION** Alaska's Prince William Sound and the town of Valdez might be remembered most for the *Exxon Valdez* oil spill, but ask anyone with an ice-axe and this is climbing central. Drive about 20km out of town to the Keystone Canyon, where you'll find arguably the best ice climbing in the United States. The waterfalls through this 5km-long canyon freeze into glorious multipitch routes such as Bridalveil Falls and, just a few metres away, Greensteps, which is ascended in four 60m pitches. Dozens of climbs, including Bridalveil Falls, begin right beside the main road, so you won't have to hump all your equipment to climbs. Stick around a while for Valdez's annual Ice Climbing Festival in early March. www.valdezalaska.org

Frozen waterfalls? Check. Easy access? Check. Is this the best ice climbing in the USA?

guides aren't essential, they will help you get the most out of the Pays Dogon. They'll show you the route, help with translation, find accommodation and food, stop you stumbling over sacred sites, and take you to the abandoned cliff dwellings that pockmark the 600m-high cliff face. Built as homes by the Tellem people, who were forced away by the Dogon, these caves are now used for Dogon burials.

The trekking options along the escarpment are numerous. The central area between Dourou and Banani is the most spectacular, but also receives the most visitors. The area north of Banani sees far fewer visitors, but the landscape is less striking. The southern section from Dorou to Djiguibombo is also very beautiful, and again popular. The far south of

the Dogon, between Kani-Kombolé and Nombori, is more tranquil but less dramatic.

Distances between villages are short, allowing you time to appreciate the people and the landscape, while escaping the midday heat.

The unusual Dogon calendar has five days per week (although villages on the plateau tend to keep a seven-day week), with once-weekly markets. These are lively and colourful, and an opportunity for beer drinking. Try to catch one during your trek.

o1 o2
o3 o4

Floating in a world of jelly ... Your *Finding Nemo* moment will be painless, as the sting of these harmless jellies is either nonexistent or mild.

↗ DO: SNORKEL IN JELLYFISH LAKE

COUNTRY Palau **TYPE OF ACTIVITY** Diving/snorkelling

FITNESS/EXPERTISE LEVEL Snorkelling has no requirements; diving covers all abilities.

WHY NOW? Palau's diving is good year-round, but come in January and you'll have seen off the wet season.

DESCRIPTION Palau is one of the world's truly spectacular dive spots, with coral reefs, blue holes, WWII wrecks, hidden caves and more than 60 vertical drop-offs. The epicentre is the Rock Islands, where 200-plus rounded knobs of limestone, covered with jungle, dot the waters for a 32km stretch southwest of Koror.

The waters surrounding the Rock Islands are teeming with more than 1500 varieties of reef and pelagic fish. There are four times the number of coral species in Palau than in the Caribbean. Divers can see manta rays, sea turtles, moray eels, giant tridacna clams, grey reef sharks and sometimes sea snakes, dugongs or chambered nautiluses. But the real fish-of-the-day is jellyfish. Among the Rock Islands' 80 marine salt lakes – former sinkholes – is Jellyfish Lake. Here, millions of harmless transparent jellyfish swim en masse following the path of the sun. Diving is not allowed but snorkelling in this pulsating mass is an unearthly sensation.

For a more traditional dive experience, head for the Ngemelis Wall, widely considered to be the world's best wall dive. From knee-deep water, the wall drops about 300m. Divers can float past a brilliant rainbow of sponges and soft corals, their intense blues, reds and whites forming a backdrop for quivering 3m orange and yellow sea fans and giant black coral trees.

Blue Corner, Palau's most popular dive, is noted for its abundance of marine life. Expect to be totally bedazzled by the variety of fish, including barracudas and schooling sharks, as well as hard and soft corals. Strong tidal currents make this a dive for the more experienced. Novice divers will prefer the German Channel and Turtle Cove; manta rays are frequently spotted in the former.

↗ DO: **PARAGLIDE AT IQUIQUE**

COUNTRY Chile **TYPE OF ACTIVITY** Paragliding
FITNESS/EXPERTISE LEVEL Not required.
WHY NOW? Savour summer as you glide along the Chilean coast.
DESCRIPTION As developers work hard to turn the northern city of
Iquique into Chile's premier beach resort (complete with glitzy casino
and beachside boardwalks), you can rise above it all by taking to the sky.
Iquique's unique geography, with its steep coastal escarpment, rising air
currents and the soft, extensive dunes of Cerro Dragón, makes it one of
South America's best paragliding destinations. It's theoretically possible
to glide all the way to Tocopilla, 240km to the south, but that's not for
novices. Tandem flights are available with a number of operators.
www.parapenteiquique.cl (in Spanish)

Walk on air in Chile and rise above the spreading concrete in Iquique.

Dare to take on a world record? In 2003, nine Tour d'Afrique riders got the gong for the fastest human-powered north–south crossing of Africa – all 11,900km of it.

↗ DO: **TOUR D'AFRIQUE**

COUNTRY Various **TYPE OF ACTIVITY** Cycling
FITNESS/EXPERTISE LEVEL High level of fitness and endurance required.
WHY NOW? The tour begins this week.
DESCRIPTION The Tour d'Afrique is an 11,900km bike race starting at the
pyramids of Giza, outside Cairo, and finishing in Cape Town, South Africa.
For four months cyclists average around 120km a day, pedalling through 10
countries and both hemispheres and past some of Africa's greatest sights,
including Luxor, Mts Kenya and Kilimanjaro, Lake Malawi and Victoria Falls.
The Tour d'Afrique is foremost a race and the pace is cracking – in 2003
nine riders were listed by Guinness World Records as completing the
fastest human-powered crossing of Africa – but you can also cycle as a
so-called 'expedition rider', trundling along at more of a touring speed. You
can also opt to ride individual sections – there are eight in total – which
range between 1000km and 2000km. www.tourdafrique.com

Inferno Race
www.inferno-muerren.ch
The world's oldest ski race, covering 15.8km in the Swiss resort of Mürren.

Dusi Marathon
www.dusi.org.za
Paddle 120km through the Valley of 1000 Hills to Durban; watch for crocodiles.

The Coastal Challenge
www.thecoastalchallenge.com
Run 250km across seven stages through the jungles, beaches and mountains of Costa Rica.

Grottenmarathon
www.taxifrenken.nl/grottenmarathon
.htm (in Dutch)
Marathon-length run in the Netherlands, 38.7km of which is through a cave at Valkenburg.

week
.03

↗ DO: **WHALE WATCH AT BAJA CALIFORNIA**

COUNTRY Mexico **TYPE OF ACTIVITY** Wildlife watching
FITNESS/EXPERTISE LEVEL Not required.
WHY NOW? To enjoy the company of California grey whales.
DESCRIPTION Even if you don't like the super-development of Los Cabos
at the height of the tourist season, the whales do, so pack everything but
your prejudices. From January to March, California grey whales have their
own winter vacation from the cold Siberian and Alaskan waters, travelling
almost 10,000km to give birth in the warmth of the Sea of Cortez. You'll
easily spot whales from the shores of Los Cabos, or you can journey
north to the shallow lagoons of San Ignacio, Ojo de Liebre and Bahía
Magdalena, mating and breeding grounds for the grey whale, where
hundreds of whales might be seen. You'll find boats for Ojo de Liebre in
the town of Guerrero Negro.

www.yearofadventures.com/january

It's adventure central at the 'end of the earth', home to the Moreno Glacier and Tierra del Fuego (Land of Fire).

January

↙ **GO: PATAGONIA,**
ARGENTINA/CHILE

week

↙ **.04**

www.yearofadventures.com/january

WHY NOW? COME TO PATAGONIA NOW WHEN IT'S AT ITS APPROACHABLE BEST, SNOW-TOPPED NOT SNOWBOUND

Patagonia is the literal end-of-the-earth, a raw and rugged place where South America tapers away to a chilly nothing. The star feature of this great southern land is the tail end of the Andes, the longest mountain chain on earth. Assaulted by wind, snow and ice for millennia, the Patagonian Andes are not especially high – they average 2000m – but they've been blasted into an array of peculiar mountain shapes, from the Torres del Paine, which look like a hand of broken fingers, to the 1.2km-high domed summit rock of Monte FitzRoy that so intoxicates climbers. Hidden beneath FitzRoy is the South Patagonian Icecap, the world's third-largest icecap (behind Antarctica and Greenland). From it springs a host of glaciers like tributaries, including the pin-up of world ice, 60m-high Moreno Glacier. Stand in awe for a while as it noisily calves seracs into the milky waters of Lago Argentino.

↗ DO: FLY TO THE SOUTH POLE

REGION Antarctica **TYPE OF ACTIVITY** Adventure travel **FITNESS/EXPERTISE LEVEL** Not required. **WHY NOW?** It's a short summer at 90° south. **DESCRIPTION** Once upon a time you had to be prepared to eat your dogs and bury your companions to set foot on the South Pole. Today you need only endure a bumpy six-hour flight, and you can be making the world's most southerly snowman. Air journeys to the South Pole begin with a preliminary flight from the Chilean town of Punta Arenas to your Antarctic base camp at Patriot Hills (at 80° south). Over the coming week you can explore your icy surrounds as you await conditions that permit flights into the Pole. You'll refuel halfway before landing beside the Amundsen-Scott Research Station at the Pole, where you will pay another price beyond the US$34,000 you have already shelled out – you will probably have a headache from the altitude as you stand atop the 3000m-thick ice. The temperature is also likely to be around -30°C.
www.adventure-network.com

A mere six-hour flight and you can be making the world's most southerly snowman...

The Andes separate two vastly different landscapes. To their rain-shadowed east is the arid Argentine steppe, which extends to the wildlife wonderland of Península Valdés, populated by Magellanic penguins, sea lions, elephant seals and rheas. To the range's west, is the fiord-slashed Chilean coast, where rivers such as Rio Serrano provide kayakers with access to iceberg-choked lakes beneath the Torres del Paine. For a more turbulent experience, think about a rafting trip on Chile's Rio Futaleufu, one of the world's wildest white-water experiences.

The full stop to this land is Tierra del Fuego, the paradoxically named 'Land of Fire', perched just above the Antarctic Circle. Split between Chile and Argentina, the Chilean side is a practically untamed expanse of massive sheep farms and mountains, sprinkled with remote lakes. The Argentine half boasts the energetic regional capital of Ushuaia and the impressive Darwin Range, which is technically the death throe of the Andes. Ushuaia is also the departure point for most Antarctica-bound ships.

o1 o2
o3 o4

Cosy up in comfort as the taiga slips past your window. At 9288km, the Trans-Siberian is the world's longest railway line.

↗ DO: **TRANS-SIBERIAN RAILWAY**

COUNTRIES Russia, China and Mongolia **TYPE OF ACTIVITY** Adventure travel
FITNESS/EXPERTISE LEVEL Not required.
WHY NOW? See Siberia as it should be seen, beneath snow.
DESCRIPTION Russia is the world's largest country, so it's only fitting it should also have the world's longest railway. Stretching 9288km from Moscow to Vladivostok, the Trans-Siberian is a great seam across Russia, and unlike most classic rail journeys it's not about luxury. Come now, as Russia slips towards winter, and it's likely your fellow travellers will be Russians and Chinese using the railway as transport not tourism. It'll be freezing outside, yet the train's heating system will be creating a microclimate more akin to the Costa del Sol.

The true Trans-Siberian Railway doesn't leave Russia, cutting across Siberia to the Pacific coast, but popular tributary lines have added the possibility of a couple of extra passport stamps. The Trans-Mongolian route breaks away into the Mongolian capital of Ulan Bator and on to Beijing. The Trans-Manchurian route journeys through northern China to Beijing – travel now and you'll pass through the city of Hǎěrbīn during its annual Ice Lantern Festival, where you'll find ice sculptures such as the Great Wall and Forbidden City.

Whatever route you choose, don't miss the opportunity to alight in the Siberian city of Irkutsk and head for the shores of Lake Baikal, the world's deepest lake. You might not appreciate its depth at this time of year, since it'll be frozen over (though a peek into the fishing holes will reveal water of remarkable clarity), but you will be able to trek across the lake's surface or among the iced-in ships at Port Baikal.

Choose from deluxe first-class compartments (two-berth en suite), soft first-class (two berth) or second class (four berth). First class doesn't necessarily mean luxury but nor does second class mean privation; four-berth compartments are perfectly comfortable.

↗ DO: STORM WATCH ON VANCOUVER ISLAND

COUNTRY Canada TYPE OF ACTIVITY Natural phenomena
FITNESS/EXPERTISE LEVEL Not required.
WHY NOW? It's the depths of the Canadian winter, with regular storms rolling in.
DESCRIPTION Each winter, Vancouver Island's west coast becomes a front-row seat to the most spectacular storms on the North American west coast. With nothing but the Pacific Ocean between the island and Japan, these well-travelled storms, driven here by a persistent low-pressure system in the Gulf of Alaska, roar ashore, bringing high winds and waves that hit harder than a boxer. Wander the beaches to experience the storms' full fury, follow the aptly named Wild Pacific Trail for a cliff-top view, take a storm-watching tour from the town of Tofino or simply watch the action from the windows of your hotel room.
www.tofino-bc.com; www.my-tofino.com

↗ DO: SURF THE SUPERBANK

COUNTRY Australia TYPE OF ACTIVITY Surfing
FITNESS/EXPERTISE LEVEL Beginners and pros alike.
WHY NOW? Cyclone swells will be lighting up the Superbank.
DESCRIPTION Until a few years ago, there was no such place as Superbank, the great white sandbar off Queensland's Gold Coast that's now home to the world's longest waves and barrels. In 1999 a 'sand bypass' project aimed to move northerly flowing sand past the mouth of the Tweed River and on to the Gold Coast. Instead it resulted in the creation of Superbank – all praise to failed bureaucracy – which stretches in a ruler-straight line from Snapper Rocks to Kirra, with summer cyclone swells creating tubes as long as an oil pipeline. So good is it at this time of year that you'll even find a handful of surfers still riding their fortune at night. The waters are always packed, but there are waves enough here for everyone.

↗ DO: TWITCH AT PARC NATIONAL DU BANC D'ARGUIN

COUNTRY Mauritania TYPE OF ACTIVITY Bird-watching
FITNESS/EXPERTISE LEVEL Not required.
WHY NOW? Mid-winter sees the highest concentration of birds.
DESCRIPTION Pinched between the Atlantic Ocean and the ocean of sand that is the Sahara, Mauritania's Parc National du Banc d'Arguin is one of the world's great bird-watching destinations. Stretching 200km north from Cape Timiris, it's the wintering site for around two million wading birds – around 30% of the waders that use the Atlantic flyway – the largest concentration of such birds in the world. Among the 108 recorded species, expect to see broad-billed sandpipers, pink flamingos, white and grey pelicans, black terns and spoonbills. The park's islands – largely formed by wind-blown sand from the Sahara – are the prime birding sites, and the only way to see them is by small boat. You'll find boats for hire in the fishing village of Twik. Bush taxis between Nouakchott and Nouâdhibou will generally stop at Ten Alloul, 14km from Twik.

Stormy weather: take a front-row seat for some spectacular tempests in North America.

The world's longest tubes are close to perfect at Superbank on Queensland's Gold Coast.

Jizerská 50
www.jiz50.cz
A 50km ski marathon at the Czech resort Bedrichov.

Raid de la Savane
http://maiarmor.free.fr/BF-accueil.php (in French)
Five-stage, 120km run through the African nation of Burkina Faso.

Rooftop Run
www.coolrunning.com.au/ultra/bogong
A 60km run through the Australian high-country, from Mt Bogong to Mt Hotham.

Regata del Rio Negro
www.regatadeirionegro.com.ar
Eight-day paddle in Argentina; said to be the longest kayak race in the world.

week
.o4

www.yearofadventures.com/january

o23

You could stay for the season and still not have skied all Whistler-Blackcomb's trails – and a quarter are black diamond runs.

February

↙ GO WHISTLER-BLACKCOMB, CANADA

week

↙ .01

www.yearofadventures.com/feburary

WHY NOW? BOTH WHISTLER AND BLACKCOMB MOUNTAINS ARE AT THEIR SNOWY BEST IN FEBRUARY

Consistently voted North America's best ski resort, and considered by many people to be the best in the world, the powder-perfect twin peaks of Whistler-Blackcomb – the principal venue for the 2010 Olympic Winter Games – contain almost 200 longer-than-average marked trails, the highest vertical drop (1609m) of any North American ski field and 29 sq km of bowls, glades and steeps. You could stay an entire season – plenty of people do – and still not explore it all.

There's plenty here for beginners, but even more to light the eyes of the adrenaline skiier or snowboarder. Around one-quarter of Whistler's runs, and 30% of Blackcomb's, are rated as black-diamond (advanced). Wander round the back of Blackcomb to Ruby Bowl and it gets even sexier. Ruby Bowl is one of 12 alpine bowls on Whistler-Blackcomb, but it's the undoubted matriarch. To reach it, ride to the top of the Glacier Express

↗ DO: ICE TREK ON THE ZANSKAR RIVER

COUNTRY India **TYPE OF ACTIVITY** Winter trekking **FITNESS/EXPERTISE LEVEL** Good fitness required – cold blood an asset. **WHY NOW?** Trek while the Zanskar River has a skin of ice. **DESCRIPTION** The extremes of cold in the Himalayan region of Ladakh mean that it's little visited in winter. The mountain passes close and the only way in and out is by air. For those hardy souls who not only take the challenge to visit in winter but want to do something even more outlandish, there's the chance to trek along the frozen Zanskar River from Chilling to Padum, sleeping in rock shelters. For Zanskaris this is a traditional route, the only way in and out when the high passes are snowed in, but for trekkers it usually means about eight days of walking, including through a canyon that's inaccessible at any other time of year. Expect severe cold (winter in Leh can reach -20°C) but be cheered by the news that Ladakh receives 300 days of sun a year, making for crisp, clear trekking days on the river.

Zanskar River – it's your chance to walk on water among Himalayan peaks and fantastic ice formations.

chairlift, then make the climb up Spanky's Ladder to confront Whistler-Blackcomb's best powder, falling in continuous steeps for more than 600m.

If you prefer to ski cross-country, more than 28km of trails wind through Lost Lake Park and the valley. You might also fancy a try at snowmobiling or dog-sledding, or you can range further afield by taking on the challenge of heli-skiing, which provides access to the untouched powder of backcountry peaks.

The centre of the mountain action is Whistler Village, built almost from scratch in the early 1980s, its resorts, hotels and stores blending together like one big ultramodern outdoor mall, mountain-style. From Vancouver, it's a 23km drive to Whistler Village along the invitingly named Sea to Sky Hwy.

Whistler-Blackcomb is not a place where you need suffer for your art. The mild Pacific air flowing around the peaks provides reliable snowfall without the truly frigid conditions of inland ski resorts.

o1 o2 o3 o4

Aconcagua, the 'stone sentinel', was first summited in 1897. Now it's your turn!

↗ DO: CLIMB CERRO ACONCAGUA

COUNTRY Argentina **TYPE OF ACTIVITY** Trekking/mountaineering
FITNESS/EXPERTISE LEVEL Good fitness (and acclimatisation) required.
WHY NOW? The climbing season is December to February; come late to avoid deep snow.
DESCRIPTION At 6960m, Cerro Aconcagua is the highest mountain outside of the Himalayas, but it yields to determined trekkers. Known as the 'roof of the Americas', the Andean peak rises above the Argentine city of Mendoza, and reaching its summit requires at least 13 to 15 days, including time to acclimatise to the altitude.

The traditional ascent on Aconcagua is the Northwest Route, approached on a 40km trail from the park entrance at Laguna los Horcones. The Polish Glacier Route is longer (76km) but more scenic and less crowded. It's also more technical, requiring the use of ropes, ice screws and ice axes. A third route, the South Face, is a demanding technical climb.

Only highly experienced climbers should consider tackling Aconcagua without the relative safety of an organised tour; even skilled climbers often hire guides who know the mountain's Jekyll-and-Hyde weather. Nonclimbers can also have a taste of Aconcagua, albeit a diluted one, by trekking to camps and refuges beneath the permanent snow line. Tour operators and climbing guides set up seasonal tents at the best camp sites, so independent trekkers and climbers usually get only the leftover spots.

From December to March, permits are obligatory for both trekking and climbing in Parque Provincial Aconcagua. They are available only in Mendoza.

Buses from Mendoza will stop at Puente del Inca, just a couple of kilometres from Laguna los Horcones, allowing easy access to the Northwest Route. Tread carefully; Aconcagua claims several lives each year.
www.aconcagua.mendoza.gov.ar

↗ DO: RIDE THE CRESTA RUN

COUNTRY Switzerland **TYPE OF ACTIVITY** Skeleton tobogganing
FITNESS/EXPERTISE LEVEL Not required.
WHY NOW? The Cresta Run opens a few days before Christmas and
operates until the end of February. **DESCRIPTION** In 1885 the Cresta
Run was first built on the slopes of the Swiss resort of St Moritz, and
continues to be reconstructed each winter season. This most famous of
skeleton (head-first tobogganing) runs is used for both competition and
play, though visitors must join the St Moritz Tobogganing Club (women not
allowed) before they can park their own skeletons on the club's skeleton
toboggans. The best in the game can reach speeds of up to 130km/h on
the Cresta Run, but beginners have trouble enough just mastering braking,
for which you use only the rakes on your boots. Fail in this and you'll
almost certainly come a cropper at the run's most famous corner, the
Shuttlecock. This at least grants you entry into the Shuttlecock Club and
the right to wear the special Shuttlecock tie. www.cresta-run.com

↗ DO: DIVE GLOVER'S REEF

COUNTRY Belize **TYPE OF ACTIVITY** Diving
FITNESS/EXPERTISE LEVEL Beginners to pros.
WHY NOW? It's the middle of Belize's dry season. **DESCRIPTION** Named
after 18th-century English pirate John Glover, Glover's Reef is the
southernmost of Belize's three atolls. Six small cayes of white sand and
palm trees are dotted along the atoll's southeastern rim, supporting a
handful of low-key resorts and diving bases. The reef sits atop a submerged
mountain ridge on the edge of the continental shelf, surrounded by
enormous drop-offs with world-class dive sites. On the east side, where
visibility is usually more than 30m, the ocean floor plummets away to
800m. Divers regularly see spotted eagle rays, southern stingrays, turtles,
moray eels, dolphins, several shark species, large groupers, barracudas and
many tropical reef fish. In the shallow central lagoon 700 coral patches brim
with marine life – brilliant for snorkellers. In a week here you could probably
manage about 17 dives, including some at other atolls.

↗ DO: VISIT THE EMPTY QUARTER

COUNTRY Saudi Arabia **TYPE OF ACTIVITY** Adventure travel
FITNESS/EXPERTISE LEVEL Not required.
WHY NOW? Come while desert conditions are bearable. **DESCRIPTION**
The Empty Quarter (Rub al-Khali), aka the Abode of Silence, is the largest
area covered by sand on the planet, encompassing 655,000 sq km (an
area larger than France). For European adventurers it conjured up all that
was romantic and forbidden about Arabia, and it has lost little of this allure.
The remarkable, sculpted dunes for which it's famous can rise more than
300m and form vast chains of longitudinal dune ridges stretching over
hundreds of kilometres. Pushed by the wind, the dunes can move at a
rate of up to 30m per year. Exploring the Empty Quarter requires more
preparation than any other destination in Saudi Arabia. Permission is free
and rarely denied, but must be obtained from the National Commission for
Wildlife Conservation and Development in Riyadh. Most Empty Quarter
expeditions start and end at either Sharurah or Sulayyil.

The record for the Cresta Run
is about 50 seconds – have
you got what it takes?

Pirate John Glover was based in
the area, but you'll find the real
treasure is below the waves.

Cole Classic
www.coleclassic.com
Rough-water swim off the Sydney
beaches: roll your arms over for 1km,
2km or 10km.

Cradle Mountain Run
www.coolrunning.com.au/ultra/cradle
Run 82km along Australia's finest
bushwalking trail, the Overland Track.

Full Monty
www.aceraces.com
Kayak 60km, cycle 100km (ascending
3000m) and run 50km through
Shropshire.

Temple to Temple
www.templetotemple.com
Seven-day, 750km bike race between
major temples in Belize.

week

.01

www.yearofadventures.com/feburary

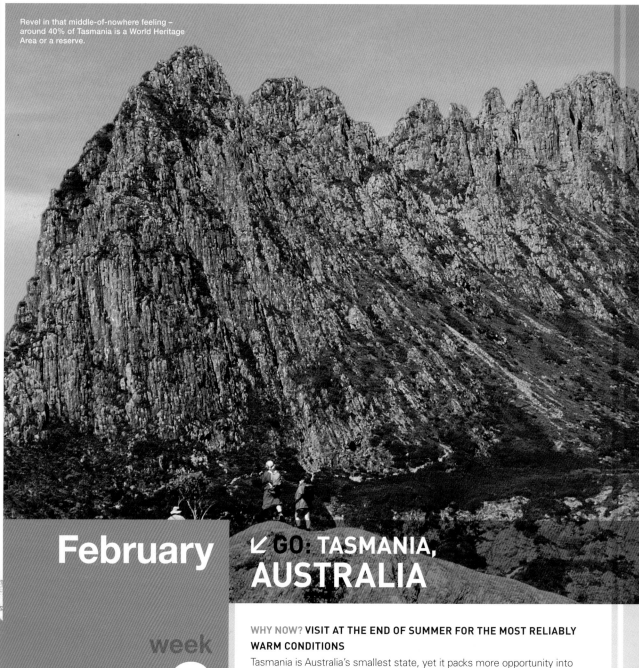

Revel in that middle-of-nowhere feeling – around 40% of Tasmania is a World Heritage Area or a reserve.

February

week
.02

www.yearofadventures.com/feburary

↙ GO: TASMANIA, AUSTRALIA

WHY NOW? **VISIT AT THE END OF SUMMER FOR THE MOST RELIABLY WARM CONDITIONS**

Tasmania is Australia's smallest state, yet it packs more opportunity into its outdoors than the other states and territories combined. Furnished with mountains shaped as peculiarly as the country's native fauna, 20% of Tasmania is made up of national parks, with most of that listed as World Heritage. Both the air and water in parts of the state are claimed to be the purest on the planet.

Suck in this air and drink the water as you discover Tassie's wealth of bushwalking trails. The Overland Track, between Cradle Mountain and Lake St Clair, is Australia's premier bushwalk, attracting summer crowds like outback flies. For an encore, you can select from a roll call of fantastic walks, such as the South Coast Track, Freycinet Peninsula, Western Arthurs, Federation Peak, Frenchmans Cap, Walls of Jerusalem or Bay of Fires.

Not only is it breath-taking, but the water in parts of Tasmania is some of the purest on the planet.

↗ DO: COMPETE IN THE COAST TO COAST

COUNTRY New Zealand **TYPE OF ACTIVITY** Adventure race **FITNESS/EXPERTISE LEVEL** Superior fitness required. **WHY NOW?** To compete in one of adventure racing's marquee events. **DESCRIPTION** The Coast to Coast is the event that gave birth to the rise and rise of adventure racing. First contested in 1980, this multisport race traverses New Zealand's South Island, beginning in Kumara Beach on the wild west coast and ending in the coastal suburbs of Christchurch. Competitors run 36km, cycle 140km and kayak 67km through the grade-two rapids of the Waimakariri Canyon. You can choose to do so individually or in teams of two, in a single day or extended across two days with an overnight rest/collapse in Arthurs Pass. Heavy rain – not uncommon on the South Island even in February – can add all sorts of surprises to the challenge. Entries to the event are accepted from 1 June of the previous year, and close on 31 December. www.coasttocoast.co.nz

Grade two rapids mean relatively easy paddling – a good breather after 36km of running and 70km of cycling.

Footsore? Tasmania still has plenty to offer. Rack up a selection of activities and the island state can knock them down.

Cycling? Tasmania is about the only place in Australia that can be comfortably circuited by bike, so each summer it becomes the scene of a wheeled migration worthy of wildebeests. Mountain bikers are not forgotten, with the Tasmanian Trail running 480km from Tassie's top to tip on back roads and trails.

Climbing? Set on the Tasman Peninsula next to Australia's highest cliffs, and rising 65m out of the Tasman Sea, is a famous and spectacular dolerite stack called the Totem Pole – your first pitch begins from your boat.

Caving? Niggly Cave near Maydena is Australia's longest explored cave at 375m, and contains the longest single pitch in the country: 191m.

Even the things that mar the Tasmanian landscape have been turned into an adventure, with the Gordon Dam, a concrete abscess in the World Heritage-listed Southwest, doubling as the site for the world's highest commercial abseil – 140m to valley floor.

All things considered, Tasmania is the kind of place you want to live, not just visit, but if you must only visit, do so at the end of summer for the most reliably warm conditions – you're nearing the Antarctic when you hit Tasmania.

For more information, visit www.discovertasmania .com.au.

01 **02** 03 04

Hit the ice and explore as the lake sets around Stockholm.

↗ DO: TOUR SKATE ON MÄLAREN

COUNTRY Sweden **TYPE OF ACTIVITY** Nordic skating

FITNESS/EXPERTISE LEVEL Some skating experience best.

WHY NOW? The skating season usually lasts from December to March; come now to coincide with the likely running of Vikingarännet.

DESCRIPTION One look at the name 'Nordic skating' and it's apparent that Sweden is a heartland for the pursuit of touring on ice skates. Whenever the ice is thick enough, Stockholm's lake and canal system is exploited by skating enthusiasts seeking the longest possible 'run'.

Stretching west from Stockholm, Mälaren is Sweden's third-largest lake (1140 sq km) and one of the country's prime Nordic skating venues. A short ride on public transport and you can be skating across the freshwater lake, covering up to 100km a day and stopping at towns, villages and cultural landmarks as you go. Among the stops you can make is the World Heritage–listed Viking trading centre of Birka on the island of Björkö, containing the largest Viking Age cemetery in Scandinavia, with around 3000 graves.

Each year – or at least those years the ice will support it – Mälaren hosts the skating race Vikingarännet. Started in 1999, this marathon event sees thousands of skaters cross the lake from Stockholm to Uppsala, a distance of around 80km – the record winning time is two hours 35 minutes. Vikingarännet is held when the lake ice is thick enough to support great numbers of skaters. The most probable date is during February.

Stockholm offers an extra skating thrill when the Baltic Sea freezes, though this occurs only once or twice every 10 years. When it does, fantastic tours of the archipelago are possible, but never skate alone.

Sharpen your blades and your Nordic skating interest at the Stockholm Ice Skate Sailing Association website (www.sssk.se). www.vikingarannet.com

↗ DO: SKI VALLÉE BLANCHE

COUNTRY France **TYPE OF ACTIVITY** Skiing

FITNESS/EXPERTISE LEVEL Good fitness and endurance required.

WHY NOW? You need a lot of snow to ski 22km, so come in deep winter.

DESCRIPTION From the evergreen Alpine resort town of Chamonix – the venue for the very first winter Olympic Games in 1924 – ride the Aiguille du Midi cable car to its needle-tip end high above the town, climb out nervously on an arête and strap on your skis for the longest run in Europe. The Vallée Blanche switches between glaciers, including the famous Mer de Glace (the Alps' second-longest glacier), as it descends 22km back to Chamonix, dropping every one of the 2760m the cable car has carried you. It's fairly easy skiing, though you'll be on your planks for up to five hours. At times you'll also be threading between crevasses so it's imperative you make the descent with a qualified guide – Chamonix is chock-full of them; begin your search at www.chamonix-guides.com.

↗ DO: WINDSURF AT CABARETE

COUNTRY Dominican Republic **TYPE OF ACTIVITY** Windsurfing

FITNESS/EXPERTISE LEVEL Beginner to pro.

WHY NOW? From December to March, the waves are big enough to make even the inner bay a bit choppy. **DESCRIPTION** Cabarete's bay seems custom-made for windsurfing. A small coral reef on the bay's upwind side protects it from waves and currents, leaving a huge area of shallow flat water. With light morning winds and mellow seas, the bay is ideal for beginners. In the afternoon, thermal winds pick up, blowing east to west and reaching speeds of 25km/h to 40km/h. About 1km out, waves break over a second coral reef, and expert windsurfers head here to practice their 360-degree spins and end-over-end flips. Don't come expecting a travelling secret because windsurfing has transformed Cabarete. Its single road, once a sandy track along the coast, is now crammed with hotels, resorts, and shops catering to wind-sport enthusiasts. Kiteboarding is also a mainstay here. www.activecabarete.com; www.cabaretewindsurfing.com

↗ DO: SNOWSHOE AT MESA VERDE

COUNTRY USA **TYPE OF ACTIVITY** Snowshoeing

FITNESS/EXPERTISE LEVEL Basic snowshoeing skills required.

WHY NOW? Snow conditions are patchy, with mid-February among the most likely snowshoeing times. **DESCRIPTION** Even if you've never been snowshoeing, you've no doubt seen images of cold people in cold places wearing what appear to be tennis racquets on their feet. Snowshoeing allows you to walk trails in the depth of winter, when all other hikers are home keeping their toes warm for summer. And at Mesa Verde National Park, nestled into the crook of the Four Corners, it comes with a surreal edge: snowshoeing in the desert, among ancestral Puebloan sites. Winter here brings unreliable snows, opening the park to snowshoeing for only a few days a year. The Cliff Palace Loop Rd offers a 10km stroll past lookouts onto the cliff dwellings, while the Morefield Campground Loop Rds offers a variety of choices, both short and long. www.nps.gov/meve

You can ski to Switzerland on these slopes – though without a cable car it's a long way back!

The price of perfect conditions is company on the waves.

Yukon Quest
www.yukonquest.com
A 1600km dog-sled race in jet-black-winter Alaska, across frozen rivers and through four mountain ranges.

Yukon Arctic Ultra
www.4ar.info/races.php
Race 42km, 160km, 480km or 750km on skis, snowshoes or mountain bike; begins a few hours after the Yukon Quest.

Patagonia Expedition Race
www.patagoniaexpeditionrace.com
Up to 10 days of mountain biking, trekking, sea kayaking, orienteering, and rope activities to cover more than 500 Patagonian kilometres.

Sapporo International Ski Marathon
www.sspc.or.jp/ski/eng_top.html
Ski 50km within seven hours on the Japanese island of Hokkaidō.

week

.o2

www.yearofadventures.com/feburary

He's no slouch, diving to depths of over 1500m in search of squid and other food. But for an elephant seal, 3.5 tonnes is a lot to lug around on land.

February

↙ GO:
STH GEORGIA ISLAND

WHY NOW? AT THIS END OF SUMMER IT HAS ONE OF THE WORLD'S MOST EXTRAORDINARY COLLECTIONS OF WILDLIFE

More than 2000km west of Tierra del Fuego, the South Atlantic island of South Georgia has been part of the adventuring psyche ever since Ernest Shackleton made his dramatic walk across the uncharted island after the *Endurance* was crushed by the Antarctic pack ice. After sailing 1300km from Elephant Island in a 6m lifeboat, across some of the world's roughest seas, Shackleton and two members of his crew trekked for 36 hours across the mountainous island on frostbitten feet (with screws from the lifeboat as makeshift crampons) to reach the whaling station at Stromness. For fit and well-equipped adventurers the possibility of following this amazing trek has become one of the key Antarctic challenges.

With its snowcapped peaks and glaciers plunging towards the sea, South Georgia has been described as an alpine mountain range rising

↗ DO: CLIMB MT KILIMANJARO

COUNTRY Tanzania **TYPE OF ACTIVITY** Trekking **FITNESS/EXPERTISE LEVEL** Good fitness and acclimatisation required. **WHY NOW?** Warm temperatures and little rain, while avoiding the New Year high season when huts may be booked out. **DESCRIPTION** The equatorial volcano Mt Kilimanjaro (5896m) is Africa's highest mountain and can be climbed along six routes. About 90% of trekkers take Kili's easiest path, the Marangu Route (so popular it's been dubbed the 'Coca-Cola Route'). Most trekkers on this route only go as far as Gillman's Point, on the crater rim at 5685m, with another two hours of high-altitude walking required to reach the summit at Uhuru Peak. Of the other routes, Umbwe is the most direct, and Lemosho the longest, while the Machame (with a descent on the Mweka Route) is probably the most scenic option. You'll go through the pain barrier on the way to the top of the mountain, but the reward is unforgettable – a sunrise view over what seems like half of Africa. All treks must be organised through a tour company.

Its height and equatorial location mean that Kilimanjaro guarantees climbers four seasons in one day.

straight out of the ocean. But at this end of summer there are swathes of green and it has one of the world's most extraordinary collections of wildlife. If you want to see king penguins or fur seals, this is the place to come – there are millions of fur seals, while single colonies of king penguins can number in the tens of thousands. There are also substantial numbers of elephant seals as well as a variety of other penguin species.

South Georgia and its outlying islands are also home to a substantial proportion of the world's albatross population, including important colonies of the largest of these astonishing birds, the gigantic wandering albatross, which can have a wing span of more than 3m.

While on South Georgia, pay homage to Shackleton's grave in the cemetery at Grytviken whaling station – Sir Ernest died in January 1922 aboard his ship moored off Grytviken.

Unless you're one of the few people who come by private yacht, the only way to reach South Georgia is by cruise ship. www.sgisland.org

You need to be a decent swimmer and in relatively good shape to keep up with the sharks.

↗ DO: **SWIM WITH SHARKS AT DONSOL**

COUNTRY Philippines **TYPE OF ACTIVITY** Snorkelling/wildlife watching
FITNESS/EXPERTISE LEVEL Good swimming skills an asset.
WHY NOW? Whale sharks visit the waters off Donsol between about February and May.
DESCRIPTION Until 1998 Donsol, on the Luzon Peninsula, was an obscure, sleepy and remote village. Then a local diver shot a video of whale sharks in the area. Days after a newspaper story about the 'discovery' was published, poachers from other provinces arrived in the area. The local and central governments quickly drafted a municipal ordinance together, prohibiting the hunting of whale sharks. Since then Donsol has quickly become one of Luzon's best-known locations, with travellers and media from around the world descending on the town to see the famous *butanding* (the local word for whale shark).

Today, Donsol is one of the world's top locations to swim with the largest fish in the sea – these gentle giants can grow to 18m in length, although it's more common to see them about half that size.

It's truly an exhilarating experience swimming along with these huge blue-grey, silver-spotted creatures. Only snorkelling equipment is allowed, with scuba diving prohibited. There's a limited supply of snorkelling equipment available for rent at Donsol's visitor centre, so it's safer to bring your own.

It's difficult to predict your chances of seeing a whale shark. The peak months are February to May, although in some years sharks migrate here as early as October and November and stay as late as June.

Upon arrival in town, stop in at the visitor centre. It will arrange a boat, spotter and a Butanding Interaction Officer for you. You'll find a small selection of accommodation in Donsol, and this once unknown town now even has a direct bus service to the capital, Manila, 11 hours away.

o1 o2
o3 o4

It's where all that glistens is ice – take a stroll along Moreno Glacier.

↗ DO: GLACIER WALK ON MORENO GLACIER

COUNTRY Argentina **TYPE OF ACTIVITY** Glacier walking
FITNESS/EXPERTISE LEVEL Not required.
WHY NOW? Stay warm atop the giant ice block. **DESCRIPTION** Discover the true meaning of the term 'cold feet' as you take a boat across the glacial melt of Lago Argentino, wander through beech forest and emerge at the edge of 15-storey-high Moreno Glacier. It's one of the few glaciers in the world not in retreat, maintaining its stability for the last 90 years. Fit your crampons and head out onto the ice, which is twisted, broken and covered in seracs like giant, blue blades of grass. Water streams across its top, disappearing into seemingly endless holes, and you walk past crevasses that yawn wider than a lion – welcome to the world of the mountaineer, without any of the requisite hardships. At the end of your walk you get a whisky with ice chipped directly from the glacier. Make base camp at the Patagonian town of El Calafate, from where buses run daily to Moreno Glacier. www.hieloyaventura.com

↗ DO: RAFT THE RÍO PACUARE

COUNTRY Costa Rica **TYPE OF ACTIVITY** White-water rafting
FITNESS/EXPERTISE LEVEL Not required.
WHY NOW? The best runs are during the November to April dry season.
DESCRIPTION Costa Rica is a paddlers' paradise and among the most developed white-water centres in Latin America. The Río Pacuare, located near the town of Turrialba, is considered among the 10 best river runs in the world. Wild and wonderful, it's home to toucans, herons, monkeys and sloths, with the river plunging through a series of spectacular canyons clothed in virgin rainforest. Rapids are separated by calm stretches that enable you to stare at the near-vertical green walls towering hundreds of metres above the river. Dozens of operators, both in Turrialba and throughout the country, arrange a variety of trips down the Pacuare in rafts or kayaks.

Close to 30km of class three rapids – enough to get you wet!

Susitna 100
www.susitna100.com
Mountain bike, ski, run or snowshoe for 160km through wintry South Central Alaska.

Tartu Maraton
www.tartumaraton.ee/tm
A 63km cross-country ski marathon in Estonia.

Kili[MAN]jaro
http://kilimanjaro-man.com
Climb Mt Kilimanjaro in eight days, cycle around it in two, then run the Kilimanjaro Marathon.

Swamp Stomp
www.wecefar.com
Bike, run and paddle for 30 hours through central Florida.

↗ DO: RACE OF HOPE

COUNTRY Cameroon **TYPE OF ACTIVITY** Mountain running
FITNESS/EXPERTISE LEVEL High level of fitness required.
WHY NOW? To compete in the Mt Cameroon Race. **DESCRIPTION** Mt Cameroon (4095m) is the highest peak in West Africa, rising direct from the Gulf of Guinea through rainforest to an alpine summit. An active volcano, it erupted seven times last century, most recently in 2000, but that doesn't deter runners from scaling it in the marathon-length Race of Hope (Mt Cameroon Race), held around this time each year. Beginning in the sprawling town of Buea, competitors follow the most direct of the mountain's trekking trails – the so-called Guinness Route – to the summit. If you dance to a slower drum, you can always just walk up the mountain. While the quickest of the runners complete the Guinness Route in 4½ hours, allow two nights to comfortably trek it.

week

.o3

Its wide range of habitats has given Costa Rica an enormous amount of biodiversity – more species per square kilometre than any other country in the world.

February

↙ GO:
COSTA RICA

week
↙ .04
www.yearofadventures.com/feburary

WHY NOW? FEBRUARY IS TRADITIONALLY THE DRIEST MONTH ACROSS COSTA RICA

Costa Rica covers less than 0.01% of the planet, yet it has almost as many birds as the USA and Canada combined, more reptiles than Europe and five times more butterflies than Australia. Measured in terms of number of species per 10,000 sq km, Costa Rica tops the list of countries at 615 species, compared to the relatively impoverished USA with its 104 species. This simple fact alone makes Costa Rica among the premier destinations for naturalists.

More than 850 animal species have been recorded in Costa Rica, but birds are the primary attraction, and they come in every imaginable colour, from the strawberry-red of scarlet macaws to the iridescent violet of sabrewings. Because many of the birds have restricted ranges, you're guaranteed to find completely different species almost everywhere you travel, too.

Scarlet eye candy for amateur ornithologists – just one of the dazzling 840 species of birds in Costa Rica.

↗ DO: CRUISE ON AN ICEBREAKER

COUNTRY Finland **TYPE OF ACTIVITY** Adventure travel/ice swimming **FITNESS/ EXPERTISE LEVEL** Not required. **WHY NOW?** To fulfil its purpose, an icebreaker must have ice. **DESCRIPTION** From the industrial Finnish Lapland town of Kemi, you can plough through pack ice on the Gulf of Bothnia on a four-hour cruise aboard the *Sampo*, an authentic Arctic icebreaker ship and the only one in the world that accepts passengers. Watch the Aurora Borealis from the ship deck, or take the option of swimming among the ice in a special watertight thermal suit. You can also take a walk on the ice, or go on a snowmobile or dog-sled trip. The *Sampo* sails at noon three to four days a week from mid-December to the end of April. As you might expect, it's not cheap, so come on a day when your pockets are feeling deep. www.sampotours.com

The secrets of successful icebreaking: a cutting bow, a strengthened hull and some serious horsepower.

Not all that's wild in Costa Rica is wildlife. If you take your inspiration from the birds and not the sloths, you can bungy jump from the Río Colorado bridge in the capital, San José. And if you're more manatee than macaw, you'll find legendary surf at Witches Rock, with its tubular 3m curls, and Ollie's Point, situated near the old airstrip used to smuggle goods to the Nicaraguan Contras in the 1980s (and named after US colonel Oliver North).

Land mammals will appreciate the dry season for some great hiking among fumaroles and tropical dry forest in Parque Nacional Rincón de la Vieja, or in the cloud forest reserves of Santa Elena and Monteverde. Those with higher ambitions can scale Costa Rica's highest mountain, Cerro Chirripó

(3820m), on a 16km trail – of the Central American countries, only Guatemala has higher peaks.

And those who want something with the lot will gravitate to Península de Osa. Largely covered by Parque Nacional Corcovado, it offers spectacular wildlife viewing at the Sirena Research Station, and the best way into Sirena is on foot. There are three trails to the station, two of which follow the coast and produce an endless pageant of birds. Scarlet macaws are guaranteed, with the tropical almond trees that line the coast a favourite macaw food. There's also the opportunity to swim with dolphins in Bahía Drake.

o1 o2
o3 **o4**

The filtering effect from the underlying limestone makes for incredible visibility.

↗ DO: CAVE DIVE AT PICCANINNIE PONDS

COUNTRY Australia **TYPE OF ACTIVITY** Cave diving
FITNESS/EXPERTISE LEVEL High level of expertise required.
WHY NOW? Freezing waters but at least the air is warm.
DESCRIPTION The ground around the South Australian city of Mt Gambier has more holes than fishnet stockings (even balls pitched to some greens at the local golf club can produce a subterranean echo) but of all the caves that puncture the so-called Limestone Coast, the Piccaninnie Ponds demand most attention.

The standout attraction at the Ponds is the Cathedral, which has a reputation as one of the world's greatest freshwater dive features. Filled by underground springs and filtered by the limestone, visibility inside this scalloped cavern reaches to 40m, and is only then impeded by the walls of the cave. The Chasm offers greater depth, plunging more than 100m, its white walls covered in algal growth.

Controls on snorkelling or diving at Piccaninnie Ponds are strict. To dive at the Ponds you must be a member of the Cave Divers Association of Australia and rated at sinkhole level. Permits are required (obtainable from the Department for Environment and Heritage office in Mt Gambier) and these are issued by timeslots – only four divers are allowed in the Ponds at any one time. All divers are allowed one hour.

Snorkellers also need to obtain permits from the DEH office, though you don't need any qualifications or affiliations to apply for them. Timeslot conditions are the same as for divers.

To experience a different sort of cave dive, head to nearby Ewens Ponds. These three ponds, connected by shallow channels, reach nowhere near the depths of Piccaninnie – their maximum depth is around 10m – but are inhabited by eels and freshwater crays. They are fed by a greater flow of spring water, creating a current that will almost imperceptibly carry you along. www.cavedivers.com.au; www.environment.sa.gov.au

01 02
03 **04**

↗ DO: SCRAMBLE TO TIGRAY'S ROCK CHURCHES

COUNTRY Ethiopia **TYPE OF ACTIVITY** Scrambling/adventure travel
FITNESS/EXPERTISE LEVEL Not required.
WHY NOW? Come at the end of the cool and dry winter. **DESCRIPTION**
Between the northern Ethiopian towns of Adigrat and Mekele lie around
120 churches carved into cliff faces or pre-existing caves. Visiting some
of these churches involves a scramble up almost sheer rock faces using
just footholds in the rock. Although daunting at first sight, the ascents
aren't difficult if taken carefully. Abuna Yemata is considered the most
challenging climb, taking about an hour, using footholds up a sheer
20-minute ascent and crossing a narrow ledge. For your effort you'll find
a church famed for its beautiful and well-preserved frescoes, and with
stunning views. Mekele makes the best base from which to explore the
churches; it can be reached by plane or bus from the capital, Addis Ababa.
Guides are available through Mekele travel agencies and are essential, not
only to locate the remoter churches, but also for tracking down the often-
elusive priests, keepers of the all-important church keys.

Avoid the lockout! Make
sure you take a guide when
visiting the churches.

↗ DO: SURF PIPELINE

COUNTRY USA **TYPE OF ACTIVITY** Surfing
FITNESS/EXPERTISE LEVEL High skill level required.
WHY NOW? About your only chance to be allowed a wave here is to come
on a February or March dawn. **DESCRIPTION** Hawaii lies smack in the path
of all the major swells that race across the Pacific Ocean, with the biggest
waves rolling into the north shores of the islands from November through
February. On Oahu's north shore, the glassy tubes of Banzai Pipeline have
become the unofficial world mecca of surfing. Winter swells can bring
in towering 10m waves, creating conditions that can be as insane as the
locals. The waves break onto a dangerously shallow reef, while equally
hazardous currents pull at the surfers, boogie boarders and bodysurfers
who crowd the sea. To find the Pipeline, head for Ehukai Beach Park
and, facing the ocean, walk about 100m to the left; come at dawn if you
want any space on a wave. Wait until summer and the Pipeline will have
mellowed into a swimmers' delight.

The great pipeline is no
easy ride – surfers have
come fatally unstuck.

Iditarod Trail Invitational
www.alaskaultrasport.com
Cycle, ski or walk 560km or 1770km
along Alaska's Iditarod Trail; a hell of a
way to finish winter.

Mt Cook – the Bloody Good Race
www.bloodygoodevents.co.nz
Kayak, cycle, mountain bike and run for
three days from Mount Cook village to
Christchurch.

Avalanche Peak Challenge
www.avalanchepeak.co.nz
Twenty-six kilometre mountain run
across New Zealand's spectacular
Avalanche Peak.

XPD
www.xpd.com.au
Australian expedition-length
adventure race; dates and
venue variable.

week
.04

www.yearofadventures.com/february

↗ DO: SAHARA MARATHON

REGION Western Sahara **TYPE OF ACTIVITY** Running
FITNESS/EXPERTISE LEVEL High level of fitness required.
WHY NOW? To run through the world's largest desert. **DESCRIPTION**
Imagine the least likely place in the world in which to run 42km, and
it'd probably be the Sahara. Now imagine running it. This annual event
between the towns of El Aaiun and Smara is staged in the disputed region
of Western Sahara to demonstrate solidarity with the local Saharawi
people, around 200,000 of whom live in refugee camps near Tindouf in
Algeria. The good news for runners is that most of the course isn't ankle
deep in Saharan sand; the bad news is that it's across hard and rocky
terrain, with the second half of the race also hilly with dunes. The Sahara
Marathon is held in the desert's coolest season, so forget heat and brace
yourself for dawn's chill. www.saharamarathon.org

Almost a third of its height was lost in the 1995 eruption of the Soufrière Hills Volcano.

March

↙ GO
MONTSERRAT

week
↙ .01

www.yearofadventures.com/march

WHY NOW? CLIMATE VARIES LITTLE ON TROPICAL MONTSERRAT, BUT THE BEGINNING OF MARCH IS ONE OF THE (MARGINALLY) COOLER TIMES, AND IS WELL REMOVED FROM THE HURRICANE SEASON

There was a time when travelling to the island of Montserrat combined two usually unrelated activities: Caribbean holiday and a death wish. You don't need a death wish to visit Montserrat anymore, just an ash mask.

After spending decades as a tight-knit community, proud of its image as an unspoiled Caribbean island with no pretensions, Montserrat was given a big how-do-you-do by the Soufrière Hills Volcano on 18 July 1995, ending 400 years of dormancy. The capital and only significant town, Plymouth, was covered in ash and subsequently abandoned. The 11,000 residents resettled around the island or emigrated, and tourists all but disappeared. In 1997 the volcano erupted again, killing 19 people. Two months later, a superheated pyroclastic flow wiped out the remainder of Plymouth.

↗ DO: IDITAROD

COUNTRY USA **TYPE OF ACTIVITY** Dog-sledding **FITNESS/EXPERTISE LEVEL** Epic endurance and sledding skills required. **WHY NOW?** To gut yourself in one of the world's toughest races. **DESCRIPTION** The greatest dog-sled event of all, and one of the blockbuster endurance events, the Iditarod is an 1850km race between Anchorage and faraway Nome on the Bering Sea. Raced along the Iditarod National Historical Trail, even-numbered years see mushers travelling north, and odd-numbered years, racing south. Known as the 'last great race', it has been held since 1973, and commemorates the role that dogs and sleds played in the settlement of remote Alaska. From a winning time of more than 20 days in the first couple of years, the record is now a smidge under nine days. If you just want to pay canine homage, visit the Iditarod Trail Headquarters in Wasilla, where the race truly starts/ends – the 80km between Anchorage and Wasilla is purely ceremonial. www.iditarod.com

Mind your *gees!* and *haws!* ('right!' and 'left!') – these dogs know exactly what they're doing.

The volcano still lets off the occasional puff of steam, but life has regained some normalcy for Montserratians, with some previously off-limit zones now welcoming back residents. Tourism in the one-third of the island left in the so-called 'Safe Zone' is low-key, but very welcome. All but two hotels were lost in the eruptions, but a half-dozen cosy B&Bs have picked up a stream of adventurous travellers.

Any visitors to Montserrat will probably witness at least a little volcanic activity, usually in the form of a small hybrid earthquake, sulphur dioxide flux or rockfall. The volcano isn't accessible, but there are several good vantage points, and you can visit the Montserrat Volcano Observatory (www.mvo.ms), set up by an international team of vulcanologists.

Although much of the ocean surrounding the southern part of the island is still off-limits, what is left of Montserrat's diving is legendary. Best of all, it's been left in near pristine condition because the volcano virtually wiped out tourism.

In July 2005 Monserrat's new airport (replacing the one destroyed by the eruption) opened, and there are now flights from Antigua and St Maarten. You can also take the one-hour Montserrat Ferry from St John's Bay in Antigua.

www.visitmontserrat.com.

Not only is it Nepal's longest and largest river, the Karnali runs through some of the country's most beautiful scenery.

↗ DO: **RAFT THE KARNALI RIVER**

COUNTRY Nepal **TYPE OF ACTIVITY** White-water rafting
FITNESS/EXPERTISE LEVEL Not required.
WHY NOW? It's high-water time, making the river significantly more challenging.
DESCRIPTION The Karnali is Nepal's longest and largest river, and a rafting trip here combines a short trek with some of the prettiest canyons and jungle scenery in Nepal. Most experienced river runners find it one of the best all-round river trips they've ever done. In high water, which you'll find now, the Karnali is a serious commitment, combining huge, though fairly straightforward, rapids with a remote location.

The trip starts with a long, but interesting, bus ride to the remote far west of Nepal. From the hill town of Surkhet a lovely two-day trek brings you to Sauli, from where it is a two-hour walk to the Karnali River. Once you start on the Karnali it's 180km to the next road access at Chisopani, on the northern border of the Royal Bardia National Park.

The river section takes about seven days, allowing plenty of time to explore some of the side canyons and waterfalls that feed into the river valley. Well-run trips also include a layover day, where the expedition stays at the same camp site for two nights. The combination of long bus rides and trekking puts some people off, but it's well worth the extra effort. You can also finish your river run with a visit to the Royal Bardia National Park for an unbeatable combination.

Even if you can't make it to the Karnali River during the high flows (September to March), it's probably the only Nepali river that offers continually challenging white water at all times of the year.

↗ DO: SKI AT CHACALTAYA

COUNTRY Bolivia **TYPE OF ACTIVITY** Skiing
FITNESS/EXPERTISE LEVEL Ski bumblers to ski bombs.
WHY NOW? It's a short ski season in Bolivia, so grab it while it's here.
DESCRIPTION The world's highest developed ski area (the term 'developed' is used loosely) is also the closest ski field to the equator. It sits atop a dying glacier on the slopes of 5395m-high Cerro Chacaltaya, 35km north of the Bolivian capital, La Paz. The steep, 700m ski piste runs from just 75m below the summit of the mountain, down to about 4900m. There is no 'bunny hill', but beginners who can cope with bumps can have a good time. The major problem is the lift, with real beginners often spending the entire day at the bottom of the hill because they can't come to grips with the utterly confounding cable tow. The ski season is from February to April.

↗ DO: VIEW LOGGERHEAD TURTLES AT MON REPOS

COUNTRY Australia **TYPE OF ACTIVITY** Wildlife watching
FITNESS/EXPERTISE LEVEL Not required.
WHY NOW? To witness hatching turtles scurry for the ocean.
DESCRIPTION The lovely Queensland beach of Mon Repos, near Bundaberg, is Australia's most accessible mainland turtle rookery and one of only two nesting sites in the South Pacific for the endangered loggerhead turtle. Every year between November and February, large numbers of loggerhead and occasional green and flatback turtles drag themselves up the beach to lay their eggs. The time to be here is when they hatch – mid-January to March – to watch the young turtles emerge and begin their often ill-fated dash for the ocean. During the laying and hatching seasons, access to the beach is controlled by staff from the Environment Protection Agency information centre, who allow visitors to see the turtles in action between 7pm and 6am. www.epa.qld.gov.au

↗ DO: TREK IN THE RWENZORI MOUNTAINS

COUNTRY Uganda **TYPE OF ACTIVITY** Trekking
FITNESS/EXPERTISE LEVEL High level of fitness required.
WHY NOW? The best trekking is in the dry season from November to March. **DESCRIPTION** Straddling the border of Uganda and the Democratic Republic of the Congo, the Rwenzori Mountains (often called the Mountains of the Moon) contain six main massifs, culminating in Margherita Peak on Mt Stanley (5109m), the third-highest point in Africa. If you want your wilderness easy this is not the place, for the paths are narrow and you must push through dense bush and bamboo forest, and wade through deep bogs. To reach the three main peaks requires technical skills and the use of ice axe, rope and crampons. The highest point normally reached by trekkers is Elena Hut (4540m), at the snout of Elena Glacier, where the technical routes up Mt Stanley begin. It's also possible for trekkers to cross two major cols, the Scott-Elliot Pass (4370m) and the Freshfield Pass (4280m). The main access town for treks is Kasese, about a 500km drive west from the capital, Kampala. www.uwa.or.ug/rwenzori.html

The high altitude means most people can manage only a couple of runs before they're gasping for oxygen.

Despite being named for their large heads, newly hatched loggerheads are just 5cm long.

Ultimate Florida Challenge
www.watertribe.com/UltimateFlorida/
UltimateFloridaOverview.aspx
Circumnavigate peninsular Florida – about 1900km – by kayak, canoe or small boat, taking up to 29 days.

Everglades Challenge
www.watertribe.com
Paddle or sail 500km of Florida water between Fort Desoto and Key Largo; nine-day limit.

Bergson Winter Challenge
www.adventurerace.pl
Trek, ski or mountain bike 400km in five days in Poland.

High Peak Marathon
www.shef.ac.uk/~hpc/hpm
A 67km overnight mountain run (or 'bog trot') along the Derwent Watershed near Sheffield, England.

week
.01

www.yearofadventures.com/march

Orang-utans – the old men of the forest – spend most of their time hauling their 80kg bodies from tree to tree.

March

week

↙ .02

www.yearofadventures.com/march

↙ GO: SABAH, MALAYSIA

WHY NOW? IN MARCH, YOU WILL FIND HAWKSBILLS LAYING EGGS ON PULAU GULISAN

On evocative Borneo, in the semi-autonomous Malaysian state of Sabah, rises the highest mountain between the Himalayas and New Guinea. The good news is that Mt Kinabalu (4095m) is one of the easiest climbs among the world's high peaks, and atop its summit you may even be greeted by an international view – on a clear day you can see the Philippines from the summit. Clear days are rare, however, and dawn on the summit is often an all-too-brief glimpse across Borneo before the clouds roll in along the mountainous spine.

Climbing Mt Kinabalu is typically a two-day exercise. Most people climb as far as Laban Rata or the nearby huts on the first day, then climb to the summit at dawn and return to park headquarters on the next day. A climbing permit and insurance are compulsory for any ascent, and guides are also mandatory for all summit attempts. March and April are the driest

↗ DO: 100KM DEL SAHARA

COUNTRY Tunisia **TYPE OF ACTIVITY** Endurance running **FITNESS/EXPERTISE LEVEL** Superior fitness required. **WHY NOW?** To race through the world's largest desert. **DESCRIPTION** Spend four days running 119km through the Sahara on a course where, if you have the energy to look up from your shuffling feet, you'll discover some of the desert's finest scenery. Beginning in the hill village of Chenini, you run three legs of the race, including a 7km night run, on the first two days, followed by a marathon-length run the following day. On the final day you'll run 28km into the oasis of Ksar Ghilane, an amazing spot surrounded by dunes and sublime desert scenery – many of the scenes from *The English Patient* were filmed here. A more leisurely approach to the 100km del Sahara is available to walkers – you set out an hour before the runners each day and can be picked up by the accompanying 4WDs at any time you've had enough. www.100kmdelsahara.com

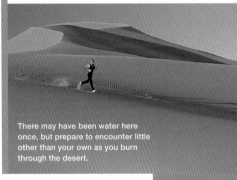

There may have been water here once, but prepare to encounter little other than your own as you burn through the desert.

times on the mountain and offer the best climbing opportunities.

Beyond the mountain, Sabah is noted for other incredible natural features. There are beautiful coral reefs to explore, and birds, animals, trees and plants to seek out. Foremost among these is the amazing rafflesia, the world's largest flower, up to 1m in diameter. A parasitic plant, you will see no roots or leaves, just the blossom…if you're lucky. It only blooms infrequently and randomly, and lasts just a few days. One of the best places to try your floral luck is the Tambunan Rafflesia Reserve, south of the Sabah capital, Kota Kinabalu. Staff at the information centre can fill you in on the latest sightings.

More reliable are Sabah's critters. Marvel at how cute unruly red hair can be at the Sepilok Orang-Utan Rehabilitation Centre, one of just four orang-utan sanctuaries in the world, or head out to the three small islands that comprise Turtle Islands National Park. Although their numbers have fallen off, two species of marine turtle – green and hawksbill – come ashore here to lay their eggs at certain times of the year. In March you will find hawksbills laying eggs on Pulau Gulisan.

o1 o2
o3 o4

The Tongariro Crossing is called 'New Zealand's finest day walk' so often it's almost an honorific.

↗ DO: TRAMP THE TONGARIRO CROSSING

COUNTRY New Zealand **TYPE OF ACTIVITY** Hiking

FITNESS/EXPERTISE LEVEL Moderate fitness required.

WHY NOW? The traditional holidays are over; you'll appreciate the quieter trail.

DESCRIPTION The Tongariro Crossing is so often called New Zealand's finest day walk that it's almost an honorific. Regularly, it's also been called the world's finest day walk.

Like a coffee-table book on vulcanism, the Tongariro Crossing, in World Heritage–listed Tongariro National Park (New Zealand's oldest national park), passes between two of the planet's most active volcanoes – Mts Tongariro and Ngauruhoe. On display, like shelf items, are dazzling lakes, belching fumaroles, lava bombs and the full spectrum of sulphuric colours. Steam fizzes from the barren earth and the perfectly conical shape of Ngauruhoe is a constant companion.

The track passes through vegetation zones ranging from alpine scrub and tussock, to higher altitudes without vegetation, to lush podocarp forest as you descend from Ketetahi Hut towards the end of the track.

Worthwhile side trips from the main track include ascents to the summits of Mts Ngauruhoe and Tongariro. Ngauruhoe can be ascended most easily from the Mangatepopo Saddle, near the beginning of the track, after the first steep climb. The summit of Tongariro is reached along a poled route from Red Crater.

The popularity of the crossing means that shuttle buses run from the town of Turangi, delivering you to the start of the walk at the Mangatepopo car park and picking you up in the evening below Ketetahi Hut. If the crossing just whets your volcanic appetite, consider continuing along the Tongariro Northern Circuit, one of New Zealand's nine listed 'Great Walks', circumnavigating Ngauruhoe and passing through the lunar landscape of New Zealand's only so-called desert. Allow four days to complete the circuit. www.doc.govt.nz/Explore

↗ DO: **SAFARI AT YALA WEST NATIONAL PARK**

COUNTRY Sri Lanka **TYPE OF ACTIVITY** Wildlife watching
FITNESS/EXPERTISE LEVEL Not required.
WHY NOW? Best time of year to see leopards and elephants.
DESCRIPTION On Sri Lanka's southeast coast, Yala West (Ruhuna) National
Park is around 1270 sq km of scrub, plains, brackish lagoons and rocky
outcrops. Lurking within the park is one of the world's densest leopard
populations – the most reliable time to see the big cats is from February
to about June, when water levels are low. For good measure, this is also
the time you're most likely to see elephants in Yala West. Most people
use a tour company or safari operator to get into the park, and you won't
have to go far to find somebody willing to take you; the coastal town of
Tissamaharama is flush with guides and drivers. There are six bungalows
and two camp sites in the park if you want the complete experience;
these can be booked through the Department of Wildlife Conservation in
Colombo.

↗ DO: **SNOWMOBILE THE MOOSEHEAD TRAIL**

COUNTRY USA **TYPE OF ACTIVITY** Snowmobiling
FITNESS/EXPERTISE LEVEL Basic snowmobiling skills required.
WHY NOW? To be mobile you'll need snow; the most reliable conditions
are from January to mid-March. **DESCRIPTION** In the rural far north of
New England, snowmobile trail systems wind throughout the woods
(much on private land and usually with the owner's blessing). Most state
parks are open for cruising and local clubs are sprinkled everywhere.
Maine's Interconnecting Trail System alone contains almost 20,000km
of trails, so it's no wonder that this state is also home to snowmobiling
heaven: Moosehead Lake. There are a number of trails around Moosehead
Lake (you can even snowmobile to a wrecked B-52 bomber) but the
standout ride is the Mooshead Trail, a 267km track that circumnavigates
the lake. If you have petrol for blood, you can tear around the trail in a day,
but you can also break it with overnight stops in the towns of Greenville,
Kokadjo, NE Carry, Seboomook, Pittston Farm and Rockwood.

↗ DO: **RIVER-TUBE IN BELIZE**

COUNTRY Belize **TYPE OF ACTIVITY** River-tubing
FITNESS/EXPERTISE LEVEL Not required.
WHY NOW? Tubing is best in the dry season (February to April).
DESCRIPTION River-tubing – sitting in an inflated inner-tube and floating or
paddling along a river – is the latest rage in Belize, blessed as the country
is with many fairly gentle and not-too-cold watercourses working their way
through gorgeous scenery. You go downstream most of the time and the
only technique that needs to be learnt is to avoid getting beached, eddied
or snagged on rocks while continuing to face in roughly the right direction!
The Mopan River near San Ignacio is a popular tubing river, but the mother
of Belizean tubing adventures is the float in and out of a sequence of
caves on the Caves Branch River, near the capital Belmopan. People come
on day trips from all over Belize for this.

Down and dirty, buffalo-style –
a sure way to beat the heat.

Keep to your right – the trail
is open to all and road rage is
best avoided.

Six Foot Track Marathon
www.coolrunning.com.au/sixfoot
A 45km foot race along a popular
bushwalking trail through the Blue
Mountains near Sydney.

Cape Argus Cycle Tour
www.cycletour.co.za
Join around 30,000 cyclists riding 110km
around Cape Town's Table Mountain.

La Ruta Maya Belize River Challenge
www.larutamayabelize.com
Paddle 274km in four days between San
Ignacio and Belize City.

ARC Winter Adventure Race
www.adventureracingcanada.com/winter
Multisport race with an icy twist;
snowshoe, ski and mountain bike
for up to six hours.

week
.02

www.yearofadventures.com/march

March

↙ GO: LA MOSQUITIA, HONDURAS

week

↙ .03

www.yearofadventures.com/march

WHY NOW? THE BEST TIME FOR SEEING BIRDS IS NOW, WHEN MANY MIGRATORY SPECIES ARE HERE

La Mosquitia – the Mosquito Coast – covers the entire northeast portion of Honduras. It has few roads and inhabitants, and a pristine natural beauty that's awe-inspiring. Manatees and other wildlife live in the eastern lagoons. Monkeys visit the forested areas along the rivers in the dawn, and there is abundant birdlife, including toucans, macaws, parrots, egrets and herons. Those who go deep into the jungle may even spot a jaguar, and crocodiles can be seen in many of the waters. As the name may suggest, mosquitoes and sand flies are even more abundant.

La Mosquitia is a genuinely remote place, of the sort that exists in very few places in Latin America and the world. At its core is the Río Plátano Biosphere Reserve, one of the most magnificent nature reserves in Central America. A World Heritage site, established jointly in 1980 by Honduras and the United Nations, it is home to abundant bird, mammal

Have a true jungle experience – La Mosquitia is one of the world's genuinely remote and wild places.

↗ DO: CAVE AT GUNUNG MULU NATIONAL PARK

COUNTRY Malaysia **TYPE OF ACTIVITY** Caving **FITNESS/EXPERTISE LEVEL** Fear of the dark a hindrance. **WHY NOW?** It's the driest month of the year, making it only seriously damp in Sarawak. **DESCRIPTION** Gunung Mulu is the largest national park in the Borneo state of Sarawak, containing abutting mountain ranges, one composed of sandstone and the other of limestone. Beneath the limestone range is a network of underground passages, stretching around 51km. A few years ago cave explorers discovered the largest chamber in the world in Gunung Mulu – the Sarawak Chamber – reputed to be the size of 16 football fields. The park's show caves are Deer, Lang, Clearwater and Wind Caves. Experienced cavers can arrange access to a few other caves, while it's also possible to explore the nooks and crannies of the show caves away from the pedestrian boardwalks. The park offers guides for adventure caving, though it doesn't supply equipment, and it requires at least a day's notice. www.mulupark.com

Some caves are closed to the public because of their fragile nature.

and aquatic life, including a number of exotic and endangered species in the river and surrounding jungle.

Large (5251 sq km) and mostly well preserved, Río Plátano consists of lowland tropical rainforest with remarkable natural, archaeological and cultural resources. Access to the southern zone is through Olancho by road, beyond Dulce Nombre de Culmí; access to the northern zone is by plane from La Ceiba to Palacios and then by motorised canoe to other destinations. The central zone is very remote and seeing it requires long expeditions.

The main jumping-off point for trips into the Mosquitia is Palacios, which has an airport and several accommodation options. Visiting La

Mosquitia is not cheap; prices are fixed at relatively high levels and are rarely negotiable.

The best time of year to visit is from November to July.

o1 o2

o3 o4

The ultimate global snapshot – get a new sense of perspective on the lonely planet.

↗ DO: BLAST OFF INTO SPACE

COUNTRY Russia **TYPE OF ACTIVITY** Space tourism
FITNESS/EXPERTISE LEVEL Large wallet required.
WHY NOW? Hit space in the month named after Mars.
DESCRIPTION Ever fancied flying into space, or at twice the speed of sound? In Russia, it can be arranged at a price. In April 2001, American billionaire Dennis Tito made history as the first paying customer of the Russian Space Agency, forking out a cool US$20 million to take a shot at space travel. After several months of training at Star City, Zvezdny Gorodok (30km from Moscow), Tito joined cosmonauts on board a Russian Soyuz spacecraft to pay a week-long visit to the International Space Station. Tito's trip, initially opposed by NASA, was considered a success and in April 2002 another millionaire, South African Mark Shuttleworth, followed in Tito's space boots.

The same journey can still be made, orbiting the earth around 120 times, and at the same price – can't be fairer than that – but there's also now the option of a shorter space trip that'll make significantly less impact on your hulking bank account. Backed by four days of intensive training, you can be blasted 100km above the earth to the point at which space begins. The rocket engines are shut down, and for five minutes you experience the sensation of weightlessness and a view that really will be out of this world. All up, you'll be off the ground for about an hour – less time than on a Moscow–St Petersburg flight.

The price for this space trip is US$102,000, which isn't so bad when you consider that it includes a lapel pin and travel bag. www.spaceadventures.com

o1 o2

o3 o4

↗ DO: VIEW THE AURORA BOREALIS

REGIONS Greenland, Scandinavia, Russia, USA, Canada
TYPE OF ACTIVITY Natural phenomena
FITNESS/EXPERTISE LEVEL Not required.
WHY NOW? Viewing of the Northern Lights is best around the spring equinox. **DESCRIPTION** Watch the northern sky turn into a Pollock canvas as the heavenly phenomenon of the Aurora Borealis (Northern Lights), wafts across the prolonged night sky. The lights form from solar particles thrown out by explosions on the sun; nearing Earth they're drawn to the magnetic poles, colliding with atmospheric gases to emit photons (light particles), of myriad shapes and colours. Often, they can look like celestial waterfalls. Viewing of the Northern Lights is best in the so-called auroral zone, which runs close to the Arctic Circle. www.northern-lights.no

↗ DO: CLIMB FANSIPAN

COUNTRY Vietnam **TYPE OF ACTIVITY** Hiking
FITNESS/EXPERTISE LEVEL Moderate fitness required.
WHY NOW? It's the driest month around the mountain. **DESCRIPTION** On the infrequent occasions it's not obscured by cloud, Vietnam's highest peak (3143m) towers above the northern hill station of Sapa. Technical skills are not required to reach Fansipan's summit, although a substantial amount of endurance, as well as proper equipment and a guide are required. The terrain is rough and adverse weather is frequent. Despite the short distance (19km) the round-trip hike to the summit will take around three to four days. After the first morning you won't see any villages; just the forest, striking mountain vistas and perhaps some local wildlife such as monkeys, mountain goats and birds. There are no mountain huts or other facilities along the way, so you'll need to be self-sufficient.

↗ DO: RESERVA FAUNÍSTICA PENÍNSULA VALDÉS

COUNTRY Argentina **TYPE OF ACTIVITY** Wildlife watching
FITNESS/EXPERTISE LEVEL Not required.
WHY NOW? To feast your eyes on an orca feast. **DESCRIPTION** One of South America's finest wildlife reserves, the Península Valdés is home to sea lions, elephant seals, llama-like guanacos, flightless rheas, Magellanic penguins and other seabirds. For most people, the biggest attraction – literally and figuratively – on the World Heritage–listed peninsula is the southern right whale, which comes to breed between June and mid-December. But if you want a true spectacle of the sea, now is the time to visit. From mid-February through mid-April, orcas come to the peninsula's northern tip, Punta Norte, to feast on unsuspecting colonies of sea lions... the spectacular and famous footage from the *Trials of Life* documentary, in which orcas beached themselves to get at sea lions, was filmed here. Chances are that you won't see a high-tide attack in all its gory glory, but the grace of the orcas in the ocean is reason enough to journey to this Patagonian peninsula. www.enpeninsulavaldes.com (in Spanish)

Scandinavians in times past dubbed the aurora *sillblixt* (herring flash), because it looked to them like a great swarm of herrings.

You're almost guaranteed to have Fansipan to yourself – few travellers make the trek.

Addo Elephant 100/50 Miler
www.extrememarathons.com
Dodge Addo Elephant National Park's 300 elephants as you run 160km or 80km.

Birkebeinerrennet
www.birkebeiner.no
A 54km Norwegian ski marathon from Rena to Lillehammer.

Goldrush
www.goldrush.co.nz
A 375km multisport event along the old gold trails of New Zealand's South Island.

Thailand Temple Run
www.thailand-temple-run.com
Run a marathon between Buddhist temples southwest of Bangkok.

week .03

www.yearofadventures.com/march

Snorkelling around the Galápagos means sharing the water with the marine iguana, which dives to feed on algae.

March

week

↙ .04

www.yearofadventures.com/march

↙ GO: GALÁPAGOS ISLANDS, ECUADOR

WHY NOW? IN MARCH THE SEA IS WARM, TURTLES ARE NESTING AND THERE'LL BE SEA-LION PUPS CRAWLING AROUND THE SHORES

Like perhaps no other place on earth, the Galápagos Islands guarantee close encounters of the wildlife kind – above and below the sea. This remote, barren archipelago was known to early explorers as Las Islas Encantadas – the Enchanted Isles – and none of its enchantment has been lost down the centuries. Visitors continue to fall under the islands' spell as they step over dozing sea lions to come face-to-face with abundant and tame birdlife and lumbering giant tortoises.

The bird-species tally in the Galápagos stands at about 140, including 28 endemic species. Two seabirds stand out: the waved albatross – the world's only tropical albatross species – and the flightless cormorant, which lost the power of flight in the absence of land-based predators.

The only land mammals that occur naturally on the islands are bats and native rats. Large marine mammals, however, are common and

The islands were actually named after the giant tortoise, but other animals have taken the name too – such as this Galapagos Hawk.

↗ DO: COCKSCOMB BASIN WILDLIFE SANCTUARY

COUNTRY Belize **TYPE OF ACTIVITY** Wildlife watching **FITNESS/EXPERTISE LEVEL** Not required. **WHY NOW?** Drying waterholes are concentrating the jaguar population into smaller areas. **DESCRIPTION** As southern Belize's waterholes dry up, you could be one of the handful of visitors each year who spot a jaguar in the world's only dedicated jaguar reserve. Cockscomb has a number of walking trails, ranging from very accessible short walks near the park headquarters to a four-day hike to Victoria Peak (1120m), Belize's second-highest point. But if it's wildlife you want, you needn't venture far from park headquarters. More than 300 bird species have been recorded here, while tame grey foxes hang around after dark at the rubbish bins behind the office. Nine-banded armadillos and striped hog-nosed skunks also sometimes turn up at the bins. Night also holds the best, if rare, chance for a cat sighting; jaguars, ocelots and pumas readily walk along the entrance road late at night. www.belizeaudubon.org/html/parks/cbws.htm

Jaguars are exceptionally elusive; only a handful of visitors a year actually see one.

abundant. Sea lions and fur seals thrive in the rich waters of the Humboldt Current and visitors are almost guaranteed close interactions. While cruising between islands keep an eye out for dolphins and whales.

Reptiles are the islands' pin-up inhabitants. The giant tortoise has a lower shell up to 1.5m long, can weight 270kg and plods around the islands of Santa Cruz, Isabela and San Cristóbal. The land iguana has skin as rough as a Florida retiree, but despite its fearsome appearance is a harmless vegetarian. The marine iguana is the world's only truly marine lizard and lives only in the Galápagos. It's found on every island and you'll see many at close range; early morning is the best time to see them on land.

The most feasible way to visit the islands is on a boat tour – day trips operate out of the town of Puerto Ayora, but most visitors go on longer tours and sleep aboard overnight.

The Galápagos can be inviting at any time of year, but in March you'll be at the tail end of the warmest (and wettest) season.

o1 o2
o3 **o4**

A quick climb before lunch? With a little training, what takes mere mortals a few days can be done in seven or eight hours!

↗ DO: CLIMB EL CAPITAN'S NOSE

COUNTRY USA **TYPE OF ACTIVITY** Rock climbing
FITNESS/EXPERTISE LEVEL Rock gods only.
WHY NOW? Spring and autumn are the best times to climb on El Cap.
DESCRIPTION The most famous route on the most famous bit of climbing rock in the world, El Capitan's Nose is where big-wall climbing was born. Guarding the entrance to the sublime Yosemite Valley, El Capitan is an imposing granite monolith rising 1000m above the Merced River. It's a rock to which most climbers can only aspire.

The first ascent of the Nose, an epochal climbing moment, was made in 1958 (one year after the first climb on nearby Half Dome) and took the combined efforts of 45 days of climbing. Most climbers now take five days to make the 31-pitch ascent, bivvying each night and hauling food up the rock with them. The elite scale it in a single day.

A combination of aid and free climbing, the Nose is not regarded as being technically difficult but it is long and more exposed than Pamela Anderson, and great numbers of climbers who set out from the Southeast Buttress fail to complete the route. That doesn't deter those with rock dreams of conquering this route; the Nose can be so 'blocked' with climbers there's often a two-day wait at the base.

For the complete El Cap experience, base yourself at Camp 4 in the Yosemite Valley. This crowded, walk-in site is as much a part of rock folklore as El Cap itself, and is now listed on the National Register of Historic Places. There's little to it but dusty clearings and bear food lockers but no self-respecting climber would be seen sleeping anywhere else in the valley. Camp 4 even comes with a built-in alarm – the sound of shotguns as rangers shoot noisemakers in attempts to chase away curious bears. www.nps.gov/yose

↗ DO: DOG-SLED IN GREENLAND

COUNTRY Greenland **TYPE OF ACTIVITY** Dog-sledding
FITNESS/EXPERTISE LEVEL Not required.
WHY NOW? Sledding high season is March to May. **DESCRIPTION** During the eight or nine months of continuous snow and frozen seas in Arctic and east Greenland, dog sled is the most common method of getting around. For visitors with money to spend, it's exciting to do a 'winter' tour. Popular dog-sledding venues include Ammassalik, Uummannaq, Ilulissat, Sisimiut and Qasigianguit. Most tours are arranged by the hotels in the respective towns, but you can also make arrangements directly with the drivers. Dog-sled trips range from one-day samplers to two-week expeditions, and some include accommodation in villages or hunting camps along the way. Greenlandic sled dogs bear little resemblance to the drippy-tongued, tail-wagging pooches most visitors probably associate with the breed. Most dogs seem only a generation or two removed from wolves and their reputation for snarling, howling and a generally ill-tempered demeanour should be taken seriously. Trying to pat adult dogs is courting disaster.

↗ DO: PARAGLIDE IN WESTERN CAPE

COUNTRY South Africa **TYPE OF ACTIVITY** Paragliding
FITNESS/EXPERTISE LEVEL From tandem tag-alongs to top guns.
WHY NOW? The strongest thermals are from November to April; March and April provide the best conditions for beginners to take a leap from Table Mountain. **DESCRIPTION** South Africa is one of the world's top paragliding destinations. For experienced pilots, airspace restrictions are minimal and the potential for long-distance, cross-country flying is tremendous. Your own transport is essential to escape the strong winds in Cape Town and reach the best sheltered sites in Porterville (a ridge site), Hermanus (a coastal site) and at Sir Lowry's Pass (a ridge site). When conditions permit, it's also possible to fly from Table Mountain, Lion's Head and Signal Hill and land on the beach at Clifton or Camps Bay. Soaring along the Twelve Apostles as the tablecloth cloud forms around you is a near-biblical experience. Mornings typically offer the best conditions for beginners. The South African Hang Gliding and Paragliding Association (www.paragliding.co.za) can provide names of operators, and plenty of schools offer courses for beginners.

↗ DO: HIKE THE ISRAEL NATIONAL TRAIL

COUNTRY Israel **TYPE OF ACTIVITY** Hiking
FITNESS/EXPERTISE LEVEL Good fitness and endurance required.
WHY NOW? Hit the desert before summer does. **DESCRIPTION** Somebody you know has beaten you to all the great trekking routes, but surely not the Israel National Trail. Rambling for 900km through Israel's least-populated and most scenic areas, from Tel Dan in the north to Taba in the south, it's a remarkably varied and beautiful route. If you want just a taste of it, head to the Eilat Mountains. From the waterfall at Ein Netafim, less than 1km off the main road, you can follow the trail to the spectacular Shehoret Canyon, 15km away. Near the mouth of Shehoret Canyon lie the impressive Amram Pillars, where there's an official camp site (no water). An excellent six- to seven-hour hike at the southern end of the trail will take you through the spectacular Nakhal Gishron gorge to the Egyptian border.

The Greenlandic sled dog is an all-weather friend, handling temperatures as low as -50°C!

You're in control when you take to the sky with a paraglider, so take your time and enjoy the view.

Polaris Challenge
www.polarischallenge.com
Two-day mountain-bike navigation event in southern England; summer and autumn events follow in the year.

Manx Mountain Marathon Challenge
www.manxmountainmarathon.co.uk
A 50km mountain running event with around 2500m of climbing.

Red Rock Rendezvous
www.mgear.com/rr06/index.aspx
Ignore the Vegas slots and head the few kilometres to Red Rock Canyon for a weekend of climbing.

International Rolex Regatta
www.rolexcupregatta.com
Four days of sailing competition in the US Virgin Islands.

week

.04

www.yearofadventures.com/march

A masterpiece of nature – the clay pans and sand dunes of Nambiax.

07 CONTINENTS

For centuries overland travel has been the epitome of adventure, recalling explorations such as Marco Polo's 13th-century journey across the Silk Road. Today, each of the seven continents is still lined with classic overland routes.

Modern overland travel has as its touchstone the so-called Hippy Trail, the great '60s and '70s overland exodus from London to Kathmandu, usually meandering through Turkey, Iran and Afghanistan. Politics and violence have long since cut the hair of the Hippy Trail, though it remains the landmark overland route.

Africa, too, has an overlanding tradition as long as its coastline, none more established than the alliterative Cape to Cairo. Beginning in Cape Town in the south and rumbling north to Cairo (or vice versa), this route easily picks off most of the list of traditional African highlights: Sossusvlei,

Etosha, Okavango Delta, Chobe, Victoria Falls, Lake Malawi, Serengeti, Kilimanjaro, Zanzibar, Aswan, Luxor and the pyramids of Giza. Most people who set out on this journey do so in the back of an overland truck. Others customise 4WDs in preparation for the rigours. And if you really want to personalise the trip, you can cycle the 11,900km route in the Tour d'Afrique (p19, January Week 3).

In North America road trips are embodied by Route 66. Stretching from Chicago to Los Angeles, Route 66 was a road as classic as the vehicles that rolled their whitewall tyres along its 4000km length. Today, in a victory of speed over sentiment, the road has all but disappeared beneath five replacement interstate highways, though it remains a cherished overland route for those who can piece together its shards.

Cyclists have shaped their own North American overland tradition by turning the US west coast into one of the great touring routes, trundling from Vancouver or Seattle to Los Angeles or San Diego, a 3000km pedal that'll take most bikers around a month.

The ultimate overland journey in the Americas – Alaska to Patagonia, along the Pan-American Hwy – is still elusive but dream-worthy. As North America thins to nothing in the Darién Gap (p62, April Week 2), the road stops at Yaviza, 88km short of the Colombian border. Travel through this transport hole is only possible on boat or foot and is extremely risky.

The only option to motorists is to somehow get to the Caribbean Sea port town of Puerto Obaldía (best done by boat), check in with the police, then boat-hop to Turbo, San Juan or Cartagena, where you can hit the road again. After the long drive along the foot of the mountains in western Colombia, you then bisect Ecuador – crossing the equator – then travel through Peru and, finally, Chile. Reach the strangely Nordic-style town of Puerto Montt, and you'll have completed perhaps the most extraordinary overland road trip possible.

Australia's open spaces are primed for road journeys. With the right equipment you can battle the bumps to Cape York, or across the Canning Stock Route (p125, August Week 1). The road that embodies overland travel here, however, is the Eyre Hwy across the Nullarbor. Although it only touches the edge of the vast treeless plain (nullarbor is dog Latin for 'no trees'), it has acquired a reputation as one of the most gruelling roads in the world. It's an undeserved title since the road is completely sealed, well serviced by roadhouses and filled with tourist and commercial traffic, but the vastness of the land is still worth experiencing. You can comfortably drive the 1219km between Ceduna and Norseman in three days, but it's also become a sleeper favourite with cyclists – ride from Norseman for the prevailing winds and allow around 10 days.

Even Antarctica has its classic overland route – the trek to the South Pole. Typically, what might be termed the Nippy Trail begins at Hercules Inlet, by Patriot Hills, and crunches through 1100km of ice to the Pole.

Don't go west young man – the 20m bronze Kim Il Sung shows the way.

April

week

.01

www.yearofadventures.com/april

↙ GO:
NORTH KOREA

WHY NOW? APRIL IS A BEAUTIFUL TIME IN KOREA, WITH MILD TEMPERATURES AND FLOWERS BLOOMING EVERYWHERE

A political stalwart if nothing else, North Korea is a land where ancient myths bend to modern political reality, where the mysterious dictator Kim Jong Il is believed to control the weather, and his father Kim Il Sung, dead for a decade, remains head of state.

North Korea is a place frozen in the Cold War. Visitors are escorted at all times outside their hotel by guides, mobile phones and the Internet are against the law and there are just a handful of international flights into the capital, Pyongyang, each week. These zealous measures to keep the country isolated make North Korea a magnet for those seeking a cultural adventure, and while travel here is not easy or cheap, the rewards are many and will instantly make you the most interesting person you know.

Once through all the North Korean red tape, trips here usually run like clockwork. Two guides will accompany you everywhere you go outside the

↗ DO: HIKE THE LYCIAN WAY

COUNTRY Turkey **TYPE OF ACTIVITY** Hiking
FITNESS/EXPERTISE LEVEL Moderate level
of fitness and good endurance required.
WHY NOW? Summer in Lycia is hot, so beat
it to the punch. **DESCRIPTION** The Lycian
Way was Turkey's first long-distance hiking
trail, created in 1999. It's a 509km trail around
the coast and mountains of Lycia, starting
at Fethiye and finishing at Antalya. It gets
progressively more difficult as it winds around
the coast and into the mountain ranges, and
can be trekked in its entirety in about 30 days,
or can be walked in smaller, easier chunks.
Good places for starting out are Ölüdeniz, Kaş,
Adrasan or Olympos. The Lycian Way offers
great views over Turkey's Mediterranean coast
and a variety of flora, and you'll find a few
pensions and hotels along the route in which
to seek some relief from your tent.
www.lycianway.com

There are over 1000 ancient
examples of the tombs the Lycians
are famed for in the region.

hotel, controlling what you see and the spiel you hear
while seeing it. Forward planning is a must – almost
everything you want to see needs to be approved
before your arrival, and ad hoc arrangements make
the guides very nervous and thus less fun to be
around. Being accompanied is non-negotiable, and if
you are not prepared to be controlled throughout the
duration of your stay, North Korea is not a destination
you should consider.

To add some adventure beyond that of simply
visiting the most reclusive member of the 'axis
of evil', plan a trip to Mt Paekdu, the highest peak
in Korea and, according to official sources, the
birthplace of Kim Jong II – in fact, he was probably
born in Khabarovsk, Russia, where his father was in

exile at the time, but the necessity of maintaining
the Kim myth supersedes such niggling facts.

Visit the Demilitarized Zone (DMZ), rolling down
a deserted six-lane highway to Panmunjeom, where
you will face off against US troops across the DMZ in
South Korea.

Visas for North Korea will not be issued to US or
South Korean citizens.

The outrigger canoes of Tokelau are made from *kanava*, a hard, water-resistant timber found on the Atafu atoll. The canoes are known for their open-water stability and safety.

↗ DO: SAIL TO TOKELAU

COUNTRY New Zealand administration **TYPE OF ACTIVITY** Boat travel/sailing
FITNESS/EXPERTISE LEVEL Not required.
WHY NOW? The best months to travel to Tokelau are from April to October, avoiding both cyclones and full cargo ships.
DESCRIPTION The three small atolls of Tokelau lie in a rough line 480km north of their nearest neighbour, Samoa. Just getting here is a major achievement and might not be available to future generations – the low-lying islands have a maximum elevation of only 5m above sea level and it's predicted that, with global warming, they'll be uninhabitable by the end of the 21st century.

Already, Tokelau is one of the most isolated spots on earth and getting here can be difficult. It has no airstrip, and a fortnightly cargo ship from Apia in Samoa is the only way travellers can get to Tokelau without a yacht. In fact, because of the hazards of anchoring, yachting to Tokelau is not much easier!

The MV *Tokelau* sails from Apia fortnightly, with the trip to Fakaofo (the closest atoll to Samoa) taking about 28 hours. There is no harbour in any of the atolls. The ship waits offshore while passengers and cargo are transferred via small boats and dinghies – a hair-raising experience if seas are heavy.

For yachties, one of the first dilemmas in finding the atolls is their low elevation, which makes them difficult visual targets. There are no harbours and anchoring offshore is difficult, especially in an offshore wind. The sea floor drops off sharply outside the coral reef and the water is too deep for most anchor chains. There's one anchorage beyond the reefs at each atoll, but leave a crew member aboard in case the anchor doesn't hold. The channels blasted through the coral are shallow and are intended for dinghies only.

01 02
03 04

Just a stone's throw from San Francisco, Marin County is home to some of the last stands of skyscraping coastal redwoods.

Come to grips with El Chorro Gorge which runs for around 4km between two limestone cliffs.

↗ DO: **MOUNTAIN BIKE IN MARIN**

COUNTRY USA **TYPE OF ACTIVITY** Mountain biking
FITNESS/EXPERTISE LEVEL Something for all levels.
WHY NOW? Spring provides ideal conditions.
DESCRIPTION Mountain biking is said to have had its beginnings in the 1970s in Marin County, out of San Francisco, where a group of riders would charge off Pine Mountain in races along Repack Rd. Today, it's a pursuit of almost global reach, even gaining admission to the Olympic Games in 1996, but if you're a sentimentalist, or just partial to a decent bit of riding, there's still plenty of good mountain biking in ancestral Marin. The county has more than 300km of trails and fire roads – not all open to cyclists – offering hair-parting descents or off-road tours. Two of the legendary rides involve circuits of Pine Mountain (where you can pay homage to Repack Rd) and Mt Tamalpais. www.marintrails.com/biking

↗ DO: **CLIMB EL CHORRO**

COUNTRY Spain **TYPE OF ACTIVITY** Rock climbing **FITNESS/EXPERTISE LEVEL** A variety of grades, but more on offer for experienced climbers.
WHY NOW? Enjoy the rock before summer turns it to hot coals.
DESCRIPTION Mountainous Andalucía is full of crags, walls and slabs that invite *escalada* (climbing), a fast-growing sport here. The sheer walls of El Chorro Gorge, one of several great sites in the north of Málaga province, are the biggest magnet, with more than 600 routes incorporating almost every degree of difficulty. El Chorro presents a great variety of both classical and sport climbing, from slab climbs to towering walls to bolted multipitch routes. The walk-ins can be lengthy but you'll find the crags more than reward the effort. There's accommodation for all budgets in the El Chorro area, and quite a climbers' scene at Bar Isabel at El Chorro train station.

↗ DO: **PARAGLIDE AT MEDELLÍN**

COUNTRY Colombia **TYPE OF ACTIVITY** Paragliding
FITNESS/EXPERTISE LEVEL Not required.
WHY NOW? Medellín claims perfect, unchanging weather year-round, but elsewhere Colombia's dry season is generally December to April.
DESCRIPTION Colombia is one of South America's best places to try paragliding, with the northern city of Medellín emerging as one of the continent's premier destinations – it's also one of the cheapest. It's home to some of the best national glide pilots, and gliding here is more popular than in any other Colombian city, Bogotá included. Thanks to the rugged topography and favourable winds, the city and the region provide good conditions for gliding. Gliding schools in Colombia's second city offer tandem flights with a skilled pilot, or you can settle in for a week-long course that'll set you on the way to becoming a pilot yourself.

Marathon des Sables
www.saharamarathon.co.uk
Six-day, 243km endurance run through the Moroccan Sahara.

Oxfam Trailwalker Melbourne
www.oxfam.org.au/trailwalker/melbourne
Run or walk (or both) through 100km of Australian bush in less than 48 hours.

Elk Mountains Grand Traverse
www.elkmountaintraverse.org
A 64km backcountry ski race between Crested Butte and Aspen, Colorado.

XTERRA Saipan Championship
www.xterraplanet.com/races
Off-road Micronesian triathlon: ocean swim, mountain-bike ride and a trail run.

week
.01

www.yearofadventures.com/april

Swim, not sing, for your supper. The Darién Gap is laced with streams feeding into larger rivers: sources of food for locals, but also one of the challenges of travelling through the region.

April

↙ GO: DARIÉN GAP, PANAMA

week

↙ .02

www.yearofadventures.com/april

WHY NOW? **VISIT NOW AND YOU'LL SNEAK IN BEFORE THE WET SEASON**

Panama's far south is one of the wildest and most ravaged areas in the Americas. It's home to the country's most spectacular national park, and the point at which North America clips onto South America. Even the Pan-American Hwy, which runs from Alaska to the south of Chile, hasn't been able to fight a way through here, earning the area the name of the Darién Gap.

Most of the region falls within Parque Nacional Darién – 5760 sq km containing sandy beaches, rocky coasts, mangrove swamps, freshwater marshes and four mountain ranges covered with double- and triple-canopy jungle. The bird-watching here is among the world's finest – there are places where you can see four species of macaw fly by with outstanding frequency. The harpy eagle, the world's most powerful bird of prey, resides here, as do giant anteaters, jaguars, ocelots, monkeys, Baird's

↗ DO: NORTH POLE MARATHON

REGION The Arctic
TYPE OF ACTIVITY Ice running
FITNESS/EXPERTISE LEVEL Superior fitness (and partiality to cold) required.
WHY NOW? To run to the geographic North Pole. **DESCRIPTION** Dubbed the 'world's coolest marathon', this is almost certainly also the only marathon run on water. Competitors in this unique event fly out of Svalbard, Norway, to a temporary camp near the North Pole. The following day they run 42km across the frozen Arctic Ocean, which may be just a couple of metres below – the course of the race is chosen a day ahead to avoid breaks in the ice. Soft conditions can force runners into snowshoes, while temperatures of around -20˚C to -30˚C can be expected. The winning time in the 2004 race was less than four hours by former Everest summiteer Sean Burch (with explorer Sir Ranulph Fiennes in second place). www.npmarathon.com

Depending on where the ice floats, a runner might travel right across 90°N – the geographic North Pole.

tapirs, white-lipped peccaries, caimans and American crocodiles.

It's an adventurer's dream, offering spectacular opportunities for rainforest exploration by trail or river, and a place where the primeval meets the present, with the scenery appearing much as it did a million years ago. Indians perfected the use of poison-dart guns here and still maintain many of their traditional practices.

The heart of this World Heritage site is the former mining valley of Cana, the most isolated place in Panama. Except for a hike of several days, the only way into the valley is by chartered aircraft.

In Darién you'll also discover the true meaning of the word 'frontier'. Southern sections of the Darién Gap are known to be frequented by Colombian paramilitaries, drug traffickers, guerrillas and bandits. The US State Department warns travellers not to cross an invisible line that extends from Punta Carreto in Kuna Yala to Yaviza and south to Punta Piña. The area from Nazaret to Punusa is like a low-intensity war zone. Cana, however, remains unaffected by the hostilities. Visit now and you'll sneak in before the wet season. You'll also witness the end of the nesting season for the mighty harpy eagle, a powerful predator that'll please any twitcher.

o1 o2
o3 o4

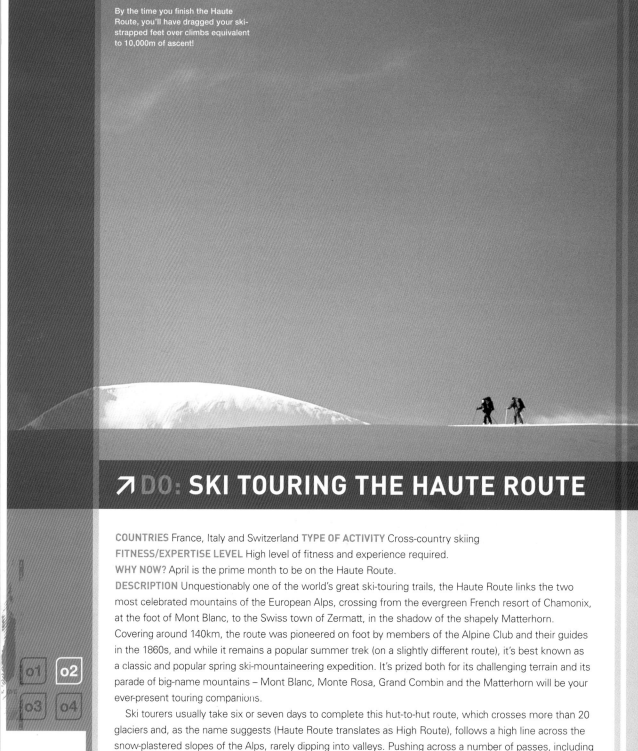

By the time you finish the Haute Route, you'll have dragged your ski-strapped feet over climbs equivalent to 10,000m of ascent!

↗ DO: SKI TOURING THE HAUTE ROUTE

01 02

03 04

COUNTRIES France, Italy and Switzerland **TYPE OF ACTIVITY** Cross-country skiing

FITNESS/EXPERTISE LEVEL High level of fitness and experience required.

WHY NOW? April is the prime month to be on the Haute Route.

DESCRIPTION Unquestionably one of the world's great ski-touring trails, the Haute Route links the two most celebrated mountains of the European Alps, crossing from the evergreen French resort of Chamonix, at the foot of Mont Blanc, to the Swiss town of Zermatt, in the shadow of the shapely Matterhorn. Covering around 140km, the route was pioneered on foot by members of the Alpine Club and their guides in the 1860s, and while it remains a popular summer trek (on a slightly different route), it's best known as a classic and popular spring ski-mountaineering expedition. It's prized both for its challenging terrain and its parade of big-name mountains – Mont Blanc, Monte Rosa, Grand Combin and the Matterhorn will be your ever-present touring companions.

Ski tourers usually take six or seven days to complete this hut-to-hut route, which crosses more than 20 glaciers and, as the name suggests (Haute Route translates as High Route), follows a high line across the snow-plastered slopes of the Alps, rarely dipping into valleys. Pushing across a number of passes, including the spectacular Val d'Arpette, with its views down onto the fractured surface of Glacier du Trient; the route tops out on the summit of Pigne d'Arolla, at around 3800m – high enough to make your head spin from more than the exertion.

All up, you'll drag your ski-strapped feet over climbs totalling around 10,000m, enough to have summited Mt Everest from sea level with Ben Nevis as a warm-down. Skiing days on the Haute Route can be long and difficult, so limber up on less gruelling tours elsewhere before slapping on the skins at Chamonix.

↗ DO: TREE CLIMB IN PEMBERTON

COUNTRY Australia TYPE OF ACTIVITY Tree climbing
FITNESS/EXPERTISE LEVEL A head for heights welcome.
WHY NOW? April is the least windy month around Pemberton; you'll appreciate it when you're 75m up a tree. DESCRIPTION Western Australia's endemic karri tree is one of the giants of the wooden world. Growing to 90m it's the tallest tree in the state and among the tallest in the world. Poking above the canopy of the thick forests of the southwest, eight karri trees were chosen in the first half of the 20th century as fire-lookout trees, with platforms built at their tops and metal spikes hammered into their trunks as ladders. Today, three of the trees have been designated as 'climbing trees', allowing visitors to climb for a windy view over hillsides thick with forest. The most popular of the trees is the Gloucester Tree, just 3km from the milling town of Pemberton, but nearby Dave Evans Bicentennial Tree is the tallest of the climbing trees at 75m. www.pembertontourist.com.au

↗ DO: WALK THE 88 TEMPLE CIRCUIT

COUNTRY Japan TYPE OF ACTIVITY Hiking/pilgrimage
FITNESS/EXPERTISE LEVEL Moderate fitness required.
WHY NOW? It's a long walk and you want to be finished before summer fully kicks in. DESCRIPTION Japan's best-known pilgrimage is the 88 Temple Circuit on the island of Shikoku. Kōbō Daishi, the most revered of Japan's saints, is said to have personally selected the circuit route. Today, most pilgrims travel it by tour bus, but many still walk. Set aside two months if you want to join them over the 1500km route. Some temples are only a few hundred metres apart, but it can be more than 100km between others. Individually, none of the temples is exceptionally interesting; it's the whole circuit that counts. The 88 temples represent the number of evil human passions defined by the Buddhist doctrine, and completing the circuit is said to rid you of these. The route begins in Tokushima and is generally walked clockwise. About half the temples have lodging facilities for pilgrims.

↗ DO: DIVE THE POOR KNIGHTS ISLANDS

COUNTRY New Zealand TYPE OF ACTIVITY Scuba diving FITNESS/ EXPERTISE LEVEL Snorkellers to advanced divers. WHY NOW? Visibility can reach to 50m in autumn. DESCRIPTION Rated by the late Jacques Cousteau as one of the world's 10 best dive sites, the Poor Knights Islands are the remnants of ancient volcanoes. Swept by the East Auckland current, which brings warm waters from the Coral Sea, you'll find fish-filled caves, archways and underwater cliffs that offer spectacular diving against a backdrop of colourful invertebrate life. And with virtually no runoff from the islands, visibility is excellent. The range of depths and dive sites promises something for everyone, including good snorkelling at most sites. Experienced divers will be drawn to Northern Archway, where schools of up to 30 large kingfish sometimes cruise through. Landing on the uninhabited, predator-free islands is prohibited. The tuatara, a reptile that roamed with the dinosaurs, and the giant weta, a fearsome-looking insect, are a couple of the unique species found here. Charter boats to the islands leave from Tutukaka.

On a windy day this tree can sway up to 1.5m. Just don't look down.

The ultimate in takeaway – pilgrims carry food on their journey to Torodo.

Sea Otter Classic
www.seaotterclassic.com
Cycling festival in Monterey, California, with races, recreational rides and a trade show.

Oxfam Trailwalker NZ
www.oxfamtrailwalker.org.nz
Cover 100km on foot near Taupo in less than 48 hours.

Three Peaks Race
www.threepeaks.org.au
Easter event in which you sail halfway around Tasmania and climb Mts Wellington, Freycinet and Strzelecki.

Dead Sea Ultramarathon
www.deadseamarathon.com
A 50km run from Amman to the Dead Sea.

week

.o2

www.yearofadventures.com/april

April

↙ GO: VANUATU

.03

www.yearofadventures.com/april

WHY NOW? THE LAND DIVING TOWERS SHOULD BE FINISHED OR NEARLY FINISHED AND READY FOR ACTION

One of the most remarkable customs you're ever likely to see is the *naghol* (land diving) on the Vanuatu island of Pentecost. Every year in early April, as soon as the first yam crop emerges, the islanders in the south build tall wooden towers in the villages. A full-sized tower is vertical for 16m, then leans backwards. Each tower takes several weeks to erect. The soil in front of the tower is cleared of rocks, then loosened to reduce the chance of injury.

Once completed, and until early June, men and boys dive from these rickety structures with only two springy vines to break their fall, a leap that is said to guarantee a bountiful yam harvest.

Between 20 and 60 males per village will dive. As a diver raises his hands he tells the crowd his most intimate thoughts; the people stop their singing and dancing, and stand quietly – these could be his last words.

Fifty feet and falling – only the men of the tribe take part in this leap of faith. It's an attempt to influence the yam harvest, but also a rite of passage.

↗ DO: VIEW TURTLES ON MASIRAH

COUNTRY Oman **TYPE OF ACTIVITY** Wildlife watching **FITNESS/EXPERTISE LEVEL** Not required. **WHY NOW?** April to June offers the best weather and plenty of turtle spotting.
DESCRIPTION With its rocky interior of palm oases and gorgeous rim of sandy beaches, Masirah is the typical desert island, and is justly fabled as a naturalists' paradise. Flamingos, herons and oyster-catchers patrol the coast by day, and armies of ghost crabs march ashore at night. But it's the island's turtle-nesting sites that have given Masirah its international renown. Four species of turtle frequent the island: hawksbill, olive ridley, green and, most numerous, loggerheads. Thirty thousand loggerheads come ashore each year, making Masirah the world's largest loggerhead-nesting site. The favourite nesting beach is by the old BERS camp. To reach 'Turtle Beach', head towards the island's northwestern tip, looking for tracks emerging from the sea or listening for the swishing of sand while the turtle is digging.

Many thousands come ashore each year to breed at the world's largest loggerhead-nesting site.

Finally the diver claps his hands, crosses his arms and leans forward. The vines abruptly stop his downward rush. Only his hair will touch the soil, to fertilise the yam crop. The crowd roars its appreciation, dancing, stomping and whistling in tribute. If it sounds vaguely familiar, it is; *naghol* was the inspiration for bungy jumping.

South Pentecost has many land-diving sites. Two in the hills behind Bay Homo are mainly for tourists, with jumps each Saturday during the season.

While you won't be allowed to make a land dive, you don't have to leave all the fun to the locals in Vanuatu. The country has several volcanoes, including the world's most accessible (very) active one, Mt Yasur, on Tanna. A night visit is recommended for sound effects and fireworks displays. Walkers can enjoy Ambrym, where the Benbow and Marum volcanoes breathe smoke and ash over an unbelievably desolate landscape.

Vanuatu is a snorkelling and diving paradise. In addition to countless coral reefs, there is terrific wreck diving: Espiritu Santo boasts the world's largest diveable WWII shipwreck: the SS *President Coolidge*.

o1 o2
o3 o4

The air may be thin, your legs may be jelly...but you can always stop for another long look at Everest.

↗ DO: CYCLE THE FRIENDSHIP HIGHWAY

REGION Tibet/Nepal **TYPE OF ACTIVITY** Cycle touring

FITNESS/EXPERTISE LEVEL Moderate fitness and good acclimatisation required.

WHY NOW? To see Mt Everest at its best as you cycle past.

DESCRIPTION See the best of Tibet as you ride between Lhasa and Kathmandu on the Friendship Hwy. This ideal cycling route takes in most of Tibet's main sights, offering superb scenery and (for those leaving from Lhasa) featuring a spectacular roller-coaster ride down from high La Lung-la (5124m) into the Kathmandu Valley. The journey is without doubt one of the most spectacular in the world. At the energy-depleting altitudes of the Tibetan desert plateau, most of which is above 4000m, it might also be one of your slowest rides.

The entire trip is just over 940km (though most people start from Shigatse, Tibet's second-largest city, about 300km west of Lhasa, knocking out the busiest section of the highway) and will take a minimum of two weeks, although to do it justice and include stopovers at Gyantse, Shigatse and Sakya, it's better to allow 20 days.

The Friendship Hwy can be cycled comfortably during several months of the year, but this is the time to ride if you want to see Tibet's star natural feature -- the north face of Mt Everest -- at its clearest. If you've come with a mountain bike, you can detour to Everest Base Camp, turning off the highway at Shegar. From here it's about a two-day ride to Rongphu Monastery, said by some to have the finest of all Everest views. Base camp is just a few kilometres on, and at this time of year you might arrive with the first of the season's mountaineers.

You can vary the return ride from base camp to the highway by taking the road to Tingri.

o1   o2

o3   o4

↗ DO: **CANYON AT WADI MUJIB**

COUNTRY Jordan **TYPE OF ACTIVITY** Canyoning **FITNESS/EXPERTISE LEVEL** Good fitness and swimming skills required. **WHY NOW?** The gorge is open April to October; come before the sun boils your brain. **DESCRIPTION** Stretching from the Desert Hwy to the Dead Sea (over 70km) is the vast and beautiful Wadi Mujib, sometimes called the 'Grand Canyon of Jordan'. There are four main walking trails in Mujib Nature Reserve, but the one through the gorge offers the most adventure. This trail follows the river as it slices through the earth, the cliffs narrowing at times to make it a slot canyon. You'll abseil past waterfalls, and at times you'll be swimming, or submerging to squeeze under rock barriers – after high water levels in 2005, ropes were fastened to the gorge walls beside some of the longer swims. The canyon trail can take up to 12 hours and can only be done with a guide from the Royal Society for the Conservation of Nature. The number of people allowed into the gorge is limited. www.rscn.org.jo

↗ DO: **DIVE BLUE HOLES**

COUNTRY Bahamas **TYPE OF ACTIVITY** Diving **FITNESS/EXPERTISE LEVEL** Novice to advanced divers. **WHY NOW?** Beat the summer hurricanes to the islands. **DESCRIPTION** For enjoyable, enthralling diving, the Bahamas has no peer, due primarily to the unbeatable repertoire of diving adventures it offers. High on the list of wonders are its blue holes, the result of changing sea levels and chemical reactions (the limestone platforms are dissolved by the combination of fresh water and carbon dioxide). Their openings resemble large, deep-blue disks, with many blue holes leading into elaborate cavern systems. Andros Island, a mere 20-minute plane hop from Grand Bahama, has become the epitome of blue-hole diving. Consider the Big Blue Hole, which originated from a collapse of the sea wall. This magical site features an enormous cavern system endowed with huge tunnels, boulders and other massive geological structures. You'll feel as though you're floating in a lunar landscape. At Turtle Cove, on Long Island, you'll find perhaps the world's deepest blue hole leading to its eighth-largest underwater cavern. www.bahamasdiving.com

↗ DO: **CLIMB MT MAYON**

COUNTRY Philippines **TYPE OF ACTIVITY** Hiking **FITNESS/EXPERTISE LEVEL** Moderate fitness required. **WHY NOW?** March and April are the best time to climb; at other times of the year it's unbearably hot and wet. **DESCRIPTION** Volcanic Mt Mayon (2462m) is one of the Philippines' most photographed sights, rising dramatically from the flat southeast Luzon terrain. It's a mesmerising sight; in fact, its name derives from the Bicolano word *magayon*, meaning 'beauty'. It's also considered one of the most dangerous volcanoes in the world, due to its relatively frequent eruptions, including in June 2001, when the lava flow formed the supposed shape of the Virgin Mary and the volcano's once perfectly symmetrical cone was cracked near the top. There are three ways for hikers to reach Mayon's crater: two routes ascend the southeastern slope via Buyuan or Lidong, while the third starts from the Mayon Skyline Hotel on the northwestern side. The southeastern side is considered the safest. Plan on two days to climb this slope.

The Wadi Mujib Gorge enters the Dead Sea at 400m below sea level – considered to be the lowest point on the surface of the earth.

At Turtle Cove, on Long Island, you'll find perhaps the world's deepest blue hole.

Tampa Bay Marathon Swim
www.distancematters.com
A 38km ocean swim across Florida's Tampa Bay.

Devizes to Westminster International Canoe Marathon
www.dwrace.org.uk
Begin paddling on Easter Saturday and stop on Easter Sunday, 200km later.

Flèche Vélocio
www.audax-club-parisien.com (in French)
Easter cycling event, with teams selecting their own 24-hour (360km minimum) route, converging at a finish point in southern France.

Costa Rica: Between Two Continents, Between Two Oceans
www.euforiaexpeditions.com
Four-day, 250km multisport race through 10 of Costa Rica's 12 microclimates.

week **.03**

www.yearofadventures.com/april

Don't rock the boat! In the Pantanal, you never know where the wildlife will pop up next.

April

↙ GO: PANTANAL, BRAZIL

www.yearofadventures.com/april

week

↙ .04

WHY NOW? ONE OF THE AREA'S TWO DRY SEASONS RUNS FROM APRIL TO MAY

The Amazon may attract more fame and glory, but the vast Pantanal wetlands in the centre of South America are a better place to see wildlife. They contain the greatest concentration of fauna in the New World, and while the Amazon's dense foliage hides its animals, the Pantanal's open spaces make the wildlife visible to the most casual observer.

The Pantanal is more than half the size of France – 230,000 sq km – of which most is in Brazil (around 100,000 sq km is in Bolivia and Paraguay). It has few people and no towns. Distances are so great and ground transport is so poor that people get around in small airplanes and motorboats. The only road that runs deep into the Pantanal is the Transpantaneira. This raised dirt road, sectioned by 118 small wooden bridges, was supposed to stretch to the Bolivian border but two-thirds of the intended route has been left incomplete for lack of funds and ecological concerns.

↗ DO: CANYONEER IN PARIA CANYON

COUNTRY USA **TYPE OF ACTIVITY**
Canyoneering/canyoning **FITNESS/
EXPERTISE LEVEL** Canyoneering experience
recommended. **WHY NOW?** Hit the slots in
spring to avoid the prospect of summer or
winter flash floods. **DESCRIPTION** Much of
Southwest USA's most stunning beauty is out
of sight, in serpentine corridors of stone. Some
of these narrow to become slot canyons, and
offer some of the best canyoneering anywhere,
involving technical climbing, swimming across
pools and shooting down waterfalls. Paria
Canyon, on the Arizona–Utah border, is one
of the most beautiful canyons – pick any six
postcards from a southern Utah gift shop, and
two will be from here. Paria's biggest attraction
is Buckskin Gulch, a deep, 19km-long canyon
only 5m wide for most of its length. Wire Pass
and Buckskin are the popular trailheads, and
serious canyoneers can tackle the five-day,
61km trek through to Lees Ferry, Arizona, with
numerous stretches of knee-deep muddy
water, some swims and many obstacles.

With access limited to just 10
people a day, you're sure to
get 'the Wave' to yourself.

April and May form one of the Pantanal's two dry
seasons, which are the best times to visit the World
Heritage–listed wetlands. The area floods in the wet
season from October to March, replenishing the
soil's nutrients, which would otherwise be very poor
due to the excessive drainage. The waters teem
with fish, and the ponds provide excellent niches for
many animals and plants. Enormous flocks of wading
birds gather in rookeries several square kilometres
in area. Later in the dry season, the water recedes,
the lagoons and marshes dry out and fresh grasses
emerge on the savanna. Hawks and alligators
compete for fish in the remaining ponds.

Guides can be arranged in the towns of Cuiabá
(in Mato Grosso), Corumbá or Campo Grande

(Matto Grosso do Sul). There's no obligation to use
a guide, but a good one can enhance your Pantanal
experience by spotting and identifying animal
and bird species, especially rarer animals such as
anteaters, anacondas, otters, iguanas and jaguars. A
guide who's familiar with the area will also know the
location of nests of rare birds.

The only way to go is up at Paklenica, and there are spectacular routes for all grades of climber.

↗ DO: **CLIMB AT PAKLENICA PARK**

o1 o2

o3 **o4**

COUNTRY Croatia **TYPE OF ACTIVITY** Rock climbing

FITNESS/EXPERTISE LEVEL Beginner routes to big-wall epics.

WHY NOW? Spring is the best climbing season, with this week coinciding with the International Meeting of Alpinists.

DESCRIPTION Rising high above the Adriatic Sea, the stark peaks of the Velebit Massif stretch for 145km in a dramatic landscape of rock and sea. Paklenica National Park covers 37 sq km of the range, circling around two deep gorges, Velika Paklenica (Great Paklenica) and Mala Paklenica (Small Paklenica), which scar the mountain range like hatchet marks, with cliffs over 400m high.

This karst landscape makes for one of Europe's premier climbing venues, offering a tremendous variety of routes from beginners' level to borderline suicidal. The firm, occasionally sharp limestone offers graded climbs, including 72 short sports routes and 250 longer routes.

You'll see the beginners' routes at the beginning of the park near Marasovići, with cliffs reaching about 40m, but the best and most advanced climbing is on Anića Kuk, which offers more than 100 routes up to a height of 350m. Nearly all routes are well equipped with spits and pitons, except for the appropriately named Psycho Killer route. The most popular climbs here are Mosoraški (350m), Velebitaški (350m) and Klin (300m).

The best base for exploring the park is Starigrad, the site of the national park office and the town with the most restaurants and accommodation options. It's also near the entrance to Velika Paklenica, which offers the most varied climbs of the two gorges.

Come this week and you'll experience the added excitement of a big-wall speed climbing competition run in conjunction with the International Meeting of Alpinists, held at Paklenica. www.paklenica.hr

↗ DO: STROMBOLI

COUNTRY Italy TYPE OF ACTIVITY Adventure travel
FITNESS/EXPERTISE LEVEL Not required.
WHY NOW? Summers can be as hot as the lava, so come in comfortable spring. DESCRIPTION In prim, proper and polite Western Europe, the Italian island of Stromboli is like the boy who sits belching at the back of the school room. The only European volcano with permanent eruptive activity, Stromboli is part of a chain of seven volcanic islands – the Aeolian Islands – off the north coast of Sicily. Recent eruptions have closed Stromboli's cratered summit to trekkers, but it's still possible to climb 400m to a point beside the remarkable Sciara del Fuoco – a lava trail cannibalising the island – to watch the volcano spit boulders into the Mediterranean Sea. In the evening, hook up with a local fisherman and take to the sea to watch the volcano's natural fireworks display and, if lucky, lava seeping down the Sciara del Fuoco.

↗ DO: WATCH CHIMPANZEES AT GOMBE STREAM

COUNTRY Tanzania TYPE OF ACTIVITY Wildlife watching
FITNESS/EXPERTISE LEVEL Not required.
WHY NOW? The chimps are often easier to find during the rainy season between about February and June. DESCRIPTION With an area of only 52 sq km, Gombe Stream is Tanzania's smallest national park. It's also the site of the longest-running study of any wild animal population in the world. British researcher Jane Goodall arrived in 1960 to begin a study of wild chimpanzees, and her research is now in its fifth decade. Gombe Stream's 150-or-so chimps are accustomed to humans, so you can sometimes get to within 5m of them. Accommodation in the park is a matter of extremes: a run-down hostel, a basic rest house or a $400-a-night luxury tented camp. You can also camp on the beach near the centre of the park, although park staff don't recommend it because of the danger from baboons. Children under seven and anybody with indications of illness are not allowed into the park. If you're really interested in chimpanzees, allow at least two days at Gombe. www.tanzania-web.com/parks/gombe.htm

↗ DO: HIKE THE SOUTH WEST COAST PATH

COUNTRY England TYPE OF ACTIVITY Hiking
FITNESS/EXPERTISE LEVEL Good fitness and endurance required.
WHY NOW? It's a long walk, so get started early in the season.
DESCRIPTION Britain's National Trail system is unequalled. Its 15 long-distance paths cover 4400km, and it's said that wherever you might stand on the island, there's a national trail within 80km. The longest, and arguably best, of the trails is the South West Coast Path, rounding Britain's spectacularly rugged southwest peninsula and crossing through three counties – Devon, Cornwall and Dorset. Walk for seven or eight weeks and you can cover its entire 1014km length. The distance is only half the battle; the peninsula's coast is decidedly hilly and following the path involves a lot of steep descents into valleys where rivers meet the sea, then just as many steep climbs out. Ascents along the route total 27,000m, or about three times the height of Mt Everest. www.southwestcoastpath.com

The naughty schoolboy of European peaks. Trek out to watch Stromboli spit boulders into the sea.

It's been suggested that human and chimp DNA is so similar, we may be in the same genus...

Patrouille des Glaciers
www.pdg.ch (in German and French)
Biannual ski-mountaineering competition – telemark 53km from Zermatt to Verbier.

Endorphin Fix
www.oarevents.com
Promising the 'toughest two-day race in the country', this multisport event passes through the Appalachian Mountains and along the New River.

Waiheke Island Challenge
www.waihekechallenge.co.nz
Sea kayak (13km), mountain bike (31km) and run (15km) on an island off Auckland.

Trento Film Festival
www.mountainfilmfestival.trento.it
The world's oldest adventure film festival, running since 1952.

week
.04

www.yearofadventures.com/april

Tamacit village has quite a backdrop – Jebel Toubkal and the High Atlas.

May

↙ GO: HIGH ATLAS, MOROCCO

week

↙ .01

www.yearofadventures.com/may

WHY NOW? **IN MAY ALPINE FLOWERS WILL BE IN BLOOM AND DAYTIME TEMPERATURES ARE USUALLY PLEASANTLY WARM**

The highest mountain range in North Africa, the High Atlas runs diagonally across Morocco, from the Atlantic coast northeast of Agadir all the way to northern Algeria, a distance of almost 1000km. There are several summits higher than 4000m and more than 400 peaks above 3000m in the range. The Toubkal region contains all the highest peaks, and is only two hours from Marrakesh and easily accessible by public transport.

Despite the wealth of high peaks it's the tallest, Jebel Toubkal (4167m) that monopolises trekking attention. From Imlil, the most popular trailhead in Morocco, it's a five-hour trek to the base of Jebel Toubkal. From here the mountain is a challenging walk rather than a climb. Most trekkers dash up and down it in two days, but you can also stretch the experience out to a rewarding week by trekking around Toubkal, passing through Berber villages as you go.

o74

↗ DO: HIKE TIGER LEAPING GORGE

COUNTRY China **TYPE OF ACTIVITY** Hiking
FITNESS/EXPERTISE LEVEL Moderate
fitness required. **WHY NOW?** For hillsides afire
with plants and flowers. **DESCRIPTION** After
making its first turn at Shígǔ, the mighty Yangzi
River surges through Tiger Leaping Gorge,
one of the deepest gorges in the world. The
entire gorge measures 16km in length, and it's
a giddy 3900m from the floor of the gorge to
the mountain tops above. There are two trails
through the gorge – the higher route is older
and is known as the 24-bend path (although
it's more like 30), while the lower route is a
new road replete with belching tour buses.
Needless to say, only the high trail is really
worth hiking. The town of Lìjiāng, 160km north
of the provincial capital, Dàlǐ, is the best base
for the hike.

Take the high road
through one of the deepest
gorges in the world.

With the High Atlas streaked with old trading
routes and well-used mules trails, it's become the
site for some of the world's best mountain biking,
whether circumnavigating Toubkal or traversing the
range to the edge of the Sahara at Ouarzazate.

For climbers, the 300m-high walls of Todra Gorge
provide some of Africa's best routes. There are some
sublime climbs here, many around French grade 5,
some of them bolted. Pillar du Couchant, near the
entrance to the gorge, offers classic long climbs,
while the Petite Gorge is better for novice climbers
with some good short routes. You'll even find a
selection of hotels inside the gorge.

It's possible to trek throughout the year in the High
Atlas, though temperatures can drop below freezing

above 2000m between November and May, when
snow covers the higher peaks and passes. Therefore,
late April to late June is the ideal time to visit.

o1 o2
o3 o4

Get into the equine spirit – not to mention frills – and time your visit to join the Feria del Caballo (Horse Fair) in Jerez de la Frontera.

↗ DO: HORSE RIDE IN ANDALUCÍA

COUNTRY Spain **TYPE OF ACTIVITY** Horse riding
FITNESS/EXPERTISE LEVEL All horse-riding abilities catered for.
WHY NOW? To be in Jerez for Feria del Caballo.
DESCRIPTION Andalucía is steeped in equestrian tradition. The horse has been part of rural life for time immemorial and Andalucía is the chief breeding ground of the elegant and internationally esteemed Spanish thoroughbred horse, also known as the Cartujano or Andalusian. Countless good riding tracks crisscross its marvellous landscapes, and an ever-growing number of *picaderos* (stables) are ready to take you on a guided ride, be it for an hour or a week. Many of the mounts are Andalusians or Andalusian-Arab crosses – medium-sized, intelligent, good in traffic and, as a rule, easy to handle and sure-footed.

The provinces of Sevilla and Cádiz have perhaps the highest horse populations and concentrations of stables, but there are riding opportunities throughout the region. Among the many highlight experiences, standouts are trail rides in the Alpujarras and Sierra Nevada, and beach and dune riding just out of Tarifa.

One of Andalucía's biggest festivals, Feria del Caballo features music, dance, bullfights and all kinds of horse competitions. Colourful parades of horses pass through the Parque González Hontoria fairgrounds in the town's north, the aristocratic-looking male riders decked out in flat-topped hats, frilly white shirts, black trousers and leather chaps, their female *crupera* (sideways pillion) partners in long, frilly, spotted dresses. It makes a tremendous end or beginning to a few days of riding through the baked Andalucían mountains.

The website www.andalucia.org has a directory of over 100 stables and other equestrian establishments.

A cycling tour means as much local beer, sauerkraut and sausage as you can handle.

You'd have to be unlucky to disappear – but surely there are worse places to be lost?

Great Saunter
www.shorewalkers.org
A 51km walk around the rim of Manhattan.

Five Boro Bike Tour
www.bikenewyork.org
The US's largest recreational ride, pedalling 67km through New York City's five boroughs.

Ridgeway 40
http://ridgeway40.org.uk
Run 65km along a hiking route through the chalk downs of Wessex.

Dirt Works
www.maxadventure.com.au/
dirtworksclassic
A 100km mountain-bike event through Yengo National Park, north of Sydney.

week

.01

www.yearofadventures.com/may

↗ DO: **CYCLE THE DANUBE TRAIL**

COUNTRIES Germany, Austria and Slovakia **TYPE OF ACTIVITY** Cycle touring **FITNESS/EXPERTISE LEVEL** Not required.
WHY NOW? Enjoy the last of spring from the seat of your bike.
DESCRIPTION Following the Danube River for more than 365km from Passau to Bratislava, the Danube Path is perhaps Europe's most popular bike route. The path is flat, the scenery (especially in the Wachau region) impressive and most towns and hotels cater well to cyclists. For most of the journey you ride along Europe's second-longest river on dedicated bike paths. Many cyclists ride only between Passau and Vienna, allowing six comfortable days to cross through northern Austria. Free booklets are available along the way, but for something with more detail, pick up Esterbauer's *Danube Bike Trail*, which contains maps, instructions and a smattering of practical tourist information.

↗ DO: **SAIL THE BERMUDA TRIANGLE**

COUNTRY Bermuda **TYPE OF ACTIVITY** Sailing
FITNESS/EXPERTISE LEVEL Good sailing skills required.
WHY NOW? A time of smooth seas, barring the paranormal.
DESCRIPTION Throw caution to the Atlantic Ocean wind and tack into the Bermuda Triangle, the name given to a notorious section of the Atlantic that's bound by Bermuda to the north, Florida to the west and Puerto Rico to the south. It's thought that as many as 100 ships and planes have vanished in the triangle, with mysterious disappearances dating back to the mid-19th century. Many of the vessels have gone down without so much as emitting a distress signal, and with no subsequent trace of the craft ever appearing. In other cases, ships have reappeared intact months after disappearing, but with no trace of the crew ever found. If you're still game, you can rent a sailboat at several places in Bermuda, or you can set sail from various points in Florida.

↗ DO: **SURF AT BELLS BEACH**

COUNTRY Australia **TYPE OF ACTIVITY** Surfing
FITNESS/EXPERTISE LEVEL High skill level and experience required.
WHY NOW? The most reliable time for Bells' waves.
DESCRIPTION For a beach with such enormous raps, Bells is surprisingly small, snuggled into the cliffs that line Australia's most famously scenic road, the Great Ocean Road. But almost nobody comes for the beach; Bells is all about waves. The powerful right-hand point break – the wave, not the movie – at Bells is a thing of surfing legend, especially when a 4m southwest swell is motoring in from the Southern Ocean. If you don't know your board from your Bells, you can always build up to this point break by taking lessons at nearby Torquay or Anglesea, or you can just wander through Surfworld, the world's largest surfing museum, in Torquay.

Réunion has 1000km of hiking trails and 1400km of biking trails – a lot of places to admire its awe-inspiring scenery from!

May

↙ GO: RÉUNION

week

.02

www.yearofadventures.com/may

WHY NOW? RÉUNION'S DRY SEASON RUNS FROM APRIL THROUGH OCTOBER, WITH MAY AND JUNE THE BEST TIMES TO HIKE

With its pavement cafés serving coffee and croissants, its French postal vans and its beret-clad bowls players, Réunion is like a slice of mainland France relocated lock, stock and wine barrel to an island in the middle of the Indian Ocean

And what an island! Sheer and lush, this overseas department of France appears to have risen dripping wet from the deep blue sea. Like Hawaii, Réunion has breathtaking natural landscapes, a live volcano and a subtly tropical climate – but on arrival, you're likely to be offered a baguette and a cup of strong black coffee rather than a palm skirt and a garland of flowers.

For many visitors, hiking is the *raison d'être* for a trip to Réunion. The island boasts more than 1000km of hiking trails, the best of which take you through an awe-inspiring landscape of jagged mountain crests,

REGION Pacific Ocean **TYPE OF ACTIVITY** Sailing **FITNESS/EXPERTISE LEVEL** Good sailing skills required. **WHY NOW?** Set sail at the start of the season. **DESCRIPTION** Between May and October the harbours of the South Pacific swarm with cruising yachts from around the world. If you have your own yacht, you've got the most flexible system for threading between the multitude of islands, but there are also options to charter or join the crew of someone else's yacht. Almost invariably, yachts follow the favourable winds west from the Americas towards Asia, Australia or New Zealand. Popular routes from the US west coast take in Hawaii and Palmyra Atoll before following the traditional path through the Samoan Islands, Tonga, Fiji and New Zealand. If you're looking to crew a yacht, ask at local yacht clubs and look at noticeboards at marinas and yacht clubs. Because of the cyclone season, which begins in November, hoist the sails now so you've got a few months in which to savour the journey.

Smooth sailing in the South Pacific – distant sails might be visible, but you'll feel like the ocean's all yours.

forested valleys, tumbling waterfalls and surreal volcanic tuff. Vast swathes of the interior of the island are accessible only on foot. As a result, the natural environment is remarkably intact, with a huge variety of flora, from tropical rainforest to gnarled thickets of giant heather.

There are two major hiking trails, known as Grande Randonnée Route 1 (GR R1) and Grande Randonnée Route 2 (GR R2), with numerous offshoots. The GR R1 does a tour of Piton des Neiges, passing through Cilaos, the Forêt de Bélouve, Hell-Bourg and the Cirque de Mafate. The GR R2 makes an epic traverse across the island all the way from St-Denis to St-Philippe via the three cirques, the Plaine-des-Cafres and Piton de la Fournaise.

In recent years Réunion has also seen an explosion of interest in mountain biking. More than 1400km of special biking trails have been established, winding through forests and scooting down mountainsides. They are graded like ski runs, according to level of difficulty.

If your French is good, you can make your hiking and biking preparations online at www.reunion-nature.com, buying maps, booking mountain lodges and checking general information.

For more information, visit www.la-reunion-tourisme.com.

o1 o2
o3 o4

Graceful giraffes are a close relative of the camel and a common sight in the park.

↗ DO: HIKE KRUGER WILDERNESS TRAILS

COUNTRY South Africa **TYPE OF ACTIVITY** Watching wildlife/hiking
FITNESS/EXPERTISE LEVEL Moderate fitness required.
WHY NOW? In May, Kruger averages around 25°C with almost negligible rainfall.
DESCRIPTION With its vast savannas, abundant wildlife and long conservation history, Kruger National Park is one of the world's best safari destinations. It's reputed to have the greatest variety of animals of any African park, with lions, leopards, elephants, Cape buffaloes and black rhinos (the big five), plus cheetahs, giraffes, hippos and antelopes. All up, there are 147 recorded mammal species and 507 bird species in the park.

The best way to get personal with this roll-call of critters is on one of Kruger's wilderness walking trails, which are a major attraction of the Southern African safari experience. They are done in small groups (maximum eight people), guided by highly knowledgeable armed guides and offer a superb opportunity to get a more intimate sense of the bush than is possible in a vehicle.

There are seven wilderness trails in the park, each with its unique attractions. The Napi Trail is known for the opportunities it offers for seeing the big five; the Bushman Trail features treks to San rock paintings; the Nyalaland Trail is most memorable for its beauty and its wilderness ambience, and is a paradise for birders; while the highly rewarding Sweni Trail is near Satara rest camp, where many lions are attracted to the herds of wildebeests, zebras and buffaloes.

The walks are not particularly strenuous, covering about 20km per day at a modest pace. The itinerary of each walk is determined by the interests of the group, the time of year and the disposition of the wildlife. Most wilderness-trail walks last two days and three nights, with departures on Wednesday and Sunday afternoon. The walks are extremely popular, so book well in advance. www.sanparks.org/parks/kruger

↗ DO: **STORM CHASE IN TORNADO ALLEY**

COUNTRY USA **TYPE OF ACTIVITY** Natural phenomena
FITNESS/EXPERTISE LEVEL Not required.
WHY NOW? May is peak tornado season. **DESCRIPTION** Tornado Alley stretches between the Rocky and Appalachian Mountains, covering central US states such as Oklahoma, Colorado, Arkansas, Texas and Nebraska. Spring here is not the time of flowers, but of tornadoes, spinning wildly with winds up to 500km/h. In May it's not uncommon for Tornado Alley to experience more than 400 twisters, which makes it probable that you will witness a twister if you join one of the growing number of tornado-chasing tours. Typically, tornado tours run for six days, beginning in twister-central Oklahoma City. Using satellite radar imaging, your guides will trace and chase the big storms across Tornado Alley, delivering you to a box-seat view of twisters or giant thunderstorms. You probably are in Kansas now, Dorothy.

↗ DO: **VISIT RIO'S FAVELAS**

COUNTRY Brazil **TYPE OF ACTIVITY** Adventure travel
FITNESS/EXPERTISE LEVEL Not required.
WHY NOW? The best time to visit Rio is between May and August, when it's cooled by balmy trade winds and the average temperature hovers around 30°C. **DESCRIPTION** Rio de Janeiro's first *favela* (slum), Morro da Providência, was founded more than 100 years ago. Today, Rocinha is indisputably the largest *favela*, with over 127,000 inhabitants. Once one of the most dangerous parts of the city, Rocinha has mellowed considerably in the last decade (though it's forbidden for residents to talk to the few police that can be found here in two tiny stations; problems are resolved within the community). In many ways Rocinha is a normal, safe and welcoming place, a reality underlined by the increasing number of tourists making the pilgrimage to the Estrada de Gávea to photograph stunning views of Corcovado Mountain and to glimpse the other side of Rio life. To see the reality behind the stereotypes, you can take one of several tours into Rocinha, including a walking tour led by the president of Rocinha's resident association. www.favelatour.com.br

↗ DO: **WALK THE CAMINO DE SANTIAGO**

COUNTRY Spain **TYPE OF ACTIVITY** Hiking/pilgrimage
FITNESS/EXPERTISE LEVEL Moderate fitness and good endurance required. **WHY NOW?** Long days matched by visual splendour – full rivers, hillsides bursting with wild flowers and swaying green cereal crops.
DESCRIPTION For more than 1000 years Europeans have taken up the age-old symbols of the Camino de Santiago (Way of St James) – the scallop shell and staff – and set off on foot to reach the tomb of James, the apostle, in the Iberian Peninsula's far northwest. Today, this magnificent long-distance walk is an appealing mix of pilgrimage and adventure, heading 783km through Spain's north from Roncesvalles, on the border with France, to Santiago de Compostela in Galicia. Testament to its importance is the fact that the walk is both Europe's Premier Cultural Itinerary and a Unesco World Heritage listing. If you walk every day, expect to be in pursuit of St James for one month.

It's the kind of adventure that makes you ask 'But why?' Here's your chance to find out.

It's hard to imagine Rocinha being gentrified, but it's not all danger anymore. Join in a walking tour and see another side of life.

Moonride
www.moonride.co.nz
Don't be afraid of the dark, mountain bike through it in Rotorua's Whakarewarewa Forest for 24 hours.

Isle of Wight Walking Festival
www.isleofwightwalkingfestival.co.uk
The largest of the UK's 20-plus annual walking festivals.

Knysna Classic Two Lagoons
http://gardenroute.org/2lagoons
A 65km (or 32km) ultramarathon near South Africa's Garden Route.

Cro Challenge Middle Dalmatia
www.crochallenge.com
Multisport event out of the Croatian city of Split.

week
.o2

www.yearofadventures.com/may

Castles, stunning landscapes, Greek and Roman ruins, and barely a tourist in sight.

May

↙ GO:
ALBANIA

week
.03
www.yearofadventures.com/may

WHY NOW? MAY IS ABOUT THE BEST TIME TO VISIT ALBANIA. YOU CAN SIGHTSEE IN THE MILD SUNSHINE, AND ENJOY THE BLOSSOMING CHERRY AND ALMOND TREES

Once the world's only officially atheist state, and the final communist domino to fall in Eastern Europe, Albania has never quite shrugged off the bad raps. For many people it's indelibly associated with its former isolation, peppered with stories of crime and poverty. The upside of these preconceptions is that travel in this Balkan country remains the monopoly of the adventurous.

In reality, visitors will find a warm and hospitable country with stunning mountain landscapes and sandy and pebbly beaches along its entire coast. Traditional villages perch on the misty mountains that cover more than 75% of the country. In Berat, families still inhabit the hill-top castle guarding the sun-bleached houses in the town below, while Apollonia and Butrint fascinate with classical ruins in rural settings you won't want to leave.

↗ DO: CLIMB IN RIO DE JANEIRO

COUNTRY Brazil **TYPE OF ACTIVITY** Rock climbing **FITNESS/EXPERTISE LEVEL** Beginners to human spiders. **WHY NOW?** With winter nearing you'll find the rock suitably cool. **DESCRIPTION** Better known for its dancing and prancing, Rio is also said to be the city with the highest number of rock-climbing routes in the world. Within an hour's drive of the city, there are around 350 documented climbs, including routes on Rio's two most famous landmarks, Sugarloaf and Corcovado, the site of the Christ the Redeemer statue. Corcovado's south face offers some of Rio's best multipitch routes, combining grunt with great views over the city. Rio de Janeiro state is blessed with further climbs if you prefer a complete escape from the city. Parque Nacional da Serra dos Órgãos, about 50km from Rio, is Brazil's climbing capital, and here you'll find the spire of Dedo de Deus (God's Finger), the country's classic piece of rock. www.climbinrio.com

Don't forget to rest and enjoy the view!

Much of the adventure comes simply with being in Albania. In the capital, Tirana, you'll still find potholes in the road up to 1m deep. At Butrint you can visit some of the Mediterranean's most evocative Greek and Roman ruins, yet there's not so much a food or souvenir stand.

Opportunities to wander through the mountains are few. There are no hiking maps of the national parks, nor are there generally any hotels or camping grounds, and the highest peak, Mt Korab (2751m), is far from any of the general travelling routes.

About the only place you'll find any mountain-style accommodation is at Llogaraja Pass in the south of the country, among some of Albania's most spectacular scenery. Here, you'll find the lamely

named Tourist Village, with wooden chalets, fresh food and pure spring water. From here, you can go for shorter hikes through thick forests where deer, wild boar and wolves roam.

The most popular outdoors excursion in Albania is to Mt Dajti (1610m), 25km west of Tirana. It's the most accessible mountain in the country and a weekend escape for many Tiranans. The hiking is gentle but you'll find lovely, shady beech and pine forests.

o1 o2
o3 o4

Cycle touring is laidback in Denmark – the highest peak is a mere 173m above sea level.

↗ DO: CYCLE IN DENMARK

COUNTRY Denmark **TYPE OF ACTIVITY** Cycle touring

FITNESS/EXPERTISE LEVEL Moderate fitness required.

WHY NOW? Roll into summer in the flattest kind of way.

DESCRIPTION Denmark is a superb country for cycling, with relatively quiet roads and an attractively undulating landscape. Here, cyclists enjoy rights that, in most countries, are reserved for motorists. There are bike lanes along major city roads, road signs are posted for bicycle traffic, and drivers are so accommodating that riding is an almost surreal experience.

There are 10 major bike routes in Denmark, all in immaculate condition. In addition to the 'top 10', each county has an extensive network of bike routes that enables you to explore every inch of the country. One classic ride, combining both national and local bike routes and taking in six islands, involves a loop of the Zealand Islands, using three of the 10 national bike routes and taking between 10 days and three weeks.

It begins by taking Route 9 south out of Copenhagen and along Zealand's east coast, passing through the historic port town of Køge, the yacht-infested Præstø and the medieval stronghold of Vordingborg. When you reach the southern tip, cross the bridge to Falster and ride around the northwest of the island before crossing another bridge to the pastorally rich island of Lolland. Once on Lolland, take in the towns of Skaskøbing and Maribo before switching onto Route 8 and heading west through Nakskov to the ferry terminal at Tårs. Sail to Spodsbjerg and cut a quick lap of the island or make a beeline for Tåsinge and the island of Funen.

On arrival at Funen head north, hugging the east coast, to the town of Nyborg, passing through a number of pretty villages and gently rolling hills. Leave Funen at Nyborg, crossing back to Zealand at Korsor. From here it's a couple of days riding on Route 6 back to the capital. For route maps, see www.trafikken.dk.

o1 o2 o3 o4

↗ DO: CAVE AT ACTUN TUNICHIL MUKNAL

COUNTRY Belize **TYPE OF ACTIVITY** Caving
FITNESS/EXPERTISE LEVEL Basic swimming skills required.
WHY NOW? The end of the dry season assures low water levels and smooth tubing. **DESCRIPTION** One of the most unforgettable and adventurous tours you can make in Belize, the trip into 'ATM' takes you deep into the underworld of this 5km-long cave. After a 45-minute hike to the cave, your subterranean journey begins with a frosty swim across a 6m-deep pool. You then walk, climb, twist and turn your way through the cave to a massive opening, where you'll see hundreds of pottery vessels and shards, along with the skeletal remains of 14 humans (seven of them children) who were almost certainly sacrificial victims. They're believed to have been offerings to the rain god Chac (who dwelt in caves) at a time of drought in the 9th century. In view of the unique value and the fragility of the cave's contents, visits are strictly controlled, and permitted only with trained guides from two San Ignacio–based companies.

↗ DO: BALLOON AT CAPPADOCIA

COUNTRY Turkey **TYPE OF ACTIVITY** Ballooning
FITNESS/EXPERTISE LEVEL Not required.
WHY NOW? Flights operate April to September; come just outside the hot summer. **DESCRIPTION** To fully appreciate an otherworldly landscape you often need to view it from above, and Cappadocia wasn't chosen as a location for *Star Wars* for its ordinariness. To best see this lunar landscape you can take to the sky in a hot-air balloon. Flight conditions are especially favourable here, and balloons operate most mornings. Flights take place at dawn (weather permitting), last for approximately 1¼ hours and are followed by the traditional champagne toast. You'll see huge stone mushrooms and fairy chimneys, all riddled with ancient cave dwellings. To add to all this, the light plays out a daily show against an outlandish landscape of vibrant hues, from gleaming white, through terracotta to bright mustard-yellow. You'll find a number of flight operators in the town of Göreme.

↗ DO: PLAY THE WORLD'S MOST DANGEROUS GOLF COURSE

COUNTRY South Korea **TYPE OF ACTIVITY** Golf
FITNESS/EXPERTISE LEVEL Straight drivers preferred.
WHY NOW? A pleasant time to be in South Korea, even if not for golfing by the Demilitarized Zone (DMZ). **DESCRIPTION** Abutting the DMZ with North Korea, Camp Bonifas is home to South Korean and American troops and a golf course now all but accredited as the most dangerous on the planet. Actually, 'course' is an exaggeration; what's here is a single par-three hole, 176m in length and ideal for the golfer who wants to cure a hook in their swing. With an artificial green and lined by barbed wire, it's also positioned beside a live minefield — an erratic drive here can have explosive results. Pay heed, then, to the entry signs that warn, 'Do not retrieve balls from the rough'. Play is restricted to the military and guests, so get cosy with somebody in fatigues.

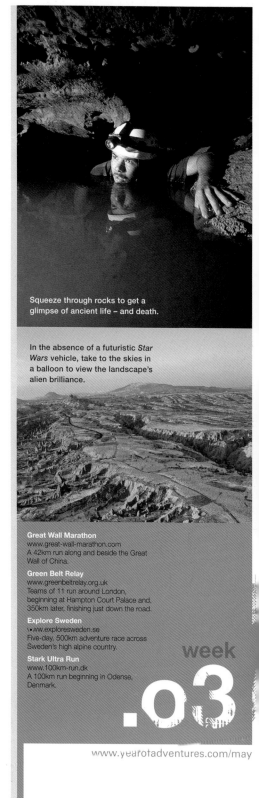

Squeeze through rocks to get a glimpse of ancient life – and death.

In the absence of a futuristic *Star Wars* vehicle, take to the skies in a balloon to view the landscape's alien brilliance.

Great Wall Marathon
www.great-wall-marathon.com
A 42km run along and beside the Great Wall of China.

Green Belt Relay
www.greenbeltrelay.org.uk
Teams of 11 run around London, beginning at Hampton Court Palace and, 350km later, finishing just down the road.

Explore Sweden
www.exploresweden.se
Five-day, 500km adventure race across Sweden's high alpine country.

Stark Ultra Run
www.100km-run.dk
A 100km run beginning in Odense, Denmark.

week
.o3

Almost 9km and rising – Everest's peak reaches 2.5cm higher every year.

May

⬋ GO: MT EVEREST, NEPAL/CHINA

week

⬋.04

www.yearofadventures.com/may

WHY NOW? THIS WEEK IS THE MOST LIKELY OPENING OF THE SO-CALLED 'EVEREST WINDOW'

The word 'Himalaya' is Sanskrit for 'Abode of Snows', and Nepal's stretch of the Himalaya has eight peaks over 8000m, including the highest of them all, mighty Mt Everest (8848m). Known to Tibetans as Qomolangma and to Nepalis as Sagarmatha, the world's highest place was the overpowering attraction for Nepal's first modern tourists – the mountaineers.

This week is the conclusive one in the Everost climbing calendar, being both the anniversary of the first ascent in 1953 by Edmund Hillary and Tenzing Norgay, and the most likely opening of the so-called 'Everest window'. This pause in winds on Everest's summit, brought about by monsoon conditions further south, allows in an expectant draft of climbers, creating the busiest time of the year on the mountain – in 2002, for instance, 154 of the year's 159 Everest summiteers reached the top between 16 and 25 May.

↗ DO: **GOBI MARCH**

COUNTRY China **TYPE OF ACTIVITY** Endurance running **FITNESS/EXPERTISE LEVEL** Superior fitness and endurance required. **WHY NOW?** To race through a vast Asian desert. **DESCRIPTION** A week-long run through the Gobi Desert in the Chinese province of Xīnjiāng. Each day you'll run or walk between 20km and 80km, covering a total of 250km across ankle-twisting rock, through slot canyons and over 300m-high dunes at altitudes certain to suck the oxygen from your lungs and energy from your thighs. As a bonus prize you can expect seasonal sand storms and temperatures nudging beyond the century (38°C). You'll also be almost fully self-reliant, carrying your own food, clothes and equipment – water and tents are supplied. Sound like a bundle of fun? www.racingtheplanet.com/gobimarch

Sound out your steps on the stone of the Gobi Desert.

If you're contemplating becoming one of the 1300-plus people to have stood atop Everest, your first piece of training should be to test the weight of your bank account. Mountaineers on the most popular route, the Southeast Ridge, pay upwards of US$10,000 per person for the permit alone.

If you lack the skills, lungs, money or inclination for this bit of high-altitude mountaineering, you can still share part of the mountaineering experience by trekking to either of Everest's two base camps, one in Nepal, the other in Tibet. The camp on the Nepali side, on the Khumbu Glacier, is by far the most popular of the two trekking destinations. Most treks into the Khumbu now begin at Lukla, passing through the Sherpa village of Namche Bazaar,

Tengboche monastery and on to base camp, at 5340m, about 11 days later.

Across the range in Tibet, the walk to the northern base camp has traditionally begun on the Friendship Hwy near Shegar, and involves a four-day trek past Rongphu monastery, but the construction of a road to the base camp (and the world's highest post box!) has dulled much of its trekking appeal.

o1 o2 o3 o4

The llamas are probably the only ones unimpressed by Machu Picchu's eerie grandeur.

↗ DO: HIKE THE INCA TRAIL

COUNTRY Peru **TYPE OF ACTIVITY** Hiking

FITNESS/EXPERTISE LEVEL Moderate fitness required.

WHY NOW? The vegetation is beautifully green and the June crowds have yet to arrive.

DESCRIPTION Run a straw poll across the globe and the Inca Trail would almost certainly win as the world's best-known hiking trail. South America's most fabled adventure attracts so many trekkers that the government has heavily regulated it in recent years – now you can only walk the trail with a guide or tour. The famous El Camino Inca is not the only Inca trail to the archaeological site of Machu Picchu, but it is the only one that winds its way past three major Inca sites in good repair. Any one of Sayacmarca, Phuyupatamarca or Huiñay Huayna would be considered a great day trip out of Cusco if they were easily accessible by road, but none can be reached without hiking all or part of the Inca Trail.

The trail is only 38km long but has steep ascents, especially to Warmiwañusca (Dead Woman's Pass), followed by swooping descents into the cloudforests bordering the Amazon Basin.

The elevation ranges from under 2000m at Aguas Calientes (the trail's end) to 4198m at Warmiwañusca, and so vegetation varies from montane rainforest, cloudforest and high-altitude *quenua* woodlands to bare *puna* grasslands. The lower reaches are a riot of different flower species, and the bird life is varied and prolific.

Curiously, the trail's end goal – Machu Picchu – is both the best known and the least known of the major Inca sites. It is not mentioned in the chronicles of the Spanish conquistadors, and archaeologists today can only speculate on its function. It is mysterious, beautifully located, extensive and expertly built, and despite its remoteness, it attracts many thousands of visitors. Savvy trekkers know to time their visit to Machu Picchu for the early morning and late afternoon, when it is relatively empty.

Meals on wheels? Armed rangers travel with you to ensure safety on the trails.

Forget the two-thirds theory, up to 90% of an iceberg can be below the surface.

Tenzing Hillary Everest Marathon
www.everestmarathon.com
A 42km run from Everest Base Camp to Namche Bazaar.

100km del Passatore
http://100km.dinamica.it
Run 100km, from Florence to Faenza, within 20 hours.

Wight Diamond Festival
www.trailbreak.co.uk
Mountain-bike festival on the Isle of Wight, including a navigation event ranging across the island.

Michigan Coast to Coast
www.infiterrasports.com
Four-day adventure race covering more than 400km.

week
.04

www.yearofadventures.com/may

↗ DO: CYCLE SAFARI AT MASHATU GAME RESERVE

COUNTRY Botswana **TYPE OF ACTIVITY** Cycling/wildlife watching
FITNESS/EXPERTISE LEVEL Moderate fitness required.
WHY NOW? The best wildlife and weather is from May to September.
DESCRIPTION Pinched between Zimbabwe and South Africa, Mashatu Game Reserve is the largest private wildlife reserve in Southern Africa, and an excellent place to view big cats and elephants (over 900 have been counted here). The reserve is only available for viewing by prebooked guests staying at one of two accommodation options, among the most luxurious in Botswana. Once here, however, you have the opportunity to add a unique twist to the traditional safari genre by touring the 300-sq-km park on a bicycle. Two styles of cycling safari are available: you can stay at the accommodation centres and ride out during the day; or you can ride by day and sleep out under the stars at night, taking turns on night watch. www.mashatu.com/cycle.htm

↗ DO: VISIT ICEBERG ALLEY

COUNTRY Canada **TYPE OF ACTIVITY** Natural wonders
FITNESS/EXPERTISE LEVEL Not required.
WHY NOW? The icebergs are beginning to flow through.
DESCRIPTION 'Iceberg Alley' is a stretch of sea along the north and east coast of Newfoundland that, in late spring and early summer, fills with well-travelled bergs. Calved from Greenland's glaciers, 10,000 to 40,000 icebergs enter the Baffin and Labrador currents each year, beginning a three-year, 1800-nautical-mile cruise south into Iceberg Alley. Fogo and Twillingate Islands in Notre Dame Bay and St Anthony on the Northern Peninsula (where you can wander the Iceberg Alley Trail) are some of the best places to witness this – ahem – titanic spectacle, though even Newfoundland's capital, St John's, gets a few hundred of the icy visitors each season. www.newfoundlandandlabradortourism.com

↗ DO: SNORKEL THE SARDINE RUN

COUNTRY South Africa **TYPE OF ACTIVITY** Snorkelling
FITNESS/EXPERTISE LEVEL No special requirements.
WHY NOW? To observe a seasonal ocean wonder.
DESCRIPTION Between late May and early July millions upon millions of sardines gather along South Africa's east coast between Port St Johns and Durban. From their spawning grounds off Cape Agulhas, the sardines have threaded a 1600km path, riding a countercurrent north along the coast. In turn, each and every predator in the oceanic food chain follows this moving feast. Dolphins, sharks, seabirds, game fish and even orcas all join the fracas. Visitors who witness the feeding frenzy will long remember the adrenaline rush as huge whales breach meters away from the boat and dolphin pods ride the bow-wave. Snorkellers score ringside views of the spectacular action, though diving should not be attempted amid the sardine shoals, as hungry predators could pose a risk to sport divers.

No mountains, but the Peak District has some of Britain's wildest and most beautiful scenery.

June

⬐ GO: PEAK DISTRICT, ENGLAND

week

⬐ .01

www.yearofadventures.com/june

WHY NOW? BEGIN THE NORTHERN SUMMER IN ONE OF THE HEMISPHERE'S PREMIER NATIONAL PARKS

So what if the Peak District takes its name from an early British tribe, the Picts, and not because of any towering summits. Or that its highest point is just 636m above sea level. Or that it's the busiest national park in Europe, and supposedly the second-busiest in the world (after Mt Fuji), receiving 22 million visitors (or more than the population of Australia) every year. If you can forgive this Midlands national park its crowds and its grandiose name, you'll be treated to some of Britain's wildest, most beautiful scenery.

Britain's first national park spills across six counties, and is surrounded by Midlands' industry. The park's own industry is adventure, much of which takes place out of sight, beneath the limestone coating, where cavers burrow through the earth in both caves and former mines. More than 100 caves and mines have been explored by spelunkers, and there

↗ DO: BUNGY JUMP AT VERZASCA DAM

COUNTRY Switzerland **TYPE OF ACTIVITY**
Bungy jumping **FITNESS/EXPERTISE LEVEL**
Not required. **WHY NOW?** Crack open the
northern summer with the world's highest
bungy jump. **DESCRIPTION** The enormous
Verzasca Dam, in Switzerland's Italian-speaking
province of Ticino, holds more than water.
From its high lip you can also make the world's
highest bungy jump, one made famous by
James Bond. In the movie *GoldenEye*, 007
plunged from this dam, a stunt that was once
voted the greatest in movie history. Thinking of
yourself as a suave secret-service agent may
be about the only thing that will give your legs
the spring they need as you stand on the lip of
the dam eyeballing a drop that looks more like
kilometres than metres. Cheer up; in another
7.5 seconds you'll be bouncing around at the
base of the dam.

Shaken, not stirred?
Follow in James Bond's
steps at Verzasca Dam.

are show caves open to the public in Castleton,
Buxton and Matlock Bath. At Poole's Cavern, near
Buxton, you'll find England's longest stalactite,
while Speedwell Cavern at Castleton is a unique
flooded tunnel you travel along by boat to reach an
underground lake called the 'bottomless pit'.

The Peak District's second piece of adventuring
fame is as the southern terminus for Britain's oldest,
second-longest and arguably most famous national
trail, the Pennine Way. Beginning in Edale, in the
national park, the trail follows the Pennine Range for
416km into Scotland. If you haven't the time or the
ticker for that, try the Limestone Way; the original
route (now altered and extended but still walkable)
covers a marathon-length chunk of the national park.

The Peak's outdoors trinity is complete with a
climb. Graced with rock stacks and tors, the Peak
offers thousands of routes on gritstone edges
and limestone. Popular climbing areas include
Millstone Edge and Stanage Edge (gritstone) and
the limestone cliff at High Tor. Burbage South offers
the unlikely combination of the Peak's most difficult
climbs and some of its gentlest bouldering.

For more information, visit www.peakdistrict-npa
.gov.uk and www.visitpeakdistrict.com.

Cool for cats. Try and track down a rare tiger in India's oldest national park.

↗ DO: TRACK TIGERS IN INDIA

COUNTRY India **TYPE OF ACTIVITY** Wildlife watching

FITNESS/EXPERTISE LEVEL Not required.

WHY NOW? The tail end of the dry season offers the most likely tiger sightings.

DESCRIPTION Corbett National Park was India's first national park, and is now home to around 10% of the country's estimated 1500 tigers. Its high forests and dense understorey make tiger sightings unreliable, but by visiting now you stand the best chance because the forest has died back, waterholes are scarce and the grass cover is minimal after winter burn-offs.

Most visitors to Corbett stay in the main camp, Dhikala, overlooking the elephant-grazed flood plains of the Ramganga River. From here safaris through the park take two forms: jeep and elephant-back. The jeeps range further, heading across to pools in the Ramganga in which tigers can sometimes be seen cooling themselves from the 40°C heat, but the elephants move more quietly, grazing on the cannabis that grows naturally and prolifically in the park. Try to arrange both if you can, though Dhikala's few elephants are in high demand.

If you miss out on sighting a tiger, you'll be appeased by a field guide worth of other creatures. Corbett is home to around 50 species of mammals, including around 85 leopards and 600 elephants, and 600 species of birds. The most commonly seen animals include langur monkeys, elephants, the ubiquitous rhesus macaques, and a variety of deer. To reach Corbett, take the overnight Ranikhet Express from Delhi to Ramnagar, where permits and accommodation must be arranged at the Project Tiger office. Jeep drivers hang about the office each morning, so don't worry about your prospects of finding a ride. Try to get a petrol vehicle as the noisier diesel jeeps can blast away any chance you have of spotting shy wildlife such as tigers. http://projecttiger.nic.in/corbett.htm

Climb every mountain. (Well, all 100 of the Famous Mountains of Japan, at least.)

↗ DO: CLIMB THE 100 FAMOUS MOUNTAINS

COUNTRY Japan **TYPE OF ACTIVITY** Hiking/climbing
FITNESS/EXPERTISE LEVEL Good fitness and endurance required.
WHY NOW? If you want to climb 100 mountains, it's going to be a long Japanese summer, so best get started.
DESCRIPTION In 1964 noted alpinist and author Fukada Kyūya released his book *Hyakumeizan*, in which he chose his 100 Famous Mountains of Japan, selecting them for a variety of reasons – height, history, shape and character. It was his wish that keen Japanese hikers would choose their own 100 and set out to climb them in their lifetimes. It didn't quite work out that way. His 100 Famous Mountains are now the accepted 100, and they have become almost every hiker's target, whether they can manage them all in one year or 30 years. The mountains stretch from Yaku-shima, an island off the southern tip of Kyūshū, to Rishiritō, an island off the northern tip of Hokkaidō.

No snow? No problem. Sand never melts.

↗ DO: SANDBOARD IN OREGON

COUNTRY USA **TYPE OF ACTIVITY** Sandboarding
FITNESS/EXPERTISE LEVEL Not required.
WHY NOW? Open year-round, the Sand Master Park offers its finest weather now.
DESCRIPTION The snows may have gone for the season but there's always sand, so head to the Oregon town of Florence to turn yourself into sandpaper at the world's first sandboarding park. Set in the Oregon Dunes National Recreation Area, the largest expanse of oceanfront dunes in the United States, sandboarding is like snowboarding for the sun worshipper – the only 'down' you need worry about at the 40-acre Sand Master Park is not in your clothing but in the descents you make through this gritty version of powder. Board rental is available at the park, as is instruction for boarding novices. www.sandmasterpark.com

week
.01

www.yearofadventures.com/june

↗ DO: RAFT THE ÇORUH RIVER

COUNTRY Turkey **TYPE OF ACTIVITY** White-water rafting
FITNESS/EXPERTISE LEVEL Not required.
WHY NOW? Fed by snowmelt, the river is at its churning best.
DESCRIPTION Çoruh River in eastern Anatolia is one of the world's best rafting rivers, offering grade four to five rapids with welcoming names such as King Kong and High Tension. But the river's great joy is scenery – tear your eyes from the rapids and you'll see 1500m gorge walls and snapshots of traditional village life. Various local operators run day trips out of the town of Yusufeli into the river's frothing Yusufeli Gorge (where King Kong awaits you), while other companies operate longer trips. To run the river's 300km length will take around a week, culminating at Yusufeli Gorge. Don't procrastinate about rafting this river, for if you wait until July, there won't be enough water to raft.

Sunset in the Serengeti, when many of Africa's animals get down to business.

June

week
↙ .02
www.yearofadventures.com/june

↙ GO: THE SERENGETI, TANZANIA

WHY NOW? THE MIGRATING WILDEBEESTS ARE MOST LIKELY TO CROSS THE GRUMETI RIVER IN JUNE

Africa's most famous park is a place that guarantees immersion in the quintessential African landscape. Here, an estimated 2800 lions roam alongside 250 cheetahs and 9000 spotted hyenas. There are zebras, giraffes, antelopes and, most famously, there's a seething mass of endlessly migrating wildebeests.

The annual migration of 500,000 wildebeests is not a single event but a continuous cycle of movement that varies from season to season. One thing is unchanging: to cross through the Serengeti towards Kenya's Masai Mara National Reserve the wildebeests must run the gauntlet of the Grumeti River. It's the most spectacular moment of the migration, with gigantic Nile crocodiles preying on the weakest of the beasts. This chancy crossing doesn't adhere to numbers on the calendar. It can occur anytime between May and July, though June is the likely month.

↗ DO: RACE ACROSS AMERICA

COUNTRY USA **TYPE OF ACTIVITY** Endurance cycling **FITNESS/EXPERTISE LEVEL** Superior fitness and endurance required. **WHY NOW?** To boast about racing in arguably the planet's toughest event. **DESCRIPTION** Pedalling your bike 5000km across the United States may sound like an enjoyable sort of cycle tour, but to do it in around nine days breeds the sort of race that *Outside* magazine once declared the world's toughest event. The route varies each year but the challenge doesn't – solo cyclists in this event will ride for up to 22 hours a day, covering around 550km each day; teams ride around the clock, averaging speeds of around 37km/h for almost six days. To compete as a solo rider, you must qualify at one of the events held by the UltraMarathon Cycling Association (www.ultracycling.com). www.raceacrossamerica.org

Coast to coast across the USA in six days. Could this be cycling's ultimate challenge?

The Grumeti crossing takes place in the Serengeti's Western Corridor, where there are several accommodation options, from a simple camp site at Kirawira to the exclusive thatched-roof tents at Grumeti River Camp. It's also easily accessed from the park centre at Seronera.

Even if you miss the drama in the Grumeti River you'll still be treated to a Serengeti show by visiting at this time of year. Wildlife concentrations in the park are greatest from December to June, and the park is one of the best places in Africa to observe big cats. The Wandamu River area in Seronera is said to hold the world's greatest density of cheetahs, and without the obstruction of trees it's almost guaranteed that you'll see them on the plains. You'll definitely sight lions, many of which have collars fitted with transmitters so their movements can be studied and their locations tracked – chances are your driver will be listening on the radio and know where the cats are.

North of Seronera, seek out hippos at Retima Hippo Pool, where you can get out of your car and picnic. If there's been recent rain, scout about for tracks of leopards and other animals and wonder what it might be like to be the picnic and not the picnicker.

o1 **o2**
o3 o4

One of the world's great rivers, the densely populated Sepik in PNG is a conduit to a world of myth, magic and ritual.

↗ DO: CRUISE THE SEPIK RIVER

COUNTRY Papua New Guinea **TYPE OF ACTIVITY** Adventure travel

FITNESS/EXPERTISE LEVEL Not required.

WHY NOW? It's best to visit early in the dry season because the mosquitoes are less numerous and the river's full.

DESCRIPTION The Sepik is one of the world's great rivers, and is to PNG as the Congo is to Africa and the Amazon to South America. However, the Sepik is more than just a river – it's also a densely populated repository of complex cultures and produces the most potent art in the Pacific. While cruising on the river, you'll still see naked kids poling dugout canoes, woven fish traps and the towering façades of spirit houses.

The Sepik is 1126km long and is navigable for almost its entire length, though a few days on the river is enough for many people. Locals prefer to travel in faster, more manoeuvrable motorboats, but most travellers favour the long dugout motor-canoes. There's nothing quite like cruising along the river sitting below the waterline in the bottom of a 20m dugout. It takes hours to get anywhere and the experience is quite calming and meditative, once you've accepted that the canoe won't tip over rounding a corner.

The most artistic villages are concentrated on the Middle Sepik and the most spectacular scenery is on the lakes or tributaries. Canoes aren't superbly comfortable but the biggest drawback is uncertainty – you can arrive at the river and find there are no canoes available for days.

Motor-canoes can be hired in Ambunti, Pagwi and Angoram, though it's better to arrange this beforehand in Wewak or, better still, before you come to PNG. River traffic is reasonably constant, and if you have an open-ended schedule and a lot of time, you can catch rides in locals' boats and with traders moving up and down the river. This is the cheapest way to go but you might be stuck somewhere for a few days waiting for a lift.

o1 o2
o3 o4

↗ DO: HIKE THE WEST COAST TRAIL

COUNTRY Canada TYPE OF ACTIVITY Hiking
FITNESS/EXPERTISE LEVEL Good fitness required.
WHY NOW? This week is the last before permits are required to hike
the trail. DESCRIPTION The 75km West Coast Trail on Vancouver Island
was originally constructed as an escape route for shipwreck survivors,
following a century of horrific maritime accidents. It's a stunning hike that
takes between five and seven days, passing through virgin spruce, cedar
and hemlock forests, across cliff tops and over suspension bridges, along
stretches of deserted beaches punctuated by clear tidal pools, and up and
down steep gullies and waterways. And every kilometre must be earned.
You'll climb hundreds of rocky steps, cross streams on slippery logs, scale
cliffs on rock-face ladders, and plough through knee-deep mud. Heavy fog
and torrential rain are *de rigueur* (as are chance encounters with bears and
even cougars). The trail is open from May through September, and walker
numbers between 15 June and 15 September are controlled by a strict
permit system. www.pc.gc.ca/pn-np/bc/pacificrim/index_e.asp

Follow in the footsteps of
shipwreck survivors along
Vancouver Island's West
Coast Trail.

↗ DO: VISIT SVALBARD

COUNTRY Norway TYPE OF ACTIVITY Adventure travel
FITNESS/EXPERTISE LEVEL Not required.
WHY NOW? See it in the endless midnight sun. DESCRIPTION The
wondrous Svalbard archipelago is around 1000km from the North Pole, and
is the world's most readily accessible bit of the polar north. It's also one of
the most spectacular places imaginable. Vast icebergs and floes choke the
seas, icefields and glaciers frost the lonely heights, and polar bears wander
the icy earth. Population estimates suggest there are around 2000 to 5000
polar bears on the archipelago, which adds a fuzzy twist to any Arctic hiking
plans. The best advice if you're trekking is to go with an organised tour.
Walk leaders will normally carry a gun and know how to use it. Standard
equipment, too, especially if you're camping out, are trip wires with flares,
as well as distress flares – these are to fire at the ground in front of the
bear, not to summon help, which could be hours away. www.svalbard.com

Into the heart of the Arctic:
the majestic ice-bound
Svalbard archipelago.

Finke Desert Race
www.finkedesertrace.com.au
Race a motorbike or buggy 230km from
Alice Springs to Finke (and return) in
central Australia.

Triangle Race
www.royaltorbayyc.org.uk
Biannual, two-week sailing (and
partying) race from Torquay (England) to
Crosshaven (Ireland), Treguier (France)
and back.

GeoQuest Adventure Race
www.gar.com.au
A 48-hour nonstop multisport event (with
snorkelling) in New South Wales.

Rat Race Bristol Urban Adventure
www.ratraceadventure.com
Adventure race through the city
of Bristol; your chance to cycle
down stairways or abseil
from buildings.

week
.o2

www.yearofadventures.com/june

↗ DO: SURF BALI

COUNTRY Indonesia TYPE OF ACTIVITY Surfing
FITNESS/EXPERTISE LEVEL From surf learners to surf legends.
WHY NOW? June offers the best surf conditions. DESCRIPTION Like a
dream-catcher, Bali's southern Bukit Peninsula droops into the Indian
Ocean, picking up swells that have journeyed across the globe just to
tumble onto its holiday beaches. From Ulu Watu, near the peninsula's
southwestern point, to Canggu, north of Seminyak, the midyear brings
trade winds from the southeast for warm water and epic waves. And
you won't have to run the gauntlet of territorial hard-heads. Kuta is Bali's
surfing nursery, with gentle beach breaks and tubes. Canggu has a good
right-hander at high tide, while an 8ft swell at Balangan can be a classic
wave. Kuta is also the place to broaden your Indonesian surf experience,
with one-week 'surfaris' on offer to other parts of the country, including
the legendary Grajagan (G-Land) on eastern Java. You'll find surfboards and
boogie boards for rent at Kuta, with variable quality and prices.

Namibia's Sossusvlei: an oasis in a 2000km sea of sand and towering dunes.

June

www.yearofadventures.com/june

↙ GO:
NAMIBIA

WHY NOW? COME NOW AND YOU'LL FIND WILDLIFE BEGINNING TO CLUSTER AROUND DRYING WATERHOLES

Wedged between the vast Kalahari and the chilly South Atlantic, Namibia has attractions that are unparalleled anywhere. Stretching more than 2000km along its central coast is the Namib Desert with its vast dune seas and the surprising oasis of Sossusvlei. This large ephemeral pan is set amid red sand dunes that tower up to 200m above the valley floor. If you experience a sense of déjà vu here, don't be surprised – Sossusvlei has appeared in many films and advertisements worldwide, and every story ever written about Namibia features a photo of it. The best way to get the measure of this sandy sprawl is to climb a dune, as most people do.

In the south, the immense Fish River Canyon dominates the stark landscape. Nowhere else in Africa will you find anything quite like this 160km-long chasm. Up to 27km wide, the dramatic inner canyon reaches a depth of 550m, forming the setting for a trekking treasure little known

↗ DO: NIGHT DIVE WITH MANTA RAYS

COUNTRY USA **TYPE OF ACTIVITY** Diving/
wildlife watching **FITNESS/EXPERTISE LEVEL**
Good diving skills recommended. **WHY
NOW?** Smooth seas and few storms in June.
DESCRIPTION Manta Ray Village, located on
the Big Island's Kona coast, is the most popular
night dive in Hawaii. Night-dive operators shine
powerful lights on the water, which attracts
plankton, which in turn attracts manta rays.
Divers have seen up to 10 mantas 'performing'
their spectacular underwater show, though it's
more common to find only a couple at a time.
Although there is no guarantee that mantas
will show up on any particular night, dives
during the new moon seem to be the best
bets for encounters. Spanish dancers, sleeping
parrotfish, sleeping goatfish and beautiful
cowries can all also be found here. Manta Ray
Village is in the middle of a boat channel and
diving here from shore isn't recommended, not
only because of possible boat traffic but also
because entering the water over the sharp lava
rocks can be extremely dangerous.

Batman beneath the
waves? Mantas wing
their way towards
the light off Hawaii's
Big Island.

outside Southern Africa. The 85km Fish River
Hiking Trail follows the sandy riverbed past a series
of ephemeral pools – in June you'll probably be
treated to the river in flow. Due to flash flooding and
heat, the route is open only from mid-April to mid-
September.

Other hiking routes can be found in the Naukluft
Mountains and Waterberg Plateau, and a growing
number of private ranches have established
wonderful routes for their guests.

Namibia is where you'll also find a 'dead' plant that
has lived for 1200 years, fields of apparently lifeless
lichen that can be resurrected with a drop of water,
and lonely beaches shared by hyenas, gemsboks,
flamingos, penguins and sea lions.

Overshadowing everything is Etosha National
Park, one of the world's pre-eminent wildlife areas.
The name of this vast park means 'Great White Place
of Dry Water'. Come now and you'll find wildlife
beginning to cluster around drying waterholes. You
might observe elephants, giraffes, Burchell's zebras,
springboks, red hartebeests, blue wildebeests,
gemsboks, elands, kudus, roans, ostriches, jackals,
hyenas, lions and even cheetahs and leopards.

For more information, visit www.namibiatourism
.com.na.

Surprisingly easy to climb, the Colossus of the Caucasus – Elbrus, Europe's tallest mountain, rises 5642m.

↗ DO: CLIMB ELBRUS

COUNTRY Russia **TYPE OF ACTIVITY** Mountaineering/hiking
FITNESS/EXPERTISE LEVEL Good fitness required.
WHY NOW? The climbing season is from around June to September.
DESCRIPTION If you've long believed that Mont Blanc is the highest mountain in Europe, allow us to introduce you to a peak named Elbrus, on the border of Russia and Georgia. A volcanic cone with two peaks – the western at 5642m and the eastern at 5621m – Elbrus bulges from the Caucasus Ridge, the geographical border between Europe and Asia, and is nearly 1000m above anything else in the vicinity. Its upper slopes are said to be coated in ice up to 200m thick, and numerous glaciers grind down its flanks. Several rivers, including the Kuban, start here.

The climb to Elbrus' summit is not technically difficult, and its beginning is made even easier by the Azau cable car, which rises in two stages, from 2350m to the Mir Bar at 3500m. A chairlift continues to 3800m. You then walk for about 1½ hours – fairly easy but slow because of the altitude and crevasses – up to Camp 11. To stay here in the peak season, you'll need to make arrangements in advance through a tour operator, or contact the rescue post. Staff here may be able to advise you.

Acclimatising at Camp 11, the final assault is made in a day – about eight hours up and eight hours down. Testament to its accessibility is the fact that in the 1980s, the Soviet regime, showing off for propaganda purposes, had groups of up to 400 climbers reaching the peak at one time. The ascent and descent have since been done in many ways: by ski, light aircraft, hang gliding and paragliding, as well as by a motorcycle with skis and, in 1997, a Land Rover.

01 02 03 04

↗ DO: **SAIL THE BLUE VOYAGE**

COUNTRY Turkey **TYPE OF ACTIVITY** Sailing
FITNESS/EXPERTISE LEVEL Sailing experience required for bareboat charter. **WHY NOW?** For a summer sail on the Mediterranean and Aegean Seas. **DESCRIPTION** Between the wars, writer and painter Cevat Şakir Kabaağaç wrote an account of his idyllic sailing excursions along Turkey's southern Aegean and western Mediterranean coasts, an area then untouched by tourism. Kabaağaç called his book *Mavi Yolculuk* (Blue Voyage), a name that has come to represent all sailing journeys along these shores. *Gülets* (wooden yachts) now sail two routes here with great frequency. Most popular is a four-day, three-night cruise between Fethiye and Kale (Demre); the less-popular route between Marmaris and Fethiye, also taking four days and three nights, is said by aficionados to be much prettier. Experienced sailors can opt for a bareboat charter and do the crewing (and cooking) themselves. Bareboats sleep between six and 11 passengers. Marmaris and Fethiye are good places to ask around about charters.

You too could sail into the blue off Turkey's coast ...

↗ DO: **TAKE THE THREE PEAKS CHALLENGE**

COUNTRY Britain **TYPE OF ACTIVITY** Walking/fell running/sailing
FITNESS/EXPERTISE LEVEL Good fitness required. **WHY NOW?** To compete in the Three Peaks Yacht Race. **DESCRIPTION** To drive between the highest peaks in Scotland, England and Wales – Ben Nevis (1344m), Scafell Pike (978m) and Snowdon (1085m) – takes around 10 hours, which helped spawn the idea that all three could be climbed in a single day. Today, it's one of the premier hill challenges in the United Kingdom, embraced as a charity event and coveted by walkers and runners. At a casual pace it's difficult to meet the 24-hour challenge, so you'll need a spring in your step across the ridges. If you want to make things more difficult still, enter the Three Peaks Yacht Race, held this week. Beginning in Barmouth at the foot of Snowdon, teams sail, cycle and run to the three summits, concluding in Fort William beneath Ben Nevis.
www.sleepmonsters.co.uk/site_3peaks

Want to bag all of Britain's highest peaks in a single day?

London to Brighton Bike Ride
www.bhf.org.uk/events
Get lost in the crowd as 27,000 cyclists ride 93km from the capital to the coast.

Lowe Alpine Mountain Marathon
www.lamm.co.uk
Spend a night in the Scottish wilds during this two-day mountain run.

Comrades Marathon
www.comrades.com
Run 80km in this South African ultramarathon between Durban and Pietermaritzburg; the 'big five' here are hills.

National 24 Hour Challenge
www.n24hc.org
Quite simply, cycle as far as you can through Michigan in 24 hours; 794km if you fancy the record.

↗ DO: **VISIT BOHOROK ORANG-UTAN VIEWING CENTRE**

COUNTRY Indonesia **TYPE OF ACTIVITY** Wildlife watching
FITNESS/EXPERTISE LEVEL Not required. **WHY NOW?** The time to visit Sumatra is during the dry season, from May to September; June and July are the best months. **DESCRIPTION** Orang-utans are found only on Borneo and the Indonesian island of Sumatra. In 1973 a rehabilitation centre was established near the Sumatran town of Bukit Lawang to help primates readjust to the wild after captivity or displacement through land clearing. 'Officially' closed to new arrivals since 1996, a new quarantine centre, just outside Medan, became operational in early 2002. The original centre at Bukit Lawang is now an orang-utan viewing area. Feedings at the centre are hugely popular and take place twice a day – 8am to 9am and 3pm to 4pm – at a platform in the jungle on the west bank of Sungai Bohorok. Most days about half a dozen orang-utans turn up to be fed, but there will be fewer if there is an abundance of forest food available. Get there early so you can see the orang-utans arrive, swinging through the trees.

week
.03

www.yearofadventures.com/june

It's like shooting through a washing machine.

June

week

↙.04

www.yearofadventures.com/june

↙ GO: BOVEC, SLOVENIA

WHY NOW? COME AS SUMMER SHRUGS THE ALPS FREE OF SNOW, AND PUMPS WATER INTO THE SOČA RIVER

Aspiring to become a Queenstown of the north, the small Slovenian town of Bovec has a great deal to offer adventure-sports enthusiasts. With the Julian Alps above, the Soča River below and Triglav National Park at the back door, you could spend a week propelling yourself through the outdoors without ever doing the same thing twice.

There are up to a dozen adventure companies organising all kinds of sporting activities in Bovec, including ice and rock climbing, skydiving, potholing, bungy jumping and, in winter, sleighing. But the holy adventuring trinity here is undoubtedly rafting, hiking and skiing. The rafting season on the beautiful 96km-long Soča River runs from April to October. Rapids on this river, which is coloured a deep, almost unreal, turquoise, range from easy to extreme (grades one to six). Rafting trips last for about 1½ hours and cover a distance of 10km. You can also go it

COUNTRY Norway **TYPE OF ACTIVITY**
BASE jumping **FITNESS/EXPERTISE LEVEL**
Minimum of 20 BASE jumps required.
WHY NOW? To witness (and participate in)
Extremesports Week. **DESCRIPTION** The town
of Voss, 100km east of Bergen, is the de facto
capital of Norway's Hardangerfjord region and
also one of Norway's adventure hotspots. In
the final week of June it hosts Extremesports
Week, which attracts adrenaline junkies with
a range of activities and competitions, with
most events open to public participation. Most
notable of the events is a BASE jump from
the 350m Nebbet cliff, open to experienced
jumpers – this imposing cliff is not a place to
indulge your curiosity about BASE jumping.
Other activities in Extremesports Week
include rafting, climbing, freeride mountain
biking, skydiving and paragliding. Even if you
miss Extremesports Week, you can come to
Voss any time to test your adventuring mettle
by bungy jumping from a parasail.
www.ekstremsportveko.com

Stop the world, I want to get off!
(But don't forget your parachute.)

solo by hiring canoes or kayaks and doing what you
can to keep your nose pointed straight in the rapids.

Hikes out of Bovec range from a two-hour stroll
south to Čezsoča and the protected gravel deposits
in the Soča, to an ascent of Rombon (2208m), five
hours away. The most popular walk in the area is
to Boka Waterfall, 5.5km southwest of Bovec. The
waterfall drops 106m from the Kanin Mountains
into the valley and is almost 30m wide – it's an
impressive sight, especially now with the last of the
snowmelt.

Paragliders need not go without in Bovec, with
the best offering being from the Mangrt Saddle
(2072m) between June and September. Skiers who
feel they've long missed the season are closer than

they imagine. The Kanin ski centre in the mountains
northwest of Bovec has runs up to almost 2300m –
the only real altitude alpine skiing in Slovenia. As a
result, the season can be long, with good spring
skiing in April and even May. It has 15km of pistes
and a similar amount of cross-country runs.
www.bovec.si

A bit of a detour and you could take in the views over the Vale of York from Kirby Bank, in the North York Moors National Park.

↗ DO: CYCLE END TO END

COUNTRY Britain **TYPE OF ACTIVITY** Cycle touring
FITNESS/EXPERTISE LEVEL Moderate fitness required.
WHY NOW? The weather favours a summer ride, with June the best month for quiet roads.
DESCRIPTION Travelling from Land's End to John o'Groats – from the extreme southwest tip to the northeast corner of the British mainland – is an ambition harboured by many, and a route cycled by around 3000 people every year. It can be cycled along numerous routes, though the Cyclists' Touring Club (www .ctc.org.uk) produces a pack containing directions for three different routes: a main road route; a scenic, Youth Hostel–based route, divided into 14 or 15 days; and a scenic B&B-based route. Each route is around 1600km in length.

Most cyclists do the trip in two to three weeks, though if you're short on time the record stands at a smidge over 41 hours. If you're not hurried, make provisions to stretch it out a little – Land's End to John o'Groats may be the United Kingdom's epic ride but there's plenty to enjoy, with the possibility of riding past places such as Dartmoor, Glastonbury, Cheddar Gorge, the Lake District and Loch Ness, and across some gruelling Grampians passes.

For the most favourable conditions, begin in Land's End and ride to John o'Groats (even if heading south to north is psychologically uphill – at least if you believe north is higher than south). Riding in this direction, the winds are more likely to be favourable and there'll be no riding into the midday sun.

Raising money for charity is very common among end-to-enders – it's estimated that around 80% of those undertaking the trip (most of them locals) are doing it in aid of a charity.

↗ DO: VISIT KRAKATAU

COUNTRY Indonesia **TYPE OF ACTIVITY** Adventure travel
FITNESS/EXPERTISE LEVEL Not required.
WHY NOW? For a smooth crossing to the island, come in the middle of
the dry season. **DESCRIPTION** Few volcanoes have such an explosive
place in history as Krakatau, the island that blew itself apart in 1883
with the loudest bang ever recorded on earth. Turning day into night and
hurling devastating tsunamis against the shores of Java and Sumatra,
Krakatau quickly became the one volcano the whole world could name.
This legendary peak lies 50km from the West Java coast, and though only
a fragment of the original Krakatau remains, it's still a menacing volcano.
In its more active phases, intermittent rumblings can be heard on quiet
nights from beaches on Java's west coast. Krakatau has been erupting
almost continuously for the past few years, but boats can sometimes land
on the eastern side of Anak Krakatau (Child of Krakatau), the peak that has
been growing out of the waters once filled by its infamous parent. Boats
can be arranged from the beach resort of Carita on Java.

↗ DO: HIKE THE TRANS CANADA TRAIL

COUNTRY Canada **TYPE OF ACTIVITY** Hiking/cycling/horse riding
FITNESS/EXPERTISE LEVEL Epic endurance required.
WHY NOW? It's going to take much of the first month of summer to pluck
up the strength.
DESCRIPTION Got a couple of years to spare? Then get started on hiking
the Trans Canada Trail, which, with 10,000km of trail constructed by 2005,
is well on its way to becoming the world's longest recreational path.
Beginning at North America's most easterly point, Cape Spear, this work in
progress will reach to Victoria on Vancouver Island, crossing through every
Canadian province on its way. At a completed length of 18,078km, it will
be half as long as the earth is round, and if you walk at a decent clip of
about 25km a day it will take almost exactly two years to finish. If you're in
a hurry, grab a bike or horse for this multi-use path. www.tctrail.ca

↗ DO: SURF IN MUNICH

COUNTRY Germany **TYPE OF ACTIVITY** River surfing
FITNESS/EXPERTISE LEVEL Basic surfing skills required.
WHY NOW? Time your visit to coincide with the Munich Surf Open.
DESCRIPTION Landlocked Munich hasn't let geography get in the way of
a good surf. At the southern tip of the Englischer Garten, in the centre of
the city, there's an artificially created wave located in a deep-chilled creek
known as the Eisbach where surfers practise their moves. The sport was
introduced here after WWII by an American GI who knew how to cruise on
a primitive waxed plank, and is now an inland fix for those who can't bear
the thought of being hundreds of kilometres from a decent wave. A little
further out from town you'll find a gentler standing wave just a stroll from
the tents at popular Campingplatz Thalkirchen. In the last week of June the
Eisbach wave hosts the Munich Surf Open, the conclusion to the river
surfing season.

Krakatau lets off some
steam – it's hard work growing
a few inches every week!

Step by step ... Banff
National Park was Canada's
first, and the world's third.

Tal-total
www.taltotal.de (in German)
Cyclist heaven, with 60km of highway
closed along the Rhine River for a day
of pedalling.

Mongolia Sunrise to Sunset
www.ultramongolia.com
Immodestly calls itself the world's most
beautiful 100km run.

Manhattan Island Marathon Swim
www.swimnyc.org
Swim 46km to circumnavigate
Manhattan.

Lapland Ultra
www.laplandultra.nu
A 100km run through the midnight sun
of northern Scandinavia.

week
.04

www.yearofadventures.com/june

105

07 SUMMITS

In some mountaineering circles it's no longer enough to simply climb Mt Everest or K2. In the past 20 years two new and more complex challenges have become the pinnacles of high-altitude mountaineering.

The most difficult of these quests is that of climbing all 14 mountains above 8000m in height – by 2005 only 12 people had achieved this lofty honour, beginning with Reinhold Messner in 1986 – but the most famous is that of the Seven Summits. To accomplish this global task, you must climb the highest peak on each continent. It's a mountain game that doesn't come cheap – climbing permits on Mt Everest alone begin at around US$10,000 a person – though it's infinitely less daunting than the challenge of the 8000m peaks. To complete the Seven Summits you need only climb one of the world's highest 100 mountains – Mt Everest (p86, May Week 4).

Second in the Seven Summits queue is South America's Cerro Aconcagua (p26, February Week 1), at 6960m. As high as it is, Aconcagua is no mountaineering ball-buster. A hardened and well-acclimatised trekker can climb the Argentine peak by its Northwest Route. The same trekker might also succeed in climbing Europe's highest summit, with 5642m Mt Elbrus (p100, June Week 3), in the Caucasus Mountains, humbled a little by the cable car that can drop you off 3800m up the mountain. From here it's a taxing but not technically difficult ascent. Ditto Mt Kilimanjaro (p33, February Week 3), the snow-drizzled volcano rising out of the Tanzanian savanna.

Depending on your interpretation of the Seven Summits, a fourth peak offers little more than a stroll. For the purists, Australia's highest peak is correctly Mt Kosciuszko (2228m) but for mountaineers

Kosciuszko is about as challenging as a walk to the shops. From the top of the Crackenback chairlift, out of the ski resort of Thredbo, it's a 6km amble, ascending just 300m, to the summit. Indeed, until 1982, when the road was closed, it was possible

to drive to Australia's high point.

In Kosciuszko's place, many climbers elect Papua's Carstensz Pyramid (aka Puncak Jaya), perhaps the most technically difficult of the summits and certainly the most logistically difficult. Permits are difficult to obtain, and in this troubled Indonesian province the entire area can be sealed off to visitors without warning. Negotiate these bureaucratic walls and you're still to be confronted by cliffs of sharp rock requiring climbing rated at 5.10 (French grade 6a to 6b; Australian 18 to 21).

In North America, the highest peak is found in faraway Alaska. From its base, Denali (6194m), or Mt McKinley, actually stands around 1000m taller than Everest and is one of the coldest mountains on

earth – the temperature on the summit regularly slips to -40°C. More than 80% of climbers use the West Buttress route, which is not considered technically difficult, and on a good season around half the climbers attempting the summit will be successful.

Which leaves the icy fin of Antarctica's Vinson Massif (4900m), a mountain discovered only in 1958 by US Navy aircraft. This Sentinel Range mountain is 20km long and 13km wide, and the time required to reach the summit ranges from two to 14 days, varying with the weather and the climber's experience and fitness level. The route has been likened in style and difficulty to Denali's West Buttress route.

The Seven Summits were first attained in 1985 by American Dick Bass. By the end of 2005, he'd been joined by almost 150 people.

Endless ice, endless space, clear Arctic air and winter sports year-round – that's Greenland.

July

week

↙ .01

www.yearofadventures.com/july

↙ GO:
GREENLAND

WHY NOW? IN THIS ARCTIC LAND, SPRING BEGINS IN JULY; WATCH AS THE FLOWERS BURST THROUGH THE MELTING SNOWS

The world's largest island (2.1 million sq km) has vast swathes of beautiful, unfenced wilderness that give adventurers unique freedom to wander at will whether on foot, by ski or by dog sled.

Greenland's dominant feature is its ice cap, the world's second-largest, covering around 80% of the island and so heavy that Greenland's interior has sunk into an immense concave basin depressed just below sea level. Very experienced cross-country skiers can emulate Fridtjof Nansen and join expeditions across the ice cap organised every year by a couple of expedition tour companies. With just white infinity ahead for three exhausting weeks, some claim it's like meditation, other that it's wanton masochism. Some crossings are accompanied by dog sled, others you drag your own supplies. If you cross the ice cap in the far south the chore is much shorter (though still very tough) and can be combined

↗ DO: HORSE RIDE ON 'UA HUKA

COUNTRY French Polynesia **TYPE OF ACTIVITY** Horse riding **FITNESS/EXPERTISE LEVEL** Not required. **WHY NOW?** July and August are the coolest, driest months in the tropical Marquesas. **DESCRIPTION** Pick all the spots in which you might fancy a journey by horse and the so-called 'Island of Horses' has to be high on the list, even if you will be made to sit on a wooden saddle. The quiet Marquesas island of 'Ua Huka earned its moniker for the semiwild horses that roam its wonderfully chaotic landscapes. The driest island in all of French Polynesia has in turn become an equestrian favourite. The most popular ride is from Vaipaee to Hane, passing the arboretum, airport and windswept arid plateaus before reaching the coastal road, which plunges down towards Hane. Ask at your pension about where to find horse owners; the good news is they'll pad the wooden saddles for cushy Western bums.

Looking for the equestrian experience of a lifetime? 'Ua Huka (Island of Horses) is it.

with trekking through more aesthetically appealing landscapes.

Away from the ice cap, Greenland offers some of the world's most marvellous trekking for those seeking a total-wilderness experience. Except for a few farm tracks in South Greenland, almost all walking is on unmarked routes. Views are magnificent and the purity of light is magical, with a profound silence generally broken only by ravens, trickling streams or the reverberating thuds of exploding icebergs.

Kayakers will find themselves in something of a paddling heartland, though if you've never kayaked before this is not the place to start. Greenland *qajaq* are the precursors of modern kayaks and few places

in the world are more mind-bogglingly beautiful for sea kayaking than Greenland's inner fjords. Great accessible areas to paddle include Tasermiut Fjord, Nuup Kangerlua and the sheltered sounds around Aasiaat. The Ilulissat area is also superb but perhaps a little too crowded with icebergs. One-way drop-off rentals mean the lovely Narsaq-to-Narsarsuaq route is especially popular.

For traditional rock climbing, Greenland's southern tip is a remarkable paradise of nearly pristine vertical granite. Walls and spires, many still unclimbed, rival those of Yosemite or Patagonia, yet are unusually accessible once you have a boat.

www.greenland-guide.gl

Accessible only by plane, Rabbitkettle Lake in Nahanni National Park Reserve sees wilderness and white water converge in Canada's far north.

↗ DO: PADDLE THE SOUTH NAHANNI

COUNTRY Canada **TYPE OF ACTIVITY** Canoeing/kayaking
FITNESS/EXPERTISE LEVEL Grade-four experience if paddling independently.
WHY NOW? The river is navigable from June to September, with July the warmest month (17°C average in Fort Simpson).
DESCRIPTION Perched just below the Arctic Circle, Nahanni National Park Reserve – Canada's first World Heritage–listed site – is a wild place that embraces its namesake, the epic South Nahanni River. Untamed and pure-blooded, the river tumbles more than 500km through the jagged Mackenzie Mountains, including a 125m drop over 200m-wide Virginia Falls. You can't get to the park by road, yet each year about 1000 people visit. Half of them are paddlers on epic white-water expeditions.

Paddling trips on the South Nahanni begin at either Rabbitkettle Lake or below Virginia Falls, simply because that's where planes can land. For the 118km from Rabbitkettle to the falls, the river meanders placidly through broad valleys. After the falls, it's another 252km to Blackstone Territorial Park, first through steep-sided, turbulent canyons and then along the broad Liard River. Moose, wolves, grizzly bear, Dall sheep and mountain goats patrol the landscape. The lower-river trip requires seven to 10 days. From Rabbitkettle it's around 14 days.

If you plan to paddle independently, you should be a capable white-water paddler (in grade-four rapids). This is no pleasure float; people have died here. Canoes are best for people with basic experience; rafts are more relaxing and are suitable for all ages. If you intend to paddle with an outfitter, trips should be prebooked, preferably months in advance.

To access the park independently, you'll need to charter an airplane into the park by contacting a flightseeing company; there are several based in Fort Simpson, east of the park. www.pc.gc.ca/pn-np/nt/nahanni

↗ DO: SWIM THE ENGLISH CHANNEL

COUNTRIES England and France **TYPE OF ACTIVITY** Swimming
FITNESS/EXPERTISE LEVEL Strong swimming ability and
endurance required.
WHY NOW? Be first out of the blocks on the Channel swimming season,
which runs from July to September. **DESCRIPTION** Sure, you can cross
the English Channel by ferry or Chunnel, but why not swim across to the
Continent? Cover yourself in grease (the water temperature is only about
15°C), dive into the sea at Shakespeare's Cliff near Dover, roll your arms
over for 32km, then step onto French soil at Cap Gris Nez to complete the
world's classic marathon swim. You won't be alone in the Channel, since
you'll be accompanied by a registered pilot and you'll pass through one of
the world's busiest shipping lanes, with around 600 tankers alone using
the Channel each day. You'll also get personal with jellyfish and whatever
flotsam is bobbing through the Channel that day. Only swims registered
with the Channel Swimming Association are recognised as official
Channel crossings. www.channelswimmingassociation.com

↗ DO: VOLCANO BOARD ON MT YASUR

COUNTRY Vanuatu **TYPE OF ACTIVITY** Volcano boarding
FITNESS/EXPERTISE LEVEL Good snowboarding skills required.
WHY NOW? Use the dry season for a marble-like run on the pumice.
DESCRIPTION Think there's nothing new in the world of adventure?
How about taking to the pumice slopes of an active volcano on your
snowboard? Mt Yasur, on Vanuatu's southern island of Tanna, is one of the
most accessible active volcanoes in the world, and one of the most active,
erupting almost continuously for eight centuries. In 2002 Zoltan Istvan
boarded the 300m slope from Yasur's crater, gliding through pumice like
stodgy snow, spawning the nascent adventure of volcano boarding. Such
is the infancy of volcano boarding, and such are the numbers of active
volcanoes, all sorts of firsts await those boarders who are prepared to
enter this brave new world.

↗ DO: SUMMER BOBSLED AT IGLS

COUNTRY Austria **TYPE OF ACTIVITY** Bobsledding
FITNESS/EXPERTISE LEVEL Not required.
WHY NOW? Summer bobsled runs begin this week (running until early
September). **DESCRIPTION** In 1976 the Olympic Winter Games journeyed
to the Austrian city of Innsbruck where, high above the city, in the ski
resort of Igls, a bobsled track snaked like plumbing across the Alpine
slopes. A few days of competition and the world moved on, ostensibly
leaving Igls and its bobsled track to slide into history. After all, what does
a city do with a slightly used bobsled track? In the case of Innsbruck and
Igls, it throws it open to the public. Bobsled runs behind professional
drivers quickly became a winter favourite in the Tyrolean city. And for the
last decade, summer visitors to Innsbruck have also been able to climb
aboard bobsleds, with wheels replacing runners for two months of the
year. What's unchanged is the speed and the G-force thrill of banking
and bending through a 1220-metre blur of Alpine country.
www.sommerbobrunning.at (in German)

Freestylin' across the Channel chop. Just mind them tankers, bro.

You thought the ski season was over? Try pumping over the pumice on a volcano board.

Wife-Carrying World Championships
www.sonkajarvi.fi
Carry your wife (or somebody else's)
through a 253m obstacle course to win
her weight in beer.

100 Miles of Namib Desert
www.100milesofnamibdesert.com
Run 150km in four days through
Namibia's major desert.

Big Five Marathon
www.big-five-marathon.com
Running race through a habitat
populated by Africa's 'big five' animals;
thinking about the lions will make you
run faster.

Tour du Canada
www.tourducanada.com
World's longest annual bike ride –
cycle across Canada for more than
two months, covering 7550km.

week
.01

www.yearofadventures.com/july

July

↙ GO: KAMCHATKA PENINSULA, RUSSIA

week

↙ .02

www.yearofadventures.com/july

WHY NOW? KAMCHATKA DANGLES JUST BELOW THE ARCTIC CIRCLE; COME IN MIDSUMMER FOR ENDLESS DAYS AND THE FINEST WEATHER

Closer to Los Angeles than Moscow, and dubbed the 'land of fire and ice', Kamchatka is one of Russia's least -explored but most spectacular regions. A 1000km-long peninsula separated from the mainland by the Sea of Okhotsk, this hyperactive volcanic land bubbles, spurts and spews in a manner that suggests Creation hasn't yet finished. The region claims more than 200 volcanoes in varying degrees of activity. Some are long extinct and grassed over, with aquamarine crater lakes, while 20 or more rank among the world's most volatile.

The volcanoes are often surrounded by lava fields, and these lunar-like cinder landscapes served as the testing grounds for Russia's moon vehicles. The thermal activity deep below the earth's surface also produces numerous hot springs, heated rivers and geysers. The most

Spectacular Kamchatka is both far from the beaten track and blessed with an abundance of volcanoes and wild animals. What more could you want?

↗ DO: BADWATER ULTRAMARATHON

COUNTRY USA **TYPE OF ACTIVITY** Ultramarathon **FITNESS/EXPERTISE LEVEL** Supreme fitness and endurance required. **WHY NOW?** To discover that madness is a foot race. **DESCRIPTION** Billed as the world's toughest foot race, the Badwater Ultramarathon puts the 'deathly' back into Death Valley. Beginning at Badwater, the lowest point in the Western Hemisphere (85m below sea level) in Death Valley's navel, the race crosses three mountain ranges to the Mt Whitney Portals, the trailhead to the summit of the highest peak in the contiguous United States. Not content to inflict 217km of running and 4000m of ascent on its competitors, the race is held in mid-summer, a time when Death Valley once suffered the second-highest temperature on record: 56.7˚C. If you're still keen, you must pass a rigorous selection process. All applicants are ranked on a scale of zero to 10, according to their previous ultramarathon achievements, with the 80 highest-ranked runners accepted into the race. www.badwater.com

I must be hallucinating. The shower's still gotta be a looong way off ...

spectacular examples are found in the Valley of the Geysers, where around 200 fumaroles sporadically blast steam, mud and water from the canyon floor.

Away from the volcanoes, Kamchatka is covered by large areas of mixed forest and plains of giant grasses, home to a vast array of wildlife, including between 10,000 and 20,000 brown bears and the sable, the animal that provided much of the impetus for early Russian explorations of the peninsula.

The entry point to Kamchatka is the town of Petropavlovsk-Kamchatsky, which is reasonably well served by air from other parts of Russia. It's possible to hike up Mts Avachinskaya and Koryakskaya, the two volcanoes that loom over Petropavlovsk. An ascent of Avachinskaya should take about four to

six hours, and you should watch for fissures in the glaciers, high winds and the thick fog that often covers the steep upper slopes in the late afternoon. Koryakskaya is more difficult and shouldn't be attempted by inexperienced climbers.

The Valley of the Geysers is 150km north of Petropavlovsk but is an expensive excursion as the only access is by helicopter, and special permission is required. If you go, the best place to touch down is the otherworldly Uzon Caldera, a 10km crater that features steaming lakes, enormous mushrooms and prolific berry bushes that are well-attended by bears.

o1 o2
o3 o4

Thirteen people have died since 1924 – with half a dozen 500kg beasts hot on your heels, tread carefully.

↗ DO: RUN WITH THE BULLS, PAMPLONA

COUNTRY Spain **TYPE OF ACTIVITY** Adventure travel/sprinting for your life
FITNESS/EXPERTISE LEVEL Bull-dodging skills handy.
WHY NOW? The bulls are about to be released.
DESCRIPTION In the Basque city of Pamplona, all hell breaks loose as Spain's best-known bull fest, Sanfermines, kick-starts a frenzy of drinking and mayhem. For visitors, the festival is best known for the chance to run with (or, more precisely, run from) the bulls as they charge through the city to the bullring.

Every morning from 7 July to 14 July, six bulls are let loose from the Coralillos de Santo Domingo to charge across the square of the same name (a good vantage point if you're not running). They continue up the street, veering onto Calle de los Mercaderes from Plaza Consistorial and then onto Calle de la Estafeta for the final charge to the ring. *Mozos* (the brave or foolish, depending on your point of view) race madly with the bulls, aiming to keep close – but not too close. The total course is 825m long and lasts a little over three minutes.

The majority of those who run are full of bravado (and/or drink), but have little idea what they're doing. It's difficult to recommend this activity, but plenty of people (mostly Spaniards) participate anyway. Try to run with someone experienced, and above all don't get caught near bulls that have been separated from the herd – a lone, frightened 500kg bull surrounded by charging humans makes for an unpredictable and dangerous animal. Keeping ahead of the herd is the general rule. As part of your preparation, familiarise yourself with the course.

To participate, you must enter the course before 7.30am from Plaza de Santo Domingo and take up your position. Around 8am two rockets are fired: the first announces that the bulls have been released from the corrals; the second lets you know they're all out and running. www.pamplona.net

o1 o2
o3 o4

↗ DO: **DRIVE THE DEMPSTER HIGHWAY**

COUNTRY Canada **TYPE OF ACTIVITY** Adventure travel
FITNESS/EXPERTISE LEVEL Not required.
WHY NOW? Under the midnight sun you can drive day or night.
DESCRIPTION Canada's 747km Dempster Hwy is a gravel hell-raiser,
pushing deep into the Arctic Circle through a remarkable slice of
mountainous terrain. Beginning 40km southeast of the infamous old
gold-rush town of Dawson City, the Dempster trails along the foot of
the Tombstone Range, passes through several First Nation towns, and
crosses the Peel and Mackenzie Rivers on ferries (or natural ice bridges
outside of summer) before heading up the Mackenzie Delta to its end
at Inuvik on the shore of the Beaufort Sea. Along the way, there are
opportunities for the adventurous to try hiking and canoeing, and there
are a number of government-run camp sites. Once a dog-sled track, the
highway is in pretty good condition but services are few and far between.
There's a service station at the southern start of the highway, and from
there it's 370km to the next one. www.yukoninfo.com/dempster

Turn left at the Arctic Circle –
the Dempster Highway is one
hell of a drive.

↗ DO: **KAYAK THE BITCHES**

COUNTRY Wales **TYPE OF ACTIVITY** White-water kayaking
FITNESS/EXPERTISE LEVEL Superior kayaking skills required.
WHY NOW? If you're going to roll in the Welsh sea, do it in summer.
DESCRIPTION As the daily tide rolls in across a line of reef and rock
between Ramsey Island and the Welsh mainland, it creates a tidal race
that has become a favourite with rough-riding kayakers. Named for its
habit of destroying ships, the Bitches can create standing waves up to 3m
in height as the tide rushes in and over the shallow reef. Kayakers surf the
waves or perform manoeuvres (what's known as playboating) in the holes
created around the waves. The Bitches are about 800m off the coast of
St Justinian, and most kayakers set out three hours before high tide for
their piece of water rodeo. To even contemplate tackling the Bitches, you
should be competent in grade-four water.

Life's a breeze? Not when you're
rough-riding the Bitches.

**World Mountain Bike Bog Snorkelling
Championships**
http://llanwrtyd-wells.powys.org.uk/
eventbogbike.htm
To a 2m-deep trench add copious mud,
a mountain bike, wetsuit and snorkel.

International Climbers' Festival
www.climbersfestival.org
Head to Lander, Wyoming, for lectures,
tips, slide shows and a bit of climbing.

7x7x7
http://7x7x7.endurancelife.com
UK seven marathons in seven days, each
by different means: road running, off-road
running, mountain biking, road biking,
kayaking, rowing and multisport.

Gigathlon
www.gigathlon.ch (in German
and French) Race 320km in
24 hours by cycling, mountain
biking, swimming, inline skating
and running.

week

.02

www.yearofadventures.com/july

↗ DO: **HIKE THE LARAPINTA TRAIL**

COUNTRY Australia **TYPE OF ACTIVITY** Hiking
FITNESS/EXPERTISE LEVEL Good fitness and endurance required.
WHY NOW? Soften the desert's extremes – temperatures in the low 20°Cs
are likely in July.
DESCRIPTION The Larapinta Trail is one of the world's great desert treks,
stretching 223km across the Australian outback from the Alice Springs
Telegraph Station to shapely Mt Sonder. Covering the virtual length of
the West MacDonnell Ranges, one of the oldest mountain chains in the
world, the trail switches between quartzite ridges, spinifex plains and
the gorges that so characterise the West MacDonnells. The trail has an
excellent infrastructure, with water sources no more than 33km apart
and camp sites well spaced along its course. If you can brave their chill,
there are even plenty of gorges for a dip. Allow between 12 and 16 days
for a comfortable trek. Trek notes and printable maps can be found on the
Northern Territory Parks & Wildlife Commission website (www.nt.gov
.au/nreta/parks/walks/larapinta.html).

July

↙ GO:
FRENCH ALPS

week

↙ .03

www.yearofadventures.com/july

**WHY NOW? FOR A FEW DAYS IN MID-JULY THE TOUR DE FRANCE
ROLLS INTO THE FRENCH ALPS**

The French Alps form the highest and most spectacular mountains in
Western Europe. Their icy spikes, needles and snowy peaks have inspired
Roman generals, Romantic poets and madcap mountaineers alike, and for
a few days in the middle of July they inspire the world's greatest cyclists.

When the Tour de France rolls its annual show into the French Alps,
most everything else is forgotten. Pelotons grind out enormous climbs,
then plummet like bobsledders, reaching speeds approaching 100km/h.
In the hours before they arrive you can see what all the sweat is about by
riding the climbs ahead of the racers (or you can just join the majority and
paint riders' names across the road).

The climb that defines the Tour's Alpine stages is the Alpe d'Huez.
This 13.8km lung-searing climb has an average grade of 8.5%, includes
21 numbered hairpin bends and is ranked *hors categorie* (above

116

Get within a hair's breadth of the heroes of Le Tour as they transcend the pain barrier.

↗ DO: **JOIN THE 300 CLUB**

CONTINENT Antarctica **TYPE OF ACTIVITY** Nude ice running **FITNESS/EXPERTISE LEVEL** Willingness to be very cold required. **WHY NOW?** When else will it hit -100˚F? **DESCRIPTION** If you ever find yourself wintering at the South Pole station, keep a careful eye on the thermometer because when it hits -100˚F (-73˚C) you'll have the opportunity for an outdoor experience about which very few people can boast. After steaming in a 200˚F (93˚C) sauna, you run naked (but for shoes) out of the station onto the snow. Some people push on even further, going around the Ceremonial Pole. While some claim that the rime of flash-frozen sweat acts as insulation, if you fall, the ice against your reddened skin will feel as rough as rock. Induction into the club requires photographic documentation. On completion, you join the elite in the 300 Club, so named for the 300˚F drop in temperature between the sauna and the Pole.

Put the locals into a flap with your 300 Club antics!

categorisation, ie *very* steep). The day the Tour visits Alpe d'Huez is a grand celebration of people, colour and sounds. Nearly 500,000 fans line the route, in touching distance of the riders in most places. Preceding this, a snake of chrome and colour inches its way to the summit as hundreds of riders painstakingly make their way to the top. Enthusiastic French spectators are usually on hand to dole out free samples of *pastis* (a liqueur) to kick riders along.

What the Alpe d'Huez is to cyclists, the Chamonix Valley is to hikers, who have their own tour of sorts. The 10-day Tour du Mont Blanc passes along the northern side of the Chamonix Valley and circuits the Alps' highest mountain in one of the world's top treks. Elsewhere in the valley, more than 300km of trails provide opportunities for walks of all difficulties. The extremely rugged Aiguilles Rouges provide some of Chamonix's classic routes, while the Grand Balcon Nord and the Montagne de la Côte take walkers as high into the mountains as they can go without becoming mountaineers.

The French Alps are at their busiest and best during July and August, when the popular trails attract tremendous numbers of walkers.

o1 o2 o3 o4

Take a hike and tackle the Munros, Corbetts and Donalds (mountains, hills and lowland hills) of Scotland.

↗ DO: BAG SOME MUNROS

COUNTRY Scotland **TYPE OF ACTIVITY** Hiking

FITNESS/EXPERTISE LEVEL Good fitness and endurance required if climbing all 284 peaks.

WHY NOW? Summer is the most practical time to be bagging Munros.

DESCRIPTION In 1891 Sir Hugh Munro, a member of the recently founded Scottish Mountaineering Club (SMC), published a list of more than 500 Scottish summits over 3000ft, a height at which they apparently became 'real' mountains. Sir Hugh differentiated between 283 'mountains in their own right' (those with a significant drop on all sides or well clear of the next peak) and their satellites, now known as 'tops'.

In 1901 all of the 'Munros' were climbed for the first time, initiating a pastime known as Munro bagging. This has grown to a national passion – there are books, CD-ROMs and even a Munro board game.

Munro's original list has since been revised by the SMC and now totals 284 summits, all of which are located north of the Highland Boundary Fault, which runs from Stonehaven, on the west coast, to Helensburgh, west of Glasgow on the shore of Gare Loch. More than 3000 people have completed the full round of Munro summits, thus earning themselves the title of Munroist.

For some, the elongated task of ticking off all 284 summits is not enough: the full round has been completed in less than 49 days; they've been done in a single winter; and they've been walked in alphabetical and height order. And once you've bagged all the Munros, there are other collections of summits you might want to tackle: the Corbetts (Scottish 'hills' over 2500ft with a drop of at least 500ft on all sides) and the Donalds (lowland 'hills' over 2000ft). Rack them all up together and you have an outing of 728 peaks. That ought keep you busy for a summer. www.mountaineering-scotland.org.uk

Pack your boards and head to 'J Bay' for some low-pressure highs when the barometer plunges.

↗ DO: SURF AT JEFFREY'S BAY

COUNTRY South Africa **TYPE OF ACTIVITY** Surfing
FITNESS/EXPERTISE LEVEL Surfing learners to the surfing learned.
WHY NOW? June to September is the best time for experienced surfers, with July also bringing the Billabong Pro championship to town.
DESCRIPTION Once a sleepy seaside town, 'J Bay' is now South Africa's foremost centre of surfing and surf culture. Boardies from all over the planet flock here to ride waves such as the famous Supertubes, once described as 'the most perfect wave in the world'. Development is raging at a furious pace in the Eastern Cape town, with clothes shopping almost overtaking surfing as the main leisure activity, but so far the local board-waxing vibe has been retained. Most beachgoers come to J Bay in December and January, handing the strong Atlantic swells to surfers in winter. Keep your eye on the low-pressure systems – anything below 970 millibars and you'll be in heaven. www.gardenroute.co.za/jbay/jbhome.htm

↗ DO: RIDE TO KHARDUNG LA

Take two wheels to their apex at Khardung La.

COUNTRY India **TYPE OF ACTIVITY** Cycling/motorcycling
FITNESS/EXPERTISE LEVEL Good fitness and acclimatisation required.
WHY NOW? It's a short snow-free season at 5600m.
DESCRIPTION Winding into the Himalaya from the Ladakhi city of Leh, the road to Khardung La (5602m) is the highest motorable road in the world, which has made it a favourite challenge among cyclists and motorcyclists. The pass is occupied by a grubby military camp and stacks of oil drums, but none of this detracts from gawking at the distant vistas and the thrill of cycling to the highest point you're ever likely to take a bike. Nor will it help the inevitable altitude aches, even if you have spent a few days acclimatising in Leh, 2100m below. The road is open for one-way traffic only: Leh to Khardung La in the morning and Khardung La to Leh in the afternoon. The miserable road-building camps of South Pullu (south of the pass) and North Pullu (on the Nubra side) have toilets, teashops and food.

↗ DO: WINDSURF AT VASILIKI BAY

COUNTRY Greece **TYPE OF ACTIVITY** Windsurfing
FITNESS/EXPERTISE LEVEL Wind and waves to suit all levels.
WHY NOW? 'Eric' is a summer creature.
DESCRIPTION Windsurfing is the most popular water sport in Greece, and little wonder when Vasiliki Bay, on the south coast of the Ionian island of Lefkada, is considered *the* place to windsurf in Europe. Nor are conditions here elitist, with many people reckoning that Vasiliki Bay is one of the best places in the world to learn the sport. You'll find a wide, sheltered bay just waiting for the afternoon winds – known locally as 'Eric' – to blow in. Along the pebbly beach, numerous windsurfing companies have staked prominent claims with flags, equipment and their own hotels. They offer all-inclusive tuition and accommodation packages. If they've got spare gear, some will willingly rent it to the independent enthusiast for a day or two. www.lefkada-greece.biz

Transalp Challenge
www.transalpchallenge.com
Eight-stage, 750km mountain-bike race for pros and amateurs, crossing the European Alps from north to south.

Rocky Mountain 1200
www.randonneurs.bc.ca/rocky/rm1200.html
Four-yearly randonnée (2008 and 2012) through the Canadian Rockies; cycle 1200km in 90 hours.

Vermont 100 Mile Endurance Run
www.vermont100.com
Run 161 hilly kilometres within 30 hours.

St Olavsloppet
www.st-olavsloppet.no
Four-day, 332km relay run from Östersund (Sweden) to Trondheim (Norway).

week
.o3

www.yearofadventures.com/july

A stairway to heaven – ice highways lead the way to seven of the world's 25 highest summits above the giant glaciers of Baltistan.

July

↙ GO: BALTISTAN, PAKISTAN

week
↙ .04
www.yearofadventures.com/july

WHY NOW? MID-JUNE TO SEPTEMBER IS THE OPTIMAL TREKKING SEASON IN BALTISTAN, AND THE ONLY TIME YOU'LL BE ABLE TO TRAVERSE GLACIERS AND CROSS PASSES

A journey through northern Pakistan is heaven for mountain lovers, a place where you can walk for days on even the most popular routes without seeing another trekker. Foremost among the trekking regions is Baltistan, the centre of the Karakoram's glaciers, peaks and rock towers, where villages are oases in a vertical wilderness of rock and ice. Five of the biggest glaciers – Biafo (65km), Baltoro (62km), Chogo Lungma (44km), Panmah (42km), and Kaberi and Kondus (36km) – offer the longest glacier traverses outside the sub-polar zones.

The ultimate in Karakoram trekking is to traverse the length of one of these Karakoram glaciers. Two treks epitomise this experience: the Hispar La trek to Snow Lake, and the Baltoro Glacier trek to K2 Base Camp. Both take you up massive ice highways lined with magnificent

↗ DO: SHARK DIVE AT GANSBAAI

COUNTRY South Africa **TYPE OF ACTIVITY** Diving/wildlife watching **FITNESS/EXPERTISE LEVEL** Diving certificate usually required. **WHY NOW?** The sharks are active in their feeding patterns. **DESCRIPTION** Cage diving to view the ocean's fiercest resident, the great white shark, is one way to get your blood flowing faster as you travel through South Africa's Western Cape. Such dives are heavily promoted in the town of Hermanus, with no less than eight operators based here, though the boats actually depart from Gansbaai, 35km along the coast (all the companies transport you there). There's no doubting the activity's popularity, but it doesn't come without controversy. Operators use bait to attract the sharks, so these killer fish are being trained to associate humans with food. It's not a pleasant idea, especially if you're a surfer. While most of the operators require that you have an internationally recognised diving qualification, some allow snorkellers. www.hermanusinfo.co.za/greatwhite; www.sharklady.co.za

So that's the daily special! Get up close and personal with great white sharks.

peaks and towers into the very heart of the Karakoram.

The Hispar La is a glaciated pass that links the Biafo and Hispar Glaciers, the Karakoram's second- and fifth-longest glaciers. Together they form the longest continuous stretch of glacier (114km). At the base of the Hispar La is Lukpe Lawo, commonly called Snow Lake, one of the world's largest glacial basins. More than a dozen 7000m peaks tower above these glaciers. To cross this technical pass is to walk through what both Francis Younghusband and HW Tilman called the finest mountain scenery in the world. The trek is extreme in its difficulty, but anyone who takes on the challenge is awed by the experience of travelling in this glacial wilderness.

Baltoro, the Karakoram's third-longest glacier, leads into the most extensively glaciated high mountain terrain on the planet. Seven of the world's 25 highest peaks rise above the glacier, including K2 (8611m), second only to Everest. All along the lower Baltoro Glacier are monumental, sheer rock walls and granite towers – Uli Biaho, the Trangos, the Cathedrals – that draw elite climbers from around the world. The trek is demanding, but is glacier travel at its best. Far and away, it is northern Pakistan's most popular trek.

John West ain't necessarily best. Alaskan brown bears wait patiently for the run of fresh salmon to begin.

↗ DO WATCH BEARS, MCNEIL RIVER

COUNTRY USA **TYPE OF ACTIVITY** Wildlife watching
FITNESS/EXPERTISE LEVEL Not required.
WHY NOW? To see what happens when bear meets fish.
DESCRIPTION Each July and August large numbers of brown bears gather in the McNeil River State Game Sanctuary, just north of Katmai National Park on the Alaska Peninsula. The majority of the bears congregate 1.5km upstream from the river mouth, where falls slow the salmon, providing an easy meal. This spot is world-renowned among wildlife photographers, and every great bear-catches-salmon shot you've ever seen was probably taken from here (or the Brooks River in Katmai National Park). Often, 20 or more brown bears will feed together below the McNeil River Falls, and up to 80 have been known to gather at one time.

The Alaska Department of Fish and Game has set up a viewing area and allows 10 visitors per day for a four-day period to watch the bears feed. From a camp, park guides lead a 3km hike across sedge flats and through thigh-deep Mikfik Creek to the viewing area on a bluff. There you can watch the bears feed less than 20m away in what is basically a series of rapids and pools where the salmon gather between leaps.

The season begins in June, when viewing is done at Mikfik Creek. Viewing switches to the bigger McNeil River in July, the prime season.

Visits to the sanctuary are by permit only, and these are issued by lottery. Your odds of drawing a permit are less than one in five, so large are the number of applications. For an application, contact the Alaska Department of Fish & Game (www.wildlife.alaska.gov/mcneil/index.cfm?); return it by March 1. You must come to the sanctuary self-sufficient, with camping equipment and food, and the entry fee, supposing you make it through the ballot, is $350 for non-Alaskans.

↗ DO: **HIKE ON CROAGH PATRICK**

COUNTRY Ireland **TYPE OF ACTIVITY** Hiking/pilgrimage
FITNESS/EXPERTISE LEVEL Basic fitness sufficient.
WHY NOW? Come for Reek Sunday.
DESCRIPTION Croagh Patrick (764m) occupies a special place in Irish tradition as the country's most hallowed place of pilgrimage and attracts tens of thousands of pilgrims to its summit every year, making it Ireland's most-climbed mountain. It has been a place of pilgrimage since at least the 12th century, and the last Sunday in July – Reek Sunday – is a national day of pilgrimage. It's the mountain's association with Patrick, the best known of Ireland's patron saints, that is Croagh Patrick's glory. It's believed that the saint fasted for 40 days and 40 nights on the mountain, emulating the biblical accounts of Moses and Christ. Legend also has it that Patrick famously evicted Ireland's snakes during his time on the mountain. The climb takes two to three hours, and concludes at the summit chapel.

↗ DO: **STAY IN A MONGOLIAN GER**

COUNTRY Mongolia **TYPE OF ACTIVITY** Adventure travel
FITNESS/EXPERTISE LEVEL Not required.
WHY NOW? Most ger camps are only open from June to mid-September.
DESCRIPTION Tourist ger camps are springing up everywhere in Mongolia. It may seem touristy, and they're usually poor value, but if you're going into the countryside, a night in a tourist ger is a great way to experience some Western-oriented 'traditional Mongolian nomadic lifestyle'. If you're particularly fortunate, you may be invited to spend a night or two out on the steppes in a genuine ger, rather than a tourist ger camp. This is a wonderful experience, offering a chance to see the 'real' Mongolia. If you're invited to stay in a family ger, in very rare cases you may be expected to pay for this accommodation, but in most cases no payment is wanted if you stay for one or two nights. If you stay longer (unless you have been specifically asked to extend your visit), you will outstay your welcome and abuse Mongolian hospitality.

Dream of being a nomad in Mongolia – it's a wonderful experience.

Arctic Team Challenge
www.atc.gl
Five-day, 250km multisport race across the Greeland island of Ammassalik.

London-Edinburgh-London (LEL)
www.audax.uk.net
The UK's premier randonnée, held every four years (2009, 2013); cycle 1400km within 118 hours.

Traversée internationale du Lac Saint-Jean
www.traversee.qc.ca
Plunge into a 32km swimming marathon in Quebec.

Atacama Crossing
www.racingtheplanet.com
Run self-supported for 250km through Chile's Atacama Desert, the driest place on the planet.

↗ DO: **PADDLE IN POLAND**

COUNTRY Poland **TYPE OF ACTIVITY** Canoeing/kayaking
FITNESS/EXPERTISE LEVEL Basic paddling skills required.
WHY NOW? Let the rivers relieve the summer heat.
DESCRIPTION The Polish towns of Augustów and Olsztyn have no great lure for tourism, but they do serve as bases for two great river trips. From Augustów, the most popular of several paddling routes is along the Czrana Hańska River. The traditional route is designed as a loop, beginning in Augustów and leading along the Augustów Canal as far as Lake Serwy and up to the northern end of this lake. Kayaks are then transported overland to Lake Wigry, from where paddlers follow the river downstream to the Augustów Canal and return to Augustów. The full loop takes 12 days. Out of Olsztyn, a 103km route runs along the Krutynia River, beginning at Stanica Wodna PTTK, 50km east of Olsztyn. You can hire kayaks at Stanica Wodna PTTK – check availability in advance.

week **.04**

www.yearofadventures.com/july

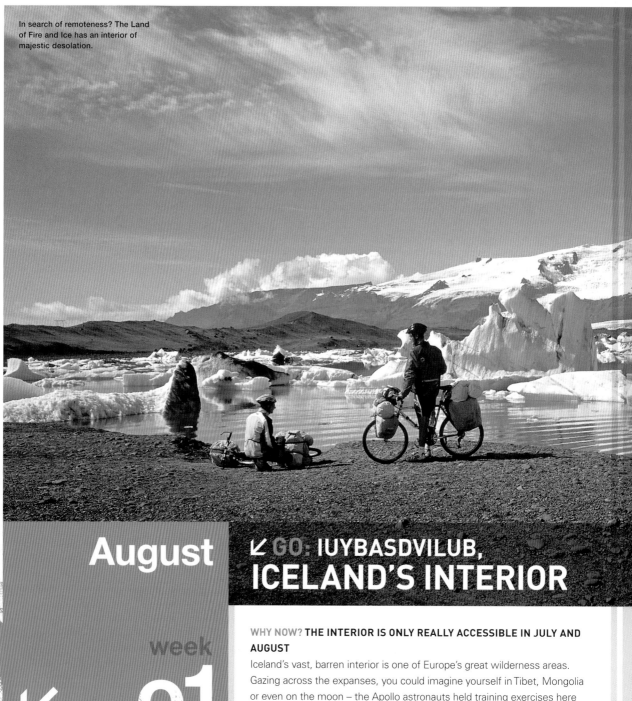

In search of remoteness? The Land of Fire and Ice has an interior of majestic desolation.

August

week

↙ **.01**

www.yearofadventures.com/august

↙ **GO: IUYBASDVILUB,**
ICELAND'S INTERIOR

WHY NOW? THE INTERIOR IS ONLY REALLY ACCESSIBLE IN JULY AND AUGUST

Iceland's vast, barren interior is one of Europe's great wilderness areas. Gazing across the expanses, you could imagine yourself in Tibet, Mongolia or even on the moon – the Apollo astronauts held training exercises here before the 1969 lunar landings. The interior is only really accessible in July and August, and this is seriously remote country. There are practically no services, accommodation, bridges, mobile-phone signals, and no guarantees if things go wrong.

There are four main routes through the interior – the Kjölur, Sprengisandur, Öskjuleið and Kverkfjöll Routes – and historically, they were places of terror to be traversed as quickly as possible. Today, they are attracting hardy visitors to such sights as Herðubreið (1682m), Iceland's most distinctive mountain, described variously as a birthday cake, a cooking pot and a lampshade; and Askja, a 50-sq-km caldera created by a

↗ DO: DRIVE THE CANNING STOCK ROUTE

COUNTRY Australia **TYPE OF ACTIVITY** 4WDing **FITNESS/EXPERTISE LEVEL** Mechanical knowledge and 4WDing skills vital. **WHY NOW?** The coolest and best time to be on the Canning. **DESCRIPTION** The world's longest and most remote stock route doubles as the most difficult road journey in Australia. Stretching more than 1700km across the arid heart of Western Australia, between Wiluna in the south and Halls Creek in the north, it crosses through uninhabited but vegetated desert country, pushing across more than 800 sand dunes. People have walked the Canning, including the eponymous Alfred Canning, and there have been rare crossings by bicycle, but it's predominantly a route for the hardiest of 4WDers. Travelling the Canning in the Australian summer is suicide. It usually begins to see the first adventurers in late April or early May. By the middle of October the season is coming to a close.

Only the most intrepid of 4WDers take on the challenge of the Canning, the world's longest stock route.

colossal explosion of tephra in 1875 and containing Iceland's deepest lake as well as a hot crater lake where the water (around 25°C) is ideal for swimming.

Also here is one of the world's finest, yet least known, trekking routes: the Landmannalaugar to Þórsmörk trek. Usually passable from mid-July to September, most people walk the trail in three to four days, though it can be stretched to six days by continuing to Skogar. The route crosses lava flows and a black pumice desert, passes belching fumaroles, makes foot-numbing stream crossings and offers views of torrential waterfalls. Most trekkers walk from north to south, losing altitude rather than gaining it. There are seven huts along the course of the trek, operated by the Iceland Touring Association (Ferðafélag Íslands; www.fi.is), so that you needn't brave Iceland's notoriously ferocious winds in a tent. Due to the trek's popularity, however, it's wise to book and pay hut fees in advance.

Any travel in the interior requires high-clearance 4WD vehicles, and it's recommended that vehicles travel in pairs.

The scene of a modern-day apocalypse, eerie Chornobyl beckons for anyone who dares to set foot in the exclusion zone.

↗ DO: VISIT CHORNOBYL

COUNTRY Ukraine **TYPE OF ACTIVITY** Adventure travel
FITNESS/EXPERTISE LEVEL Not required.
WHY NOW? Go the double – get sunburned and contaminated at the same time.
DESCRIPTION It's the world's weirdest day-trip, one for extreme tourists and a once-in-a-lifetime experience that you probably won't want to repeat. A package tour to the Chornobyl exclusion zone – the site of the world's worst nuclear accident, on 26 April 1986 – will take you to the heart of an apocalypse.

Tours are operated by several travel agencies in the Ukraine capital, Kyiv, and they'll assure you that you receive no more radiation on your three hours or so in the zone than you would on a New York–London flight (but they would say that, wouldn't they?).

Usually, no overalls or special shoes are supplied and you really don't need them. Just keep off the absorbent moss and watch where you put your hands. You'll be closely accompanied by a guide with a Geiger counter. At brief moments – including near the reactor or near moss – this will beep its way up to 600 or 800 micro-roentgens, when normal background radiation is 14. Reportedly, no-one has received an accidental dose since 1992, but guides venturing out alone admit to sometimes having to throw away their shoes.

Tours usually visit the reactor information centre and the giant catfish in the river (reportedly this big because of a lack of predators and competitors, not through mutation). They also pass the graveyard of helicopters, fire trucks and other rescue vehicles used in the clean-up operation, and can drop in on one of the 358 zone residents. The most sobering sight is the ghost town Pripyat, where Chornobyl workers and their families once lived. Today, deserted buildings and overgrown streets present a truly post-apocalyptic scene.

Some of the agencies supply a bottle of red wine as 'the best protection against radiation'.

↗ DO: HIKE TO THE VALLEY OF FLOWERS

COUNTRY India **TYPE OF ACTIVITY** Hiking
FITNESS/EXPERTISE LEVEL Moderate fitness required.
WHY NOW? For the valley's full floral display.
DESCRIPTION In 1931 British mountaineer Frank Smythe wandered into the Himalayan Bhyundar Valley to find many hundreds of species of wild flower carpeting the earth. He named the place – and it remains – the Valley of Flowers. Begin trekking from near the Uttaranchal town of Joshimath, a long, uncomfortable drive into the Himalaya from the yoga centre of Rishikesh, and follow the crowded pilgrims' trail towards the holy lake of Hem Kund. Branching away from the trail 6km before the lake, you enter the Valley of Flowers, which is about 10km long and 2km wide. At this time of year it's also a palette of colour. To protect the valley, camping is not allowed, but accommodation is available in Ghangaria, on the Hem Kund path, about 7km from the Valley of Flowers.

↗ DO: WINDSURF THE COLUMBIA RIVER GORGE

COUNTRY USA **TYPE OF ACTIVITY** Windsurfing
FITNESS/EXPERTISE LEVEL Beginners to pros.
WHY NOW? The winds are only suitable in summer.
DESCRIPTION In the Columbia River Gorge, forming the border between Oregon and Washington State, the 1.6km-wide river has carved a 1000m-deep chasm through the Cascade Range. What has formed (beyond a spectacular array of waterfalls) is a natural wind tunnel, with 30-knot winds pushing through the gorge from the cool, coastal west in summer. These westerlies, which directly oppose the river's flow, create optimal windsurfing conditions, and are generally strongest at the eastern end of the gorge. Experienced windsurfers head for a couple of heavy-duty sites near Maryhill, while the Wall is a small launch spot that attracts expert windsurfers who can handle huge swells. If you're new to windy ways, you'll find windsurfing schools in the town of Hood River. www.fs.fed.us

↗ DO: SWIM WITH FUNGIE

COUNTRY Ireland **TYPE OF ACTIVITY** Swimming/wildlife watching
FITNESS/EXPERTISE LEVEL Basic swimming skills required.
WHY NOW? Let the Atlantic get some summer warmth before you dive into it.
DESCRIPTION If any one thing rivals Dingle's pubs for fame it is Dingle Bay's resident dolphin, Fungie. In the winter of 1984 Dingle fishing crews began to notice a solitary bottlenose dolphin that followed their vessels, jumping about in the water and sometimes leaping over smaller boats. In the subsequent years Fungie has become an international celebrity and the world's most famous wild dolphin. A daily two-hour boat trip, operated by the Dingle Boatmen's Association, allows visitors the opportunity to swim with the 4m dolphin. Book well ahead for this is one very popular cetacean. One-hour boat trips also offer a drier look at Fungie.
www.dingle-peninsula.ie

Feast your eyes on wild flowers just a pleasant stroll from Ghangaria.

Wave jumping on a river? Yes, it can be done – and you can surf the Wall while you're at it.

AuSable River Canoe Marathon
www.ausablecanoemarathon.org
Race a canoe 190km along this Michigan River; expect to take about 16 hours.

Descenso Internacional del Sella
www.descensodelsella.com
Race a canoe 19km down the Sella River in northern Spain.

Avon Descent
www.avondescent.com.au
Paddling and power-dinghy race along 134km of Western Australia's Avon and Swan Rivers.

Boston Light Swim
www.bostonlightswim.org
USA's oldest marathon swim; stroke 13km across Boston Harbour.

week
.01

www.yearofadventures.com/august

Ladakh will leave you breathless in every sense of the word, however you choose to explore its high-altitude lunar landscape.

August

INDIA

week

↙ .02

www.yearofadventures.com/august

WHY NOW? THE POPULAR LEH TO MANALI ROAD IS USUALLY OPEN ONLY FROM MID-JULY TO MID-SEPTEMBER

Ladakh, literally 'the land of high passes', separates the peaks of the western Himalaya from the vast Tibetan plateau. Opened to tourism in 1974, Ladakh is often called 'Little Tibet', due to the similarities in topography and culture.

Access to Leh (3505m), the Ladakhi capital, is via one of two very different experiences: you can take a one-hour flight from Delhi for one of the most spectacular air journeys in the world, or you can drive for two days from Manali or Srinagar across high Himalayan passes. The popular Leh to Manali road is usually open only from mid-July to mid-September but dates depend on the passes being clear of snow. If you fly in, prepare to be greeted by altitude sickness. Take it easy for a couple of days, drinking water and not alcohol. At the end of this time you should be twitching to explore the desert foothills and snowcapped

↗ DO: CYCLE FROM BAÑOS TO PUYO

COUNTRY Ecuador **TYPE OF ACTIVITY** Cycling **FITNESS/EXPERTISE LEVEL** Moderate fitness required. **WHY NOW?** The highlands' dry(ish) season – June to September – offers the most comfortable cycling conditions. **DESCRIPTION** When it comes to incredible views of the upper Amazon Basin, it doesn't get much better than the stretch of road from Baños to Puyo in the central highlands of Ecuador. The bus ride is great, but taking in the views from the seat of a mountain bike is even better. It's mostly downhill – the road follows the Río Pastaza canyon as it drops steadily from Baños, at 1800m, to Puyo, at 950m – but there are some definite climbs, so ready those legs for the 60km ride. Along the way you'll pass Pailón del Diablo, one of Ecuador's most impressive waterfalls. Parts of the road are unsealed, and there's passport control at Shell, so carry your documents. From Puyo (or earlier), you can simply take a bus back to Baños, putting your bike on the roof. Several companies in Baños rent mountain bikes.

Bike down the Amazon – the best view may well be from the seat of your trusty treadly.

peaks that enclose this side chamber of the mighty Indus Valley.

Mountain trekking is king in Ladakh, where you can wander over passes and between the Buddhist gompas (monasteries) that balance atop sharp-edged rocky spurs. You'll find myriad trekking agencies in Leh willing to guide you through this starkly beautiful land. Most enticing of the trekking opportunities is the ancient kingdom of Zanskar, a haven for trekkers cut off from the rest of Ladakh by frozen passes for eight months of the year. Beautiful and dramatic, the high altitude will leave you short of breath in more ways than one.

White-water rafting trips on the Indus and Zanskar Rivers are possible from July to September. A popular taster is the three-hour thrill from Phey to Nimmu (grade two to three rapids), or you can arrange longer, customised trips.

Cyclists have also discovered Ladakh as the springboard for one of the great touring routes. Although only 475km in length, the raw and elemental road between Leh and Manali crosses four high passes (including Taglang La at 5328m), with high-altitude scenery that will most certainly astound and impress. Riding from Leh to Manali (2050m) means a net loss of altitude, but cycling from Manali means you can work on acclimatising as you ride. Take your pick.

o1   **o2**

o3   o4

Icebergs dead ahead! Lose yourself among the blue hulks of Glacier Bay National Park.

↗ DO: KAYAK IN GLACIER BAY

COUNTRY USA **TYPE OF ACTIVITY** Sea kayaking
FITNESS/EXPERTISE LEVEL Newcomers to experts.
WHY NOW? Cold seas, warm summer.
DESCRIPTION Ten tidewater glaciers that spill out of the mountains and fill the sea with icebergs of all shapes, sizes and shades of blue have made Glacier Bay National Park & Preserve an icy wilderness renowned worldwide. It's also a kayakers' paradise, despite the expense of getting there.

Using the tour boat MV *Spirit of Adventure* to drop you and your kayak off means your paddling options around Glacier Bay are extensive because you can be put ashore at one of several spots up bay. The landing sites are changed periodically in order to avoid habituating bears to human presence at any one spot.

Sebree Island, near the entrance of Muir Inlet, is a good spot to be dropped off because it allows you to avoid the long paddle from the park headquarters at Bartlett Cove. Many kayakers then travel the length of the inlet to McBride, Riggs and Muir Glaciers at the north end before returning to Sebree Island for a pickup. Such a trip would require five or six days of paddling. Those with more time but less money can book just a drop-off and then paddle back to Bartlett Cove, an eight- to 10-day trip. A round-trip paddle out of Bartlett Cove to the glaciers of Muir Inlet is a two-week adventure for most people. Whatever your paddle, keep a watch for humpback whales, which are migratory residents here over summer.

The most dramatic of Glacier Bay's eponymous blocks are in the West Arm, but the upper areas of this inlet are usually closed to campers and kayakers due to seal-pupping and brown bear activity.
www.nps.gov/glba

↗ DO: KITEBOARD ON MAUI

COUNTRY USA **TYPE OF ACTIVITY** Kiteboarding
FITNESS/EXPERTISE LEVEL Kite kids to kite kings.
WHY NOW? Expect the best winds from June to September.
DESCRIPTION The relatively new water sport of kiteboarding has become
so popular at the western end of Kanaha Beach on Maui's north shore
that they've renamed the place 'Kite Beach'. There are even areas set
aside solely for kiteboarders. A little like skateboarding or snowboarding
on water, kiteboarding is actually a form of surfing. While it may be
impressive to watch, it's hard to master. Instruction is available at Kite
Beach in three hour-long lessons. First you learn how to fly the kite, then
you practice body-dragging (letting the kite pull you across the water)
and finally you step on board. A reef keeps waters near the shore flat
for beginners, while the more experienced can head beyond the reef for
breaking waves.

↗ DO: MUDWALK IN GRONINGEN

COUNTRY Netherlands **TYPE OF ACTIVITY** Mud walking
FITNESS/EXPERTISE LEVEL Moderate fitness required.
WHY NOW? Buried knee-deep in a sea of mud, you're going to want a
warm time of year.
DESCRIPTION At low tide in the northern Dutch province of Groningen,
mud flats stretch from the coast all the way to the Frisian Islands.
Undeterred by this sloppy mess, the locals have turned it to their
advantage, creating the unique activity of *wadlopen* (mud walking). Treks
of up to 12km from the mainland to the islands are possible, though
the 7km walk to Schiermonnikoog is the most popular. The centre for
wadlopen is the tiny village of Pieterburen (22km north of Groningen),
where you'll find several groups of trained guides. Don't head out without
a skilled guide as it's easy to get lost on the mud flats, and without a good
knowledge of the tides you can end up under water, permanently.
www.wadlopen.net (in Dutch)

↗ DO: HIKE THE KOKODA TRAIL

COUNTRY Papua New Guinea **TYPE OF ACTIVITY** Hiking
FITNESS/EXPERTISE LEVEL Good fitness required.
WHY NOW? The coolest, driest and best months to trek are from May to
September.
DESCRIPTION Every one of the steep, slippery steps you take on the
Kokoda Trail's 96km natural rollercoaster requires concentration. Imagine,
then, how tough it must have been carrying a pack, rifle and ammunition,
constantly ill with dysentery and waiting to be ambushed by enemy
troops. Such was the trail's origin, with Japanese troops attempting a
sneak attack on Port Moresby, repelled eventually by Australian forces
and Papua New Guineans. Today, the trail attracts around 1100 hikers a
year, many to honour its history and many simply for a damn good hike.
You should use local guides and carriers, never walk with less than four
people, and allow between six and 11 days.

Nothing will quite prepare
you for the elemental thrill of
kiteboarding on Maui.

The perfect excuse to
wallow in the mud.

TransRockies
www.transrockies.com
Week-long, 600km mountain-bike event,
with around 12,000m of climbs.

**Atlantic Island – Around the Island
Marathon Swim**
www.acswim.org
Swim 36km around Absecon Island,
including a 16km ocean leg.

Sierre-Zinal
www.sierre-zinal.com (in French)
A 31km mountain run through the Swiss
Alps, with views on to five 4000m peaks.

Leadville Trail 100
www.leadvilletrail100.com
Mountain bike 161km through the
Colorado Rockies, or come a week
later to run the same course.

week
.02

www.yearofadventures.com/august

Not just another 'stan – Kyrgyzstan is home to the highest and most beautiful peaks of the Tian Shan mountain range, so pack your trekking boots.

August

↙ GO ↙ **CENTRAL TIAN SHAN,**
KYRGYZSTAN

week
↙ **.03**

www.yearofadventures.com/august

WHY NOW? MOST HIGH-ALTITUDE TREKS OR CLIMBS TAKE PLACE IN JULY OR AUGUST

This highest and mightiest part of Central Asia's Tian Shan mountain system is at the eastern end of Kyrgyzstan. It's an immense knot of ranges, with dozens of summits above 5000m, which culminates in Pik Pobedy (Victory Peak, 7439m) and Khan Tengri (7010m) – it's one of the most beautiful peaks in the world, and is often likened to the Matterhorn.

The best selection of treks is out of the town of Karakol. The Terskey Alatau range that rises behind the town offers a fine taste of the Tian Shan. Of numerous possible routes that climb to passes below 4000m, the best take in the alpine lake Ala-Köl above Karakol, and the Altyn Arashan hot springs above Ak-Suu.

Of the Tian Shan's thousands of glaciers, the grandest is 60km-long Inylchek, rumbling westward from both sides of Khan Tengri. Across the

Icy-cold lake Ala-Köl is worth feasting your eyes upon, but we don't recommend a dip!

↗ DO: CLIMB SVOLVÆRGEITA

COUNTRY Norway **TYPE OF ACTIVITY** Rock climbing **FITNESS/EXPERTISE LEVEL** Climbing experience (and a head for heights) required. **WHY NOW?** Who wants to climb this far north at any time other than summer? **DESCRIPTION** The small but modern port town of Svolvær is as busy as it gets on Norway's Lofoten Islands, and much of the activity centres on a pinnacle of rock. Svolværgeita, (the Svolvær Goat), is one of the symbols of Lofoten, a distinctive two-pronged peak that towers above the town. Climbing it is claimed as one of Norway's great adrenaline rushes, not so much for the climb but for the challenge once you reach its top. Having scaled the Goat, it's almost compulsory that you then jump from one 'horn' to the other. Nearly anyone can get to the base of Svolværgeita, but reaching the horns, Storhornet and Lillehornet, requires a 40m technical climb before you make the 1.5m jump between them. Don't look down if you think a view of the town cemetery might be off-putting.

Look, no ropes! Take a death-defying leap across the void at the pinnacle of Svolværgeita.

glacier's northern arm, where it joins the southern arm, a huge, iceberg-filled lake – Lake Merzbacher – forms at 3300m every summer. Some time in early August, the lake bursts its ice-banks and explodes into the Inylchek River below.

The most common walking route to the Inylchek Glacier is a remote and wild five- or six-day trek from Jyrgalang. You'll need the support of a trekking agency to guide you over the glacier, keep you in supplies and let you stay in its base camps. With an experienced guide it's possible to continue over the glacier for one long day to Lake Merzbacher and continue the next day to the camps. Most groups take in a stunning helicopter route around the valley and out to Inylchek town.

Nearby Lake Issyk-Kul is arguably Kyrgyzstan's biggest attraction. At 170km long, 70km across and a maximum depth of 695m, it's the second-largest alpine lake, after South America's Lake Titicaca, and has an astonishing array of ecosystems, from desert and semidesert to steppe, meadow, forest, subalpine and glacial. Plans are afoot to create a reserve the size of Switzerland around the lake.

The best walking season is June through to September, with most high-altitude treks or climbs taking place in July or August.

o1 o2
o3 o4

Remember not to hyperventilate as you sink into sharkdom off the Isla del Coco (Cocos Island).

↗ DO: **DIVE WITH HAMMERHEAD SHARKS**

COUNTRY Costa Rica **TYPE OF ACTIVITY** Diving/wildlife watching
FITNESS/EXPERTISE LEVEL Experienced divers only.
WHY NOW? For the sharks, school is in.

DESCRIPTION In the opening minutes of the film *Jurassic Park*, a small helicopter swoops over and around a lushly forested island with dramatic tropical peaks descending straight into clear blue waters. That island is Isla del Coco (Cocos Island), around 600km southwest of the Costa Rican mainland in the eastern Pacific Ocean. It's extremely wet, with about 7000mm of annual rainfall, and legend has it that a band of pirates buried a huge treasure here – despite more than 5000 treasure-hunting expeditions, it's never been found.

For divers, however, there is indeed a great treasure chest here, one reflected in the title of an IMAX film shot here: *Island of the Sharks*. This film wasn't fantasy; the waters around Cocos Island offer probably the best shark diving in the world and some of the most memorable underwater experiences on the planet.

Though it's the wet season in Central America, it's also the busiest time for sharks. Due to Cocos Island's isolation and the fact that you cannot stay on the island, live-aboard boats are your ticket to the sharks – two companies, Undersea Hunter and Okeanos Aggressor, operate eight- to 10-day diving trips out of San Jose.

The customary first dive is in the protected waters around Manuelita Island, a shark cleaning station off the northern tip of Cocos, but it's the submerged mountain at Alcyone that is the great drawcard. Here the largest schools of hammerheads are found, white-tip reef sharks mill about like ants and whale sharks have been known to cruise by. You'll wonder if Jacques Cousteau was looking above or below the ocean surface when he described Cocos as the 'most beautiful island in the world'.
www.aggressor.com; www.underseahunter.com

Coasteering – that cliff-hanging, cutting-edge adventure sport calls the Pembrokeshire coast in Wales its home.

Quttinirpaaq (even the name has a mysterious ring) is a destination truly out of the ordinary – with a price tag to match.

↗ DO: COASTEER IN PEMBROKESHIRE

COUNTRY Wales TYPE OF ACTIVITY Coasteering
FITNESS/EXPERTISE LEVEL Good swimming skills required.
WHY NOW? You're going to be leaping into the Irish Sea, so you want summer at full beam. DESCRIPTION Coasteering is Wales' private piece of adventuring, pioneered on the Pembrokeshire coast in the 1980s and still comfortably at home here. It's something of a superhero sport, like canyoning along a cliff-rimmed coast. Equipped with wetsuit, flotation jacket and helmet, you traverse along the coastal cliffs by a combination of climbing, traversing, scrambling, cliff jumping and swimming. Routes are graded, so you can choose your dunking according to the level of difficulty. Give coasteering a try around its birthplace, St Davids, or head north to Snowdonia. Your only regret will be that coasteering wasn't created in a place with warmer water.

↗ DO: HIKE ON MT OLYMPUS

COUNTRY Greece TYPE OF ACTIVITY Hiking
FITNESS/EXPERTISE LEVEL Good fitness required.
WHY NOW? For the most favourable mountain conditions.
DESCRIPTION Mt Olympus, chosen by the ancients as the abode of their gods, is Greece's highest and most awe-inspiring mountain and the country's first national park. It takes two days to climb to Olympus' highest peak, Mytikas (2918m), with one night spent in a refuge, though it's worth spending more time if you really want to explore the mountain. The village of Litohoro is the best base for Olympus; it has bus connections to Athens and Thessaloniki. The most popular trail up the mountain begins at Prionia, a tiny settlement 18km from Litohoro. Most people drive or take a taxi to Prionia, but you can trek there along an 11km marked trail, which follows the course of the Enipeas River. The strenuous 4½-hour trek is over sharply undulating terrain, but offers glorious views. From Prionia, it's a 2½-hour walk to Refuge A, which can accommodate 140 people.

↗ DO: VISIT QUTTINIRPAAQ NATIONAL PARK

COUNTRY Canada TYPE OF ACTIVITY Adventure travel
FITNESS/EXPERTISE LEVEL Not required.
WHY NOW? Arctic Canada...better come in summer.
DESCRIPTION If you have a fortune to squander, a fun way to do it would be to visit Quttinirpaaq, Canada's second-largest and most northerly national park, tucked into the end of faraway Ellesmere Island. A charter plane from the town of Resolute costs around $32,000 round-trip for up to six people. What you get for your buck is the chance to visit Cape Columbia, North America's northernmost point (located above 80° north); 2616m Mt Barbeau; and Lake Hazen Basin, a thermal oasis where the animals, due to their unfamiliarity with humans, appear strangely tame. It's a place for the person who thinks they've been everywhere.
www.pc.gc.ca/pn-np/nu/quttinirpaaq/index_E.asp

Boston-Montreal-Boston (BMB)
www.geocities.com/b-m-b
North America's major 1200km randonnée, with a 90-hour time limit. Held every year that Paris-Brest-Paris is not.

Grand Raid Cristalp
www.grand-raid-cristalp.ch
Mountain bike 131km while climbing around 4700m through the Swiss Alps.

Björkliden Arctic Mountain Marathon
www.bamm.nu/en
Two-day (50km or 70km) mountain orienteering race 200km north of the Arctic Circle.

Pikes Peak Marathon
www.pikespeakmarathon.org
Ascend almost 2400m over 21.5km to reach one of the USA's highest summits.

week
.03

www.yearofadventures.com/august

Step outside the stereotypes of modern Japan and trek wild Hokkaidō's land of volcanoes.

August

↙ GO: HOKKAIDŌ, JAPAN

www.yearofadventures.com/august

WHY NOW? COME AT THE END OF AUGUST AND YOU CAN WITNESS THE BEGINNING OF THE WAVE OF AUTUMN COLOURS

The northernmost of Japan's islands, Hokkaidō accounts for more than 20% of the country's land area yet it contains just 5% of the population. The real beauty of the island lies in its wilderness regions, where there are no cultural monuments but there is superb scope for outdoor activities. There are 10 active volcanoes on Hokkaidō, and while some are occasionally closed to hikers, it can be an intriguing experience to scale a volcano with sulphur shooting out of cracks in the rocks.

Daisetsuzan National Park – Japan's largest national park – is both the island's crown and its jewel, covering Hokkaidō's highest peaks and dominating the tourist scene. Most visitors, however, only travel around its boundaries, riding the gondolas and taking little more than a glance at its beauty. To really appreciate this landscape you must walk – a five-day traverse can take you across the summits of more than a dozen alpine

↗ DO: SURF AT PUERTO ESCONDIDO

COUNTRY Mexico **TYPE OF ACTIVITY** Surfing **FITNESS/EXPERTISE LEVEL** Good surfing skills and experience required. **WHY NOW?** The May to September wet season brings the best waves. **DESCRIPTION** Mexico's Pacific coast has some awesome waves. Among the very best are the summer breaks at spots between San José del Cabo and Cabo San Lucas in Baja California, and the 'world's longest wave' on Bahía de Matanchén, near San Blas. Most famous and cherished are the barreling waves at Puerto Escondido, a place that has become known as the 'Mexican Pipeline'. Escondido's barrels roll into long, straight Zicatela Beach, which doubles as the town's hip hang-out, with its enticing cafés, restaurants and accommodation. The heavy beach break here will test the mettle of most surfers and can be matched by the heavy locals. Celebrate a day of waves with a customary bit of Puerto partying.

¡Arriba! Take a ride on the Mexican Pipeline.

peaks, including Hokkaidō's highest, the active volcano Asahi-dake (2290m).

Eight more Hokkaidō national parks will continue to challenge any preconceived ideas you have about an urban, neon-powered Japan. In Shiretoko National Park you can choose your poison: the active volcano Iō-san, or Japan's highest concentration of brown bears (numbering around 600). Akan National Park contains several volcanic peaks, and while there aren't many extended hikes, there are plenty of day-walk options and postcard-perfect crater lakes. Shikotsu-Tōya National Park offers an even more personal look at volcanoes – Shōwa Shin-zan erupted in 2000 – with fast and easy access to the island's major airport if you're in a hurry.

A welcome by-product of all this thermal indigestion is the presence of so many *onsen*, or natural hot springs. Soaking in one is an activity as Japanese as sumo. You'll even find a spring at the end of your Daisetsuzan traverse.

Hokkaido's relative sparseness also makes it a great cycling destination, as you can pedal 2500km around its perimeter roads.

The lively city of Sapporo is Hokkaidō's major centre, with good air and rail connections to Tokyo. Hokkaidō summers are fleeting things, with July and August the best months.

o1 o2
o3 **o4**

Cyclists, pull on your knicks and start training! You'll want to be in good shape to attempt the Paris-Brest-Paris, the pinnacle of endurance cycling.

↗ DO: PARIS–BREST–PARIS

COUNTRY France **TYPE OF ACTIVITY** Endurance cycling

FITNESS/EXPERTISE LEVEL Supreme endurance required.

WHY NOW? Grab the chance, for it comes around only once every four years.

DESCRIPTION The PBP, as it is affectionately known, is the most prestigious event in the world of non-competitive long-distance cycling, running since 1891. The 1200km event is held every four years (2007, 2011) in the last week of August and attracts around 3500 riders from all over the world.

The PBP starts at St Quentin-en-Yvelines, near Versailles, southwest of Paris, and meanders west through Normandy and Brittany on a convoluted series of tiny, hilly roads to Brest (613km) before returning to Paris.

Participants are required to finish the course within 90 hours, thereby averaging at least 13.3km/h. The large bunches charge off the starting line as if in a short time trial. Despite using roads open to normal traffic, the peloton often occupies the full width of the carriageway. If traffic appears from the opposite direction, the whole bunch suddenly squeezes on to the right-hand side, where riders on the outside can be squeezed off the bitumen, ending up ignominiously in a muddy ditch.

Cyclists ride for much of the day and night. The resulting sleep deprivation is a major hazard and a reason for many abandonments. Riders have been known to fall asleep, crash and be unable to continue.

Riders pass through around 10 *contrôle* (checkpoint) towns, where the town's residents turn out to watch, cheer or set up unofficial wayside feeding stations, creating an atmosphere not unlike the Tour de France. Prospective participants must qualify by completing a series of Audax Club Parisien–sanctioned lead-up rides involving randonnées of 200km, 300km, 400km and 600km in the year prior to PBP. These must be ridden within time limits based on an average speed of 15km/h. www.audax-club-parisien.com

↗ DO: **ANGEL FALLS**

COUNTRY Venezuela **TYPE OF ACTIVITY** Adventure travel
FITNESS/EXPERTISE LEVEL Not required.
WHY NOW? The best time to see Angel Falls is during the wettest months
of August and September.
DESCRIPTION The world's highest waterfall, Angel Falls has a total height
of 979m and an uninterrupted drop of 807m, 16 times the height of
Niagara Falls. It's in a distant wilderness without any road access. The
village of Canaima, about 50km northwest, is the major gateway but it
also doesn't have any overland link to the rest of the country. A visit to the
falls is normally undertaken in two stages, flying into Canaima and then
taking a light plane or boat to the falls. In the wet months of August and
September the falls will be voluminous and spectacular, though frequently
covered by cloud.

↗ DO: **HIKE THE KALALAU TRAIL**

COUNTRY USA **TYPE OF ACTIVITY** Hiking
FITNESS/EXPERTISE LEVEL Good fitness required.
WHY NOW? Kauai is one of the world's wettest places, but August sees
an average of just 45mm of rain in Lihue. **DESCRIPTION** By reputation the
Kalalau Trail is Hawaii's premier hiking trail. It's also a heartbreaking path,
both beautiful and brutal, following an ancient Hawaiian footpath along
the valleys of Kauai's famous Na Pali Coast. It passes hidden waterfalls,
wild beaches and visions of traditional Hawaii, ending below the steep
fluted *pali* (cliffs) of Kalalau, where the sheer green cliffs drop into brilliant
turquoise waters. Though these cliffs aren't Hawaii's highest, they are
indeed the grandest. The classic hike involves walking 18km into Kalalau
Valley on the first day, camping at Kalalau Beach for two nights and then
hiking back out the third day. Permits are required to hike the Kalalau
Trail, and the campgrounds are often booked up months ahead, so apply
for your permit as far in advance as possible (up to one year is allowed).
www.kauai-hawaii.com

↗ DO: **CLIMB TAVAN BOGD UUL**

COUNTRY Mongolia **TYPE OF ACTIVITY** Mountaineering
FITNESS/EXPERTISE LEVEL Mountaineering skills required.
WHY NOW? The best time to climb is August and September, after the
heaviest of the summer rains. **DESCRIPTION** At 4374m, Mongolia's
highest mountain forms the borders of three nations, and for this reason
it's also known as Nairamdal (Friendship) Peak. Atop the summit you
can simultaneously be in Mongolia, China and Russia. Tavan Bogd is also
one of Mongolia's most spectacular peaks, and the only one in the area
to be permanently covered with large glaciers (including the 19km long
Potanii Glacier, the longest in Mongolia). To climb it, you need to be with
an experienced group equipped with ice axes, crampons and ropes. Don't
even consider attempting it solo. If you have your own vehicle, you can
drive to within about 40km of the base of the mountain. From here, it's a
17km trek to the first glacier, where most climbers set up base camp. The
climb up the glacier is about 25km, and you can expect to encounter icy
temperatures, crevasses and very volatile weather.

Watch water cascade nearly
1000m at the world's highest
waterfall, remote Angel Falls.

Everything you ever
imagined Hawaii to be
is encapsulated in the
devastatingly beautiful
Kalalau Trail.

Oxfam Trailwalker Sydney
www.oxfam.org.au/trailwalker/sydney
Run or walk (or both) through 100km of
Australian bush in less than 48 hours.

**World Bog Snorkelling
Championships**
http://llanwrtyd-wells.powys.org.uk
Ever wondered what it would be like to
stick your head down a dirty toilet?

Birkebeinerrittet
www.birkebeiner.no/ritt_eng
Billed as the world's largest mountain-
bike race (12,500 riders in 2005); pedal
89km from Rena to Lillehammer.

Ultra Trail Mont Blanc
www.ultratrailmb.com
Run 158km through three
countries, ascending 8500m
as you loop around Mont
Blanc within 45 hours.

week
.04

www.yearofadventures.com/august

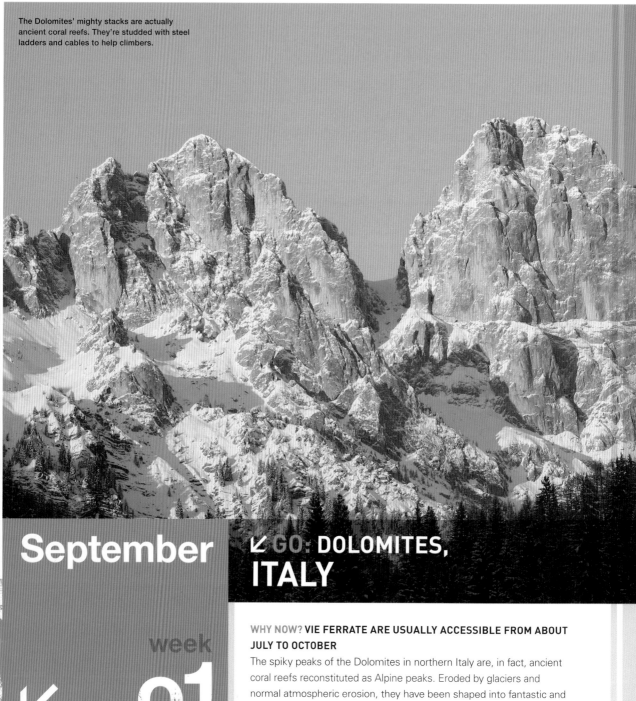

The Dolomites' mighty stacks are actually ancient coral reefs. They're studded with steel ladders and cables to help climbers.

September

week

.01

www.yearofadventures.com/september

↙ GO: DOLOMITES, ITALY

WHY NOW? VIE FERRATE ARE USUALLY ACCESSIBLE FROM ABOUT JULY TO OCTOBER

The spiky peaks of the Dolomites in northern Italy are, in fact, ancient coral reefs reconstituted as Alpine peaks. Eroded by glaciers and normal atmospheric erosion, they have been shaped into fantastic and spectacular formations. Appropriately, such unique Alpine mountains have spawned a unique mountain pastime.

Via ferrata (iron way), is the Dolomites' gift to mountain lovers. Neither hiking nor mountaineering, it is, like scrambling, a middle ground for those who seek something more or less than these two common Alpine pursuits. A *via ferrata* uses intriguing and often ingenious combinations of ladders, metal brackets, chiselled footholds and even bridges to allow progress on steep or vertical cliffs. Steel cable is bolted to the rock at waist level. The cable acts as both a handhold and security, with walkers clipping onto it with a lanyard and karabiner system.

↗ DO: HIKE IN THE RILA MOUNTAINS

COUNTRY Bulgaria **TYPE OF ACTIVITY** Hiking **FITNESS/EXPERTISE LEVEL** Good fitness recommended for Rila's steep slopes. **WHY NOW?** Catch the tail end of the summer hiking season. **DESCRIPTION** The Rila Mountains might be small (2629 sq km) but they are beautiful, boasting 180 perennial lakes and streams and numerous mineral springs (*rila* comes from the Thracian word for 'mountains of water'), and Mt Musala (2925m), the highest peak in the Balkans. The mountains are steep but the spectacular views, flora and fauna make the hard work worth it. One popular three-day hike starts at Malîovitsa, visits the magnificent Sedemte Ezera (Seven Lakes) and finishes at Rila Monastery, Bulgaria's largest and most renowned monastery. A more sustained seven-day outing involves a north–south crossing of the range from Klisura to Hizha Predel. Mountain huts (*hizha*), provide dormitory accommodation. Many serve meals but these can be basic, so it may be advisable to bring food: inquire first. www.rilanationalpark.org/en

No wonder it's known as the 'mountains of water' – the Rilas have over 180 lakes and streams and countless mineral springs.

The first *vie ferrate* were created as military tools to move troops and equipment quickly and safely over difficult terrain, and there are now more than 80 routes through the Dolomites. The most popular is probably Ivano Dibona, a spectacular but technically straightforward route to the summit of Monte Cristallo above Cortina d'Ampezzo.

The standout *via ferrata*, however, is the Bocchette Alte (High Bocchette) in the Brenta Dolomites. This advanced route is probably the most difficult in the Brenta Dolomites, requiring basic alpine skills to cope with crossing steep snow gullies. The popular Bocchette Centrali offers an excellent intermediate route. It is well protected, featuring spectacularly exposed ledges and ladders. The Bocchette routes can be accessed by cable car from Madonna di Campiglio.

The Dolomites can also be seen by more conventional methods. Hiking paths crisscross the mountains, included four Alte Vie (High Routes), each taking up to two weeks. These routes link existing trails and incorporate new trails that make difficult sections easier to traverse. Other summer pastimes include mountain biking, hang-gliding and rock climbing.

For more information, visit www.dolomiti.org.

Look into those eyes and tell me you wouldn't secretly yearn to pat this pint-sized Río Madidi monkey.

↗ DO: PARQUE NACIONAL MADIDI

COUNTRY Bolivia **TYPE OF ACTIVITY** Wildlife watching
FITNESS/EXPERTISE LEVEL Not required.
WHY NOW? Bask in the dry season.
DESCRIPTION The Río Madidi watershed is one of South America's most intact ecosystems. Most of it is protected by the 18,000-sq-km Parque Nacional Madidi, which takes in a range of habitats, from steaming lowland rainforests to 5500m Andean peaks. This little-trodden utopia is home to a mind-boggling variety of Amazonian wildlife, including 44% of all New World mammal species, 38% of tropical amphibian species, over 10% of the world's bird species and more animal and plant species than any other South American reserve.

Most of the park is effectively inaccessible, which is why it remains such a treasure, but Madidi also has a special Unesco designation permitting indigenous inhabitants to use traditional forest resources. There's only one accommodation option in the park: Chalalán Ecolodge, on the idyllic oxbow lake, Laguna Chalalán. This simple but comfortable lodge, surrounded by relatively untouched rainforest, allows visitors to amble through the jungle and appreciate its incredible richness. Although the flora and fauna are lovely, sounds more than sights provide the magic here: the incredible dawn bird chorus, the evening frog symphony, the collective whine of zillions of insects, the roar of bucketing tropical rainstorms and, in the early morning, the thunder-like chorus of every howler monkey within a 100km radius.

If all this sounds too primeval, be comforted: Madidi is also home to the world's first dot-com animal. With the discovery of a new titi monkey in 2004, park authorities saw on a unique fundraising opportunity – they auctioned the naming rights. An internet gaming company secured the rights for US$650,000, and the monkey's common name officially became GoldenPalace.com monkey. www.chalalan.com (in Spanish)

o1 o2
o3 o4

↗ DO: **SWIM WITH HUMPBACK WHALES**

COUNTRY Tonga **TYPE OF ACTIVITY** Swimming/wildlife watching
FITNESS/EXPERTISE LEVEL Good swimming skills required.
WHY NOW? It's the middle of the whale season.
DESCRIPTION Whale-watching tours are offered throughout the world, but only on the Tongan island group of Vava'u can you actually swim beside the whales, a controversial if exhilarating brush with nature. Humpback whales come to these waters between July and November, and visitors to the town of Neiafu can board boats, cruise up to the whales and snorkel around them. It's a controversial practice – some say the regular presence of boats and humans in the water disturbs the mothers and calves just when they are most vulnerable, and may force them to abandon the area before they are ready. One tour operator in Neiafu refuses to allow swimming for this reason. But many people who have swum with whales say they experience a sense of mutual curiosity, rather than alarm or distress.

Want a once-in-a-lifetime chance to swim with humpbacks and their calves? The choice is yours.

Untangle the strands of the Silk Road, an ancient network of caravan tracks once used to bring Chinese silk west.

↗ DO: **TRAVEL THE SILK ROAD**

REGION Central Asia **TYPE OF ACTIVITY** Adventure travel
FITNESS/EXPERTISE LEVEL Not required.
WHY NOW? To cross through Central Asia after its baking summer.
DESCRIPTION Geographically, the famed Silk Road was never a single road, but rather a fragile network of shifting intercontinental caravan tracks that wended through some of the highest mountains and bleakest deserts on earth, and along which the prized thread silk travelled west from China. The network had its main eastern terminus at the Chinese capital, Ch'ang-an (modern Xi'an), and frayed like rope as it crossed Central Asia to Constantinople or Antioch in Syria. Today, almost any overland crossing between Xi'an and the Middle East will follow strands of this celebrated trading route. Classic Silk Road stops include Kashgar (China), Samarkand (Uzbekistan) and Bukhara (Uzbekistan).

Marathon of Britain
www.marathonofbritain.com/mob
Run 280km in six days across a variety of
British landscapes.

Liffey Descent
www.liffeydescent.com
Paddle 28km on Ireland's Liffey River;
do it in earnest or just for the craic, but
watch out for the Straffan Weir.

Maui Channel Swim
www.mauichannelswim.com
Team relay swim, crossing the 15.3km
channel between the Hawaiian islands of
Lanai and Maui.

Durango MTB 100
www.gravityplay.com/MTB100
Mountain bike 161km, climbing across
the Colorado Rockies.

↗ DO: **CYCLE THE ICEFIELDS PARKWAY**

COUNTRY Canada **TYPE OF ACTIVITY** Cycle touring
FITNESS/EXPERTISE LEVEL Moderate fitness required.
WHY NOW? Cracking weather and cracking views without the bumper-to-bumper midsummer traffic.
DESCRIPTION Opened in 1940, the 230km Icefields Parkway that links Lake Louise with Jasper remains one of Canada's most spectacular stretches of road. The highway follows a lake-lined valley between two chains of the Eastern Main Ranges, which make up the Continental Divide. The mountains here are the highest, craggiest and maybe the most scenic in all the Rockies; little wonder that often there are more hikes than cars on the road. Some have even called this the most beautiful cycling route in the world. You'll find a host of well-spaced camping grounds and hostels along the Parkway, outnumbered only by the wildlife – in addition to the gawking tourists (you'll be one of them), goats, bighorn sheep and elk often linger beside the road or even on it. Because of the terrain, it's easier to begin at Lake Louise and cycle to Jasper.

week

.01

www.yearofadventures.com/september

143

In Xīnjiāng, northeast China, civilisations collide and a 1000km expanse of desert meets a mighty mountain range.

September

week

.02

www.yearofadventures.com/september

↙ **GO:** XĪNJIĀNG,
CHINA

WHY NOW? HIT THIS DESERT PROVINCE BETWEEN THE BLAZE OF HIGH SUMMER AND THE BITE OF WINTER

Xīnjiāng is like a whole other country enclosed within China's borders. Vast deserts stretch over 1000km before ending abruptly at the foot of towering mountain ranges, and its extreme climate has been a defining aspect of its culture throughout the centuries. Abandoned Buddhist cities lie along the treacherous trade routes of times past, while in newer oasis towns, Islamic monuments point the way to the future.

Gone are the trifling regional differences between Beijing and Guangzhou – here the language is not just a different dialect, it's a completely different linguistic family; it's no longer about whether you dip your dumplings in soy sauce or vinegar, it's how you want your mutton cooked. However you look at it, the province is a world apart, more Central Asian than East Asian, but nevertheless with a fate that's always been inextricably tethered to the Middle Kingdom.

↗ DO: OKAVANGO DELTA BY MOKORO

COUNTRY Botswana **TYPE OF ACTIVITY** Adventure travel/wildlife watching **FITNESS/ EXPERTISE LEVEL** Not required. **WHY NOW?** From July to September water levels are high and the weather is dry. **DESCRIPTION** The Okavango River is Southern Africa's third-longest waterway, the 'river that never sees the sea', with more than 18 billion cubic metres of water spreading and sprawling annually through the inland delta, a maze of lagoons, channels and islands covering an area of almost 16,000 sq km. The abundant water attracts vast numbers of wildlife – elephants, zebras, buffaloes, wildebeests, giraffes, hippos, kudus and innumerable birds. The best way to see them is by *mokoro*, a traditional dugout canoe ideally suited to the shallow delta waters. They can accommodate two passengers and some limited luggage, and are propelled by a poler who stands at the back of the canoe. Day trips can be taken from the city of Maun, or you can glide across the delta for several days.

Glide across the 16,000 sq km Okavango Delta, a waterworld where wildlife thrives.

Xīnjiāng is China's most arid province; it contains the country's hottest and coldest places; it has the longest inland river, the Tarim; the largest desert; and the second-lowest lake in the world, Aydingkul Lake.

It's also a place from where you can set out to explore two of the world's great overland routes: the Karakoram Hwy and the Silk Road. The former heads south over high Khunjerab Pass, while the latter runs east from Kashgar, splitting into two in the face of the huge Taklamakan Desert. Within Xīnjiāng, this ancient route is marked by a ring of abandoned cities deserted by retreating rivers and swallowed by encroaching sands. Cities such as Niya, Miran and Yotkan remain covered by sand.

This is a great time of year to explore. You can fly to the provincial capital, Ürümqi, from Beijing, or if you want an adventurous approach to an adventurous destination, follow the southern Silk Road in through Charklik to Ali in Tibet.

o1 **o2**
o3 o4

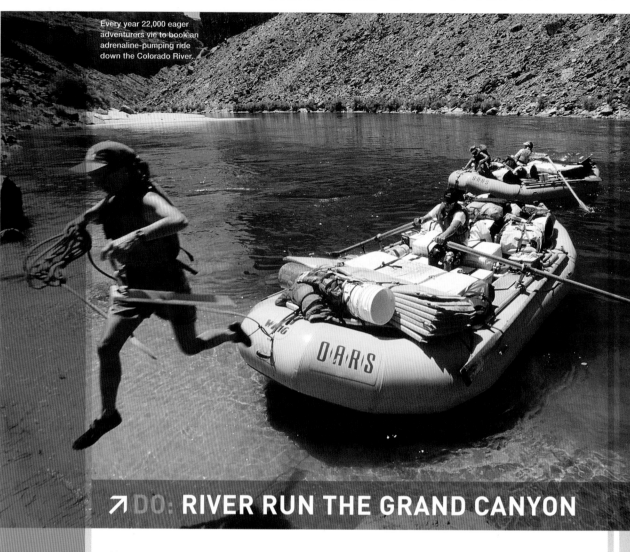

Every year 22,000 eager adventurers vie to book an adrenaline-pumping ride down the Colorado River.

⊅ DO: RIVER RUN THE GRAND CANYON

COUNTRY USA **TYPE OF ACTIVITY** White-water rafting
FITNESS/EXPERTISE LEVEL Not required for commercial trips; extensive experience needed for private trips. **WHY NOW?** Travel outside the peak summer season and you stand some chance of securing a place on a trip. **DESCRIPTION** If standing on the South Rim peering at the dark line of the Colorado River has you twitching for a more intimate canyon experience, join the 22,000-plus people who run the river in rafts and inflatable boats each year.

A run down the Colorado River is an epic, adrenaline-pumping adventure. 'Normal' rapids are rated one through five (with five being pretty damn tough), but the 160-plus rapids on the Colorado are rated one to 10, with many five or higher. Two merit a 10! The biggest single drop is at Lava Falls, which plummets 11 stomach-churning metres in less than 300m.

Rafting the Colorado independently is so popular that a hold was placed on applications in 2003. On a commercial trip, your biggest decision is picking a boat – oar, paddle or motorised. Motorised inflatable boats go twice as fast as oar or paddle boats, and tend to be the most stable (meaning you'll probably still fall out, but there is less chance of the boat flipping). For more excitement, take an oar boat (the most common raft on the river), which still provides stability, but feels more like a raft. The guide does all the rowing (thus retaining control on big rapids). For heart-attack fun, take a paddle trip. You, your shipmates and a guide paddle. Overturning is almost guaranteed and you're dependent on your shipmates' paddling skills.

Given two or three weeks, you can run the entire 446km of river through the canyon. Three shorter sections (each 160km or less) take four to nine days. Trips fill up months (even a year) in advance, so plan early. www.nps.gov/grca

↗ DO: **PONY TREK IN LESOTHO**

COUNTRY Lesotho **TYPE OF ACTIVITY** Pony trekking
FITNESS/EXPERTISE LEVEL Not required.
WHY NOW? Cool and comfortable trekking ahead of the wet season.
DESCRIPTION Pony trekking is one of Lesotho's top drawcards. It's done
on sure-footed Basotho ponies, the result of crossbreeding between
short Javanese horses and European full mounts. Lesotho's revered King
Moshoeshoe the Great is recorded as having ridden a Basotho pony in
1830, and since that time these animals have become the preferred mode
of transport for many villagers. Malealea is arguably the best pony trekking
centre, with popular routes that include Ribaneng Waterfall (two days);
Ribaneng and Ketane Waterfalls (four days); and Semonkong (five to six
days). The Basotho Pony Trekking Centre, atop the delightfully named God
Help Me Pass, is more no-frills and do-it-yourself, and the place to come
if you want to ride away from the crowds for up to a week. For overnight
treks, you'll need to bring food (stock up in the capital, Maseru), a sleeping
bag and warm, waterproof clothing.

↗ DO: **HIKE AROUND MT KAILASH**

COUNTRY Tibet **TYPE OF ACTIVITY** Hiking/pilgrimage
FITNESS/EXPERTISE LEVEL Moderate fitness required.
WHY NOW? Get here before the winter snows do (usually October).
DESCRIPTION The 52km circuit *(kora)* of Mt Kailash (6714m) is one of the
most important pilgrimages in Asia, holy to Hindus, Buddhists, Bon-pos
and Jains. Tibetan Buddhists believe that a single circuit cleanses the sins
of one life, while 108 circuits brings nirvana in this life. The hike isn't easy,
since it crosses a 5630m pass, though some devout pilgrims walk it in a
day. Four days is more comfortable, and if you think you're doing it tough,
look out for the pious pilgrims who circuit by prostrating themselves –
lying on the ground, standing and walking to the point their hands reached
on the ground before lying down once again.

↗ DO: **DIVE IN EAST TIMOR**

COUNTRY East Timor **TYPE OF ACTIVITY** Diving
FITNESS/EXPERTISE LEVEL Some diving experience is best.
WHY NOW? For clear water and the prospect of manta rays and whale
sharks. **DESCRIPTION** Scuba diving and snorkelling has been the most
successful adventure activity to develop in East Timor since the country
gained its independence in 2002. Coral reefs run close to shore, and
divers only have to wade in and swim a few strokes to reach spectacular
drop-offs. The reefs offer a colourful array of hard and soft corals with a
vivid assortment of reef fish. Pelagics and open-water species such as
tuna, bonito and mackerel are also regularly encountered, along with
harmless reef sharks, manta rays, dolphins and dugongs. The water is
clearest from April to September, with visibility typically 20m to 35m and
water temperature around 26°C to 28°C. Dive operators can be found in
the capital, Dili, with some dive sites very close to the city. Atauro Island,
30km north from Dili, also has superb diving and day trips can be made
from Dili.

Take the donkey work out of exploring Lesotho – ride through this rolling land on a Basotho pony.

One of the world's most sacred sites, Mt Kailash is circled by countless pilgrims in search of enlightenment.

Paris–Dakar by Bike
www.bike-dreams.com
Inaugurated in 2006; 10 weeks, 7000km
from Paris to Dakar on two wheels,
not four.

Three Peaks Alpine Marathon
www.dreizinnenmarathon.com
A 21km road and mountain-track run
through the Dolomites, ascending to a
snowy 2575m at Büllelejoch Hut.

Colorado Relay
www.coloradorelay.com
Teams of five or 10 run 273km in a day.

Jungfrau Marathon
www.jungfrau-marathon.ch
Marathon-length Swiss trail run
from Interlaken to Kleine Scheidegg,
ascending around 1500m.

week

.02

www.yearofadventures.com/september

Six thousand kilometres of sparkling Adriatic coastline sprinkled with islands makes an enticing prospect – in, on or out of the water.

September

↙ GO: CROATIA

week ↙ .03

www.yearofadventures.com/september

WHY NOW? IN SEPTEMBER, THE CROWDS WILL HAVE THINNED OUT AND OFF-SEASON ACCOMMODATION RATES ARE IN PLACE

In 2005 Croatia was voted both the 'hot' travel destination by Lonely Planet staff and the *National Geographic Adventure* destination of the year, which makes this Balkan nation difficult to resist.

With almost 6000km of coastline and 1185 islands (of which only 66 are inhabited), it's little surprise that much of the activity in Croatia takes place on the water. The long, rugged islands off the mountainous coast stretch all the way from Istria to Dubrovnik, making this a yachting paradise. Fine, deep channels with abundant anchorage and steady winds attract sailors from around the world, and throughout the region, yachts can tie up right in the middle of everything.

There are countless possibilities for anyone carrying a folding sea kayak, especially among the Elafiti Islands and the Kornati Islands, while serious windsurfers gravitate to the town of Bol on Brač Island, where

↗ DO: **MONITOR TSAVO LIONS**

COUNTRY Kenya **TYPE OF ACTIVITY** Wildlife monitoring **FITNESS/EXPERTISE LEVEL** Not required. **WHY NOW?** It's warm and dry, bringing wildlife to the waterholes. **DESCRIPTION** Join Earthwatch for a scientific expedition gathering information about the maneless lions of Tsavo. You will identify individual lions, record their behaviour and study their prey in an effort to protect the livestock of the local people (and, ergo, protect the declining lion population). Reward for your effort comes in a camp site that overlooks a waterhole where elephants, buffalos, baboons and other wildlife come to drink. If maneless lions aren't your thing (or you're troubled by their past reputation as man-eaters), you can pick from more than 100 other year-round, worldwide expeditions operated by Earthwatch, a nonprofit organisation that sponsors conservation research by placing paying volunteers alongside scientists. You might prefer to observe whale sharks off the Western Australian coast or survey wetlands in Belarus. www.earthwatch.org

Strike a blow for the future of the planet while having the holiday of a lifetime.

the wide bay perfectly catches the *maestral* (strong, steady westerly wind) that blows from April to October.

The varied underwater topography of the Croatian coast has spurred a growing diving industry. From Istria to Dubrovnik, nearly every coastal resort has a dive centre. Although there's a bit of everything along the coast, the primary attractions are shipwrecks and caves. The porous karst that forms the coastal mountains has created an astonishing variety of underwater caves, especially in the Kornati Islands. Shipwrecks are also a common sight, most notably the *Baron Gautsch* wreck near Rovinj. Remains of Roman wrecks with 1st-century amphorae can be found within reach of Dubrovnik, but special permission is necessary since they are protected cultural monuments.

Climbers will find some of Europe's best rock-climbing crags in Paklenica National Park (one of eight national parks that cover 7.5% of the country), which is also a great hiking drawcard. For the best views of the barren coastal mountains, climb Mt Ilija (961m) above Orebić, or Sveti Jure (1762m) from Makarska.

September is the best month to visit Croatia since it's lost some of its summer heat, though the sea remains warm, the crowds will have thinned out and off-season accommodation rates are in place. www.croatia.hr

o1 o2 o3 o4

Take to the rolling uplands of Wales on two wheels for a world-class cycling adventure.

↗ DO: MOUNTAIN BIKE IN WALES

COUNTRY Wales **TYPE OF ACTIVITY** Mountain biking
FITNESS/EXPERTISE LEVEL Trainer wheels to disc brakes.
WHY NOW? Good weather, firm tracks.
DESCRIPTION Wales has become something of a mountain-biking mecca in recent years, with its trails dubbed the best in the world by the International Mountain Bicycling Association. Stunning all-weather single-track radiates from seven excellent mountain-biking centres, five of which have world-class ratings.

In North Wales head for some of the Britain's best purpose-built tracks at Coed Y Brenin Forest Park and epic rides at Gwydyr Forest Park, at the edge of outdoors-central Betws-y-Coed. Here, you'll find the 25km Gwydyr Trail, with some excellent technical single-track bookended by a few sustained climbs.

Explore the wilds of Mid-Wales on some excellent networks by basing yourself at Machynlleth or Llanwrtyd Wells, two towns where mountain biking has almost become a way of life. Other good facilities in this area include wild Nant-y-Arian near Aberystwyth and the Hafren Forest near Llanidloes.

In South Wales, Afan Forest Park, east of Swansea, is also in the world-class rankings. Its newest offering, the White's Level Trail, has added rocky outcrops to the cycling challenge. There's also a superb new specialist downhill course – the 15km Trwch Trail – at Cwmcarn, northeast of Caerphilly.

If you fancy cycling on a bit of horizontal as well as vertical, or perhaps even riding between your mountain-biking outings, consider riding 420km across Wales on Lôn Las Cymru, a cycle trail with a reputation as the most difficult on the UK's National Cycle Network. Starting from the Anglesey port of Holyhead, it passes through mountainous Snowdonia before hitting the green hills and mountains of rural Mid-Wales, and then on into the formerly industrial Welsh Valleys and finally to the capital, Cardiff. www.mbwales.com

↗ DO: **KOMODO DRAGONS**

COUNTRY Indonesia **TYPE OF ACTIVITY** Wildlife watching
FITNESS/EXPERTISE LEVEL Not required.

WHY NOW? Enjoy your reptiles in the dry season. **DESCRIPTION** Komodo
is a hilly, desolate yet beautiful island in eastern Indonesia with a name
all but usurped by its most famous inhabitants, the gargantuan monitor
lizards, 3m long and 100kg in weight, known as Komodo dragons. Dragons
also inhabit the islands of Rinca, Padar and coastal western Flores, but
there's still something undeniably attractive about seeing Komodo dragons
on Komodo itself. You're most likely to see dragons at Banu Nggulung,
a dry river bed about a 30-minute walk from the tourist accommodation
camp of Loh Liang. A little 'grandstand' overlooks the river bed where
the dragons gather. Spectators are fenced off from the dragons, so don't
expect to walk up to them and have them say 'cheese'. Ferries no longer
stop at Komodo; to reach the island you will need to arrange a boat
charter. www.komodonationalpark.org

Dragons are alive and well on
Indonesia's Komodo Island,
in the form of these 3m-long,
100kg beasts.

Look out for relics
from *Apocalypse Now*
on the banks as you
pit yourself against the
Pagsanjan current.

↗ DO: **CANOE THE RAPIDS OF PAGSANJAN**

COUNTRY Philippines **TYPE OF ACTIVITY** White-water canoeing
FITNESS/EXPERTISE LEVEL Not required.

WHY NOW? The wet season (August to September) creates the best
rapids. **DESCRIPTION** Canoe rides through the rapids of the Pagsanjan
River, near Manila, are one of Luzon's major tourist attractions. The rides
begin with a paddle up to Magdapio Falls, with two *banceros* (boatmen)
guiding each canoe for about 1½ hours against the fearsome flow of
the river, through an awesome gorge hemmed by towering cliffs and
vegetation – some of the final scenes of Francis Ford Coppola's epic
Vietnam War movie *Apocalypse Now* were filmed along this stretch of
river (a few relics from the movie can still be seen along the banks). At the
top, the *banceros* will take you under the 10m-high falls on a bamboo raft
(for an additional fee). From here, you let the water do the work. The trip
downstream is fast and exhilarating. Avoid weekends, when half of Manila
seems to descend on Pagsanjan.

Mourne Mountain Marathon
www.mourne2day.com
Two-day orienteering run through the
mountains of Northern Ireland.

Colorado Last Chance
www.rmccrides.com/lastchance.htm
A 1200km randonnée out of Boulder and
crossing into Kansas.

Xtreme Terrain Triathlon
www.allabouttriathlons.co.uk
A Surrey triathlon for the bush lover, with
a lake swim, mountain-bike ride and
cross-country run.

Terra Incognita
www.adventurerace.hr
Five-day relay adventure race in
Croatia, part of the Adventure
Racing World Series.

week
.03

↗ DO: **HIKE IN JAPAN'S NORTH ALPS**

COUNTRY Japan **TYPE OF ACTIVITY** Hiking
FITNESS/EXPERTISE LEVEL Moderate fitness required.

WHY NOW? Let summer (and the August crowds) melt the snows.
DESCRIPTION The hiking route from Tate-yama to Kamikōchi is Japan's
ultimate long hike. Running the length of the North Alps – Japan's hiking
hotspot – it's the one walk every Japanese walker wants on his or her
resumé, and although long, it's not especially difficult and no technical
skills or special equipment are required. The hike's start at Murodō (below
Tate-yama) is at 2450m, the maximum altitude reached is 3190m at
Ōku-hotaka-dake (Japan's third-highest peak) and you won't drop below
2000m until you descend on the final day. In five or six days you'll cover
65km, and it's possible to stand atop more than 20 summits. The most
interesting way to reach Murodō is along the Tate-yama Kurobe Alpine
Route, a combination of train, cable-car and bus from Toyama railway
station 30km away.

Corsica is crisscrossed with trails linking the coast with its mountainous interior, but a Pernod is never far away at the end of the day!

September

↙ **GO: CORSICA, FRANCE**

week

↙ **.04**

www.yearofadventures.com/september

WHY NOW? THE HIGH TOURIST SEASON IS OVER, THE BAKING SUMMER HEAT IS ON THE SLIDE AND THE SEA'S AT A PLEASANT 23°C

For such a small island, less than 200km long and less than 90km wide, Corsica offers adventure in large doses. The lush mountains and multitude of well-marked trails are ideal for hiking and horse riding alike, while 1000km of coastline with clear warm waters and top diving makes it a water-lover's paradise.

As famous as Corsica itself is the trans-island GR20 trekking route, stretching 168km through the granite ridges of the island's interior. To walk its entirety you'll need at least two weeks, but if you fancy something shorter, you can try the selection of Mare e Monti (Sea to Mountains) and Mare e Mare (Sea to Sea) trails that crisscross the island. Although less publicised than the GR20, these routes take in some spectacular mountain and coastal scenery, with the added bonus of ending each day comfortably in a village.

↗ DO: **VISIT THE MINARET OF JAM**

COUNTRY Afghanistan **TYPE OF ACTIVITY** Adventure travel **FITNESS/EXPERTISE LEVEL** Not required. **WHY NOW?** This route is best attempted between June and October; at other times, snow and spring melt can make the roads difficult or impossible to traverse. **DESCRIPTION** A trip to see the 65m-high, World Heritage–listed Minaret of Jam is one of the most adventurous things to do in Afghanistan. The roads are appalling, the region very remote and there's no governmental rule; check the security situation beforehand. From Bamiyan, take a minibus west to Yawkawlang, then another to the provincial capital, Chaghcheran. Take any transport heading west to Garmao. Trucks regularly go north to Kamenj and will drop you at Jam. The approach to the minaret is beautiful. The road descends to the Hari Rud river and the mountain walls close in, until the minaret is revealed, hidden in the narrow cleft of the valley. There's a *chaikhana* near the minaret where you can eat and sleep. Unesco is also building a guesthouse.

Just making it to the World Heritage-listed Minaret of Jam is a minor miracle.

The variety of landscapes in Corsica also makes it an ideal place to see on horseback. There are 1900km of bridle tracks open to riders, and whether you choose an hour-long trek or a two-week tour, there are a whole host of reputable riding schools to cater to most needs and abilities.

If you're a diver, Corsica will show you about as good a time as you'll find anywhere in the Mediterranean. The dramatically rugged landscape continues underwater in the form of more mountains and canyons, needles, sharp peaks, rocky masses and scree, while the sea bed is a handsome carpet of yellow flowering anemone, red coral and gorgonian. Of the island's 30 diving centres, the Golfe de Porto, with its granite walls plunging to abysses 800m beneath the surface and its teeming marine life, is Corsica's little-visited jewel; the Golfe de Valinco is home to the Mediterranean's great underwater wonder, red coral; and the Baie de Calvi contains one of the most highly rated sites in all Corsica in the wreck of a B-17 bomber (experienced divers only).

o1 o2
o3 **o4**

Surfers, watch out when the Silver Dragon roars! This 3km-wide, 7m-high wall of water travels at up to 40km/h.

↗ DO: SURF THE QIANTANG BORE

COUNTRY China **TYPE OF ACTIVITY** Bore surfing

FITNESS/EXPERTISE LEVEL Surfing supremos only.

WHY NOW? To coincide with the year's largest wave.

DESCRIPTION A spectacular natural phenomenon occurs when the highest tides of the lunar cycle cause a wall of water to thunder up the narrow mouth of the Qiantang River from Hangzhou Bay in southeastern China. It is the largest such tidal 'bore' in the world, creating a wave so mythical the Chinese call it the Silver Dragon.

Up to 3km wide and more than 7m high, the wave travels up to 40km/h, and the roar of it can be heard from about 20km away. The Qiantang Bore occurs regularly through the year, when the highest tides occur at the beginning and middle of each lunar month, though the traditional time to witness it is as part of the Mid-Autumn Festival, around the 18th day of the 8th month of the lunar calendar. This date varies on Gregorian calendars but falls around the end of September a number of times before 2015. This is usually one of the highest bore tides of the year.

The Qiantang Bore can be dangerous enough to watch – it was once said to have swept 10,000 people away – but it's also been attempted by surfers. Nobody has stood for more than 11 seconds, and that rider's support boat was capsized by the wave.

The Qiantang River is one of up to 100 rivers around the world that experience these surge waves. Others include the Amazon, Dordogne and Severn Rivers. The latter, near Gloucester in England, is the heartland of bore surfing. Waves occur here over a four- or five-day period each month, and have been surfed for almost 10km. www.boreriders.com

01 02 03 **04**

↗ DO: **SIMPSON DESERT CYCLE CHALLENGE**

COUNTRY Australia **TYPE OF ACTIVITY** Mountain biking
FITNESS/EXPERTISE LEVEL High level of fitness and endurance required.
WHY NOW? To race a bunch of other nutters through the Australian desert.
DESCRIPTION Australia might be the land of sand and beaches but after five days of pedalling through the interior sands of the Simpson Desert you might think this less appealing than you once did. Billed as the country's toughest mountain-bike race, the Simpson Desert Cycle Challenge leaves the oasis of Purnie Bore in northern South Australia and crosses around 580km (and 750 sand dunes) to another form of oasis – the classic outback pub at Birdsville. Each day you'll pedal through around 120km of sand – get comfortable with having your bike slung over your shoulder – and still you must average 12km/h to escape the ignominy of being gathered up by the sweep van. www.sdcc.org.au

↗ DO: **WHALE WATCH AT HERMANUS**

COUNTRY South Africa **TYPE OF ACTIVITY** Wildlife watching
FITNESS/EXPERTISE LEVEL Not required.
WHY NOW? See whales and a whale festival.
DESCRIPTION Between June and November, southern right whales migrate to Western Cape's Walker Bay to calve. By timing your whale pilgrimage to coincide with the Hermanus Whale Festival, usually held this week, you'll not only get to see the southern rights, you can also take part in the Welcome the Whales Wave, a 5km-long chain of people waving hello to the marine mammals (which are yet to wave back). Whale watching at Hermanus on the bay is a simple affair, for the town calls itself the world's best land-based whale-watching site, and whales are readily visible from the cliff paths that run from one end of Hermanus to the other – Castle Rock, Kraal Rock and Sievers Point are the best spots. The town even has a whale crier who blows a kelp horn to signal the whereabouts of whales – different morse codes refer to different points along the coast. www.hermanus.co.za; www.whalefestival.co.za

↗ DO: **SWIM THE CATALINA CHANNEL**

COUNTRY USA **TYPE OF ACTIVITY** Marathon swimming
FITNESS/EXPERTISE LEVEL Superior fitness and endurance required.
WHY NOW? You'll probably be in the water for 12 hours, so let summer warm it up first. **DESCRIPTION** Second only to the English Channel in the minds of marathon swimmers, the Catalina Channel separates Catalina Island from Los Angeles and was first crossed by swimmers in 1927 in a race created as a response to the heavy publicity of English Channel swims. At its shortest point, it's around 34km from the mainland to the island, comparable to (if warmer than) its celebrity European equivalent. It has been crossed in little more than seven hours, and by people as young as 12, but attracts few people willing to challenge it – between 1927 and 2004 little more than 100 people swam the channel. www.swimcatalina.org

Only for those with true grit – Simpson Desert cyclists forge on across the sand.

Whale watchers of the world unite at the world's best vantage point, Hermanus, South Africa.

3 Peaks Cyclo-Cross
www.3peakscyclocross.org.uk
A 61km cyclo-cross race, climbing 1500m across three Yorkshire Dales' mountains.

Fish River Canoe Marathon
www.fishmarathon.org.za
Two days (81.8km) of white-water paddling through South Africa's semidesert Karoo.

MaXx Exposure
www.trailbreak.co.uk/maxx_exp
Begin at sunset and try to mountain bike 129km of England's South Downs Way walking track by sunrise.

Cro Challenge Dubrovnik
www.crochallenge.com
Multisport meets mega-walls as competitors kayak, swim, run, climb and abseil the Dubrovnik city walls.

week
.04

www.yearofadventures.com/september

155

The world is filled with natural wonders, but somehow seven natural features have come to be regarded as more wondrous than the rest.

Visiting the seven natural wonders would be a global adventure of its own, ranging across five continents and travelling from the highest point on earth to below the surface of the Pacific Ocean. Along the way you might become an expert mountaineer, vulcanologist and diver, and you'll get to play at one of the planet's great activity centres.

The wonder of Mt Everest (p86, May Week 4) is in its numbers – 8850m above sea level, 239m higher than the mountain world's second-in-charge, K2. You can become your own living wonder by climbing through the death zone to

07 NATURAL WONDERS

its summit, or you can just gaze upon its summit by trekking towards the base camps. Two monasteries, Tengboche in Nepal and Rongphu in Tibet, command arguably the best views.

A second mountain appears on the list also, but it's no sky-scratching Himalayan peak. Paricutín, about 320km west of Mexico City, is one the planet's youngest mountains, emerging from a cornfield during a nine-year volcanic eruption that started in 1943. A 410m-high cone was created, and lava flows covered an area of around 20 sq km, engulfing the villages of San Salvador Paricutín and San Juan Parangaricutiro.

Today, Paricutín's large black cone stands mute, emitting gentle wisps of steam. Near the edge of the lava field, the top of San Juan's church protrudes eerily from the sea of solidified, black lava, and is the only visible trace of the two buried villages.

From the town of Angahuan, you can wander to the San Juan church and climb on to the summit of the mountain.

It's a relatively short journey from Paricutín to the Grand Canyon, from something that grew out of the ground to something carved into it. The world's most famous canyon is up to 1.6km deep and averages 16km across. Snaking along its floor is 446km of the Colorado River. You can raft through the canyon (p146, September Week 2) for a perspective from within, or you can stroll the 21km Rim Trail for a traditional South Rim view. For a bit of both, the ultimate Grand Canyon adventure is a rim-to-rim crossing, hiking the South Kaibab Trail down to the river, then ascending the North Kaibab Trail to the North Rim. Allow about three days.

From here, the seven natural wonders go to water. Victoria Falls (p186, November

Greet the day with a spectacular view of canyons in the USA.

Week 4) rumble with such force they've earned themselves the nom de plume 'the smoke that thunders', and double as one of the world's premier adrenaline destinations. When you're done admiring this wonder, you can begin wondering whether to bungy jump, raft, jet boat, ride an elephant...

Rio de Janeiro's mountain-squeezed harbour is another of the seven natural wonders, and one you can admire as you scale one of the city's many rock faces (p83, May Week 4) before heading for the Great Barrier Reef.

Stretching more than 2000km along and beyond Australia's east coast, the Great Barrier Reef is the world's most extensive coral system, composed of around 2900 separate reefs. At times it runs up to 300km off the coast, but it's not difficult to access – there's something like 730 certified tourism operators visiting the reef. Hardy Reef and Knuckle Reef are among the best snorkelling spots in the world. There's great diving throughout, especially at Cod Hole, where you can swim with the resident giant and docile potato cod, which can grow to weigh as much as 60kg, and the SS *Yongala*, a shipwreck that has been cultivating a vivid marine community for more than 90 years. You can also hoist a sail or dip a paddle to thread between the 74 Whitsunday Islands (p166, October Week 1).

If you've made the journey this far, you're probably deserving of rest. End your quest, then, inside the perpetual Polar Night, with the final wonder, the Northern Lights (p51, March Week 3), as your psychedelic bed lamp.

Buddhism and Bhutan form a synthesis of old and new in this trekker's paradise tucked high in the Himalayas.

October

↙ GO
BHUTAN

WHY NOW? THE SNOWMAN TREK CAN ONLY BE ATTEMPTED BETWEEN LATE SEPTEMBER AND MID-OCTOBER

The Himalayan kingdom of Bhutan is not an ordinary place. It has one foot in the past and one in the future. Its farsighted leaders recognise the necessity of being part of the modern world, but they realise that once their forests and culture are destroyed, they can never be recovered. They have maintained their traditional culture, yet they have adapted what they need from modern technology. You'll find monks transcribing ancient Buddhist texts onto computers and traditionally dressed archers using the most high-tech bows and arrows.

Bhutan is a country of rolling hills and towering crags, with only small patches of cultivation and very little deforestation. It's often compared to Switzerland, not only because they're similar in size, but also because many parts of Bhutan look like the Swiss Alps, with green hills, chalet-like houses and snow peaks sticking out of nowhere.

COUNTRY Tanzania **TYPE OF ACTIVITY** Hiking/wildlife watching **FITNESS/EXPERTISE LEVEL** Moderate fitness required. **WHY NOW?** Walks operate through the dry season (June to October). **DESCRIPTION** Selous Game Reserve is one of the last great wild places: 55,000 sq km of untamed bushland, untouched forests, crocodile-filled lakes and emerald green floodplains. It's slightly larger than Switzerland, four times as big as the Serengeti, and the second-largest protected natural area in the world. Only the northern section of the park is open for tourism. Here you'll find hippos, elephants, wildebeests and zebras in abundance. The Selous is also one of the few wildlife areas in Tanzania that you're allowed to explore on foot. Walking safaris are conducted from all the reserve's hotels: a fantastic opportunity to see Africa up close without engine noise and diesel fumes. You can take three-hour hikes near the hotels or trek for days among dangerous animals, resting each night in catered camps. www.tanzania-web.com

Is that the rumble of thunder I hear? Watch out for the wild inhabitants of the Selous.

Virtually the entire country is mountainous, and to see the best of Bhutan you should spend a week or more on foot, trekking through the great forested wilderness that covers most of the country. There are 13 officially permitted trekking routes in Bhutan, including what's sometimes described as the world's most difficult trek. Fewer than half the people who attempt the Snowman Trek actually finish it, either because of problems with altitude (you climb to passes above 5300m) or heavy snowfall on the high passes. Its season is short – late September to mid-October – and its commitment is long, covering around 25 days in country so remote that if you find the passes blocked by snow, the only way out is by helicopter.

Bhutan's most popular route, walked by around 40% of trekkers to the country, is the nine-day Jhomolari Trek I, taking you to a high camp at Jangothang (4080m) for spectacular views of 7314m Jhomolhari. The trek is possible from April to early June and September to November, but the best chance of favourable conditions is in October or April.

Fancy yourself as a runner? You'll never know if you pass muster unless you run up Mt Kinabalu.

↗ DO: MOUNTAIN RUN ON MT KINABALU

COUNTRY Malaysia **TYPE OF ACTIVITY** Mountain running
FITNESS/EXPERTISE LEVEL Superior fitness and good acclimatisation required.
WHY NOW? To compete in the Mt Kinabalu International Climbathon.
DESCRIPTION The British may cherish fell running, or mountain running, as something of a national pastime, but to find its most extreme challenge you must travel to Sabah for the annual Mt Kinabalu International Climbathon. Created in 1987 as a training exercise for park rangers to test their rescue skills, it began the following year as an international race, one that's now promoted as the 'world's toughest mountain race'.

In the Climbathon, competitors run up and down Mt Kinabalu (4095m), Southeast Asia's highest peak. From the race start at Timpohon Gate, runners ascend 2230m to Kinabalu's highest point, Low's Peak, before turning around and running back. The race covers a total distance of 21km, and the winner usually returns to Timpohon Gate in just under three hours; the cut-off time for stragglers is 4½ hours. Expect high temperatures and bath-like humidity at the base of the mountain and whatever the mountain gods throw at you on the top.

If this sort of high-altitude running sounds like just your thing, you needn't limit your experiences to Mt Kinabalu. The Climbathon is one of between six and eight races that make up the annual Sky Runner World Series. The season begins in May (and concludes on Kinabalu), and you can starve your running body of oxygen in places such as Switzerland, Mexico, Japan and Andorra. Each race contains significant climbs and most are run above 2000m. One of the long-standing races is the International Skyrace Valmalenco-Valposchiavo, usually held in June and following former smugglers' tracks from Italy to Switzerland.
www.sabahtourism.com; www.buffskyrunner.com

o1 o2 o3 o4

↗ DO: RAFT THE GAULEY RIVER

COUNTRY USA **TYPE OF ACTIVITY** White-water rafting
FITNESS/EXPERTISE LEVEL Experience needed for independent trips.
WHY NOW? Get there as the water does. **DESCRIPTION** They call it the
Gauley Season and it is quite simply one of the world's great white-
water moments. For 22 days each autumn, there are scheduled releases
of water from the Summersville Dam in West Virginia to lower the
Summersville Lake to its winter level. Up to four million litres a minute
pours from the dam, and waiting for it are a host of rafters to ride its
sudden, gut-churning rapids. As the Upper Gauley drops around 100m
in little more than 15km, it provides more than 40 rapids to negotiate,
including several grade-five rapids, the highest grade a raft can run. Grab
a paddle and brace for the deceptively named Sweet's Falls, a 5m plunge
that helps make the Upper Gauley about the best white-water run in the
United States.

↗ DO: TRAVEL THE KARAKORAM HIGHWAY

COUNTRY China and Pakistan **TYPE OF ACTIVITY** Adventure travel/cycling
FITNESS/EXPERTISE LEVEL High level of fitness if cycling.
WHY NOW? For clear skies and moderate temperatures, the best time to
travel is September and October. **DESCRIPTION** The Karakoram Highway
connects the Silk Road oasis of Kashgar, in China's Xīngjiāng province,
with Islamabad, Pakistan's modern capital, via the 4730m Khunjerab Pass,
the semimythical Hunza Valley and the trading post of Gilgit. It's been
open to travellers only since 1986 and has assumed legendary status
as one of the world's great adventure road trips. Within reach of the
highway is some of the most awe-inspiring mountain scenery anywhere
– the Karakoram boasts the highest concentration of lofty peaks and long
glaciers in the world. A favourite way to make the 1300km crossing is by
bicycle. It's a spectacular trip for cyclists who are super fit and have an
appetite for the unexpected.

↗ DO: SAIL THE WHITSUNDAY ISLANDS

COUNTRY Australia **TYPE OF ACTIVITY** Sailing
FITNESS/EXPERTISE LEVEL One person in your group must be
competent in operating a yacht.
WHY NOW? Warm weather, cool seas and helpful winds.
DESCRIPTION A chain of 90-plus islands – all but four of which are
protected in at least some part as a national park – the Whitsundays
epitomise tropical Queensland. Stiff breezes and fast-flowing tides can
produce tricky conditions for small craft, yet with a little care the islands
offer superb sailing, and bareboat charters have become enormously
popular. Superseded racing maxis and antique tall ships vie for a place
among the islands, and it doesn't matter if you can't remember the last
time you spliced a mainbrace, or if you have sailed into too many ports
to recall, there'll be a boat to suit. Most companies have a minimum hire
period of five days. There's also a bamboozling array of sailing tours that
supply professional crew and catering – just about every second store in
Airlie Beach is an 'information centre' willing to set your dollars sailing.
www.whitsundaytourism.com

The washing machine effect –
hold on tight and let the river
take its course.

In search of the Silk Road
via the simply spectacular
Karakoram Highway.

Jungle Marathon
www.junglemarathon.com
Run 100km or 200km through the
Amazon region of northern Brazil.

Whitney Classic
www.summitadventure.com/courses
_whitney.htm
Cycle almost 220km through Death
Valley to Mt Whitney Portal, with climbs
totalling more than 4500m.

**Kalahari Augrabies Extreme
Marathon**
www.extrememarathons.com
Seven-day, 250km self-sufficient run
through South Africa's Great Kalahari
Desert.

Triple Crown
www.triplecrownbouldering.org
The first of three bouldering competitions
in southeast USA; series two and
three are held in November and
December.

week
.01

www.yearofadventures.com/october

161

Cast yourself adrift with 3000 karst islands on Halong Bay – just one of Vietnam's attractions for adventurers.

October

↙ GO:
VIETNAM

WHY NOW? OCTOBER OFFERS ONE OF THE BEST BALANCES BETWEEN HEAT AND COLD, DRY AND WET

Vietnam is a place of coast and mountains – there's 3451km of the former and 75% of the country is covered by the latter. Karst formations have been shaped into striking landscapes, with mountain tops sticking out of the sea like bony fingers. It sounds custom-made for exploration and adventure, though Vietnam is only just beginning to realise its potential.

Cyclists were among the first to add Vietnam to their wish-list. The Mekong Delta is cycling heaven, with barely a bump in its silted surface. The coastal route along Hwy 1 is an alluring and popular achievement, though the insane traffic makes it tough and dangerous. Better is the new inland trunk road, Hwy 14, which offers stunning scenery and little traffic.

Halong Bay is undoubtedly Vietnam's natural wonder. Picture 3000 incredible islands rising from the emerald waters of the Gulf of Tonkin and you have a vision of greatness – it's been likened to Guilin and

week

↙ .02

www.yearofadventures.com/october

↗ DO: KAYAK THE YASAWA ISLANDS

COUNTRY Fiji **TYPE OF ACTIVITY** Sea kayaking **FITNESS/EXPERTISE LEVEL** Basic kayaking experience required. **WHY NOW?** The Fijian winter is warming up, while the cyclone season is still a few weeks away. **DESCRIPTION** After the famous mutiny on the *Bounty* in 1789, Captain William Bligh paddled through Fiji's Yasawa Islands on his way to Timor. Given that he was being chased by Fijian canoes, he may not have enjoyed the experience as much as you will along this 90km-long chain of 20 ancient volcanic islands off the northwest corner of Viti Levu. Famed for lovely white-sand beaches, crystal-blue lagoons and rugged volcanic landscapes, the group forms a roughly straight line within the Great Sea Reef. Islands are no more than 10km apart, making for short paddles between landfalls. You'll find the best paddling along the western side of the islands, where you'll be sheltered from the prevailing southeast winds.

Make like an old-time Fijian warrior and paddle the clear waters off the Yasawa Islands.

Krabi. Paddling among the karsts is an activity that has taken off in recent years and Halong Bay is now following hard behind Krabi as Southeast Asia's kayaking capital. Climbers are yet to really stamp their chalk on the bay, though it's only a matter of time before the word gets out. Ninh Binh and Phong Nha could also offer some climbing competition.

The most popular diving area in Vietnam is Nha Trang, where there are around 25 dive sites, both shallow and deep. There are no wrecks, but some sites have good drop-offs and there are a few small underwater caves to explore. The waters support a good variety of soft and hard corals, and a reasonable number of small reef fish.

Surfing is also a new arrival on the Vietnamese scene – Mui Ne Beach is among the best spots, while experienced surfers head for China Beach in Danang.

Picking a best time to begin a Vietnamese adventure is a tough call, with monsoons hitting different parts of the country at different times. October offers one of the best balances between heat and cold, dry and wet.

When the tough get going ... vie for the privilege of competing in the legendary Hawaii Ironman (stricly for fitness fanatics).

↗ DO: HAWAII IRONMAN

COUNTRY USA **TYPE OF ACTIVITY** Ironman triathlon

FITNESS/EXPERTISE LEVEL Superior fitness required.

WHY NOW? To swim, run and cycle among 1500 super-athletes.

DESCRIPTION It began as an argument in 1978 about who was fitter – cyclists, runners or swimmers – and morphed almost immediately into one of the world's great endurance events. Competitors must swim 3.8km, cycle 180km and then run a marathon-length 42km, all inside 17 hours. The best in the game complete the course in less than nine hours, with the record time of eight hours and four minutes set in 1996 by Belgian Luc van Lierde.

Harsh *kona* (leeward) conditions on the appropriately named Kona Coast on Hawaii's Big Island make the event the ultimate endurance test, even by triathlon standards. Heat reflected off the lava landscape commonly exceeds 100°F, making dehydration and heat exhaustion major challenges. Many contenders arrive weeks before the race just to acclimatise. On the day of the race, nearly 7000 volunteers line the course to hand out around 50,000 litres of water – more than 30 litres for each racer! Such are its challenges, the Hawaii Ironman was labelled 'lunatic' by *Sports Illustrated* as far back as 1979. In reward for all this punishment, the top male and female winners walk (or crawl) away with US$100,000 each.

To race at Kona you must first qualify, and each year around 50,000 triathletes attempt to snare one of the 1500 spots. There are 26 qualifying events held around the world, from Brazil to Australia to the Canary Islands, and each race is allocated a number of qualifying slots. Miss these and you can enter a lottery draw for US citizens (150 race positions available) or international competitors (50 positions).

www.ironmanlive.com

Live life on the edge. No, your eyes aren't deceiving you – that pencil-thin line is indeed a road.

↗ DO: CYCLE THE WORLD'S MOST DANGEROUS ROAD

COUNTRY Bolivia **TYPE OF ACTIVITY** Mountain biking
FITNESS/EXPERTISE LEVEL Good bike control recommended.
WHY NOW? Come at the end of the dry season to avoid a muddy run.
DESCRIPTION The Yungas Hwy between the Bolivian capital La Paz and
the town of Coroico is officially the world's most dangerous road, at least
according to a 1995 Inter-American Development Bank report. Given that
an average of 26 vehicles disappear over its edge each year, the title is
well deserved. It's a gravel track only 3.2m wide – just enough for one
vehicle – with sheer 1000m drops, hulking rock overhangs, waterfalls
that spill across and erode the highway, and a growing reputation among
cyclists keen for an adrenaline rush. Bike hire is available in La Paz. Now all
you need do is watch those edges, drunk drivers and marauding trucks.

↗ DO: WATCH POLAR BEARS IN CHURCHILL

COUNTRY Canada **TYPE OF ACTIVITY** Wildlife watching
FITNESS/EXPERTISE LEVEL Not required.
WHY NOW? To share your holiday with big white bears.
DESCRIPTION There are no roads to Churchill, set on the shores of frigid
Hudson Bay, but that doesn't stop people getting here. What draws
almost every one of them is the town's status as the supposed polar-bear
capital of the world. Churchill is on the bears' migration route between
winters spent hunting on the frozen bay and summers spent on land,
and it's through October that they pass by the Manitoba town. You can
take day tours in purpose-built buggies, or you can stay (for a hefty fee) in
transportable 'tundra lodges'. Where you hope not to see a polar bear is
in town itself. Local authorities maintain a 24-hour vigil from September
to November, with gunshots fired at night to shoo away any town-bound
bears. You can reach Churchill by air or rail from Winnipeg.

Embrace polar bears on the shores of Hudson Bay...well, not literally perhaps!

Polar Circle Marathon
www.polar-circle-marathon.com
Greenland marathon that includes 8km
across the ice cap.

Furnace Creek 508
www.the508.com
Only 48 hours to cycle 817km, climbing
10,000m around a little place called
Death Valley.

Smoky Mountains Adventure Race
www.racedaycompany.com/WENCAR/
siteupgrade/home.php
Gruelling 40 hours of paddling, running,
mountain biking and abseiling in the
USA's most popular mountain range.

Ecomotion Pro
www.ecomotion.com.br
Six-day, 450km adventure race
in Brazil.

week

.02

↗ DO: MORNING GLORY CLOUDS

COUNTRY Australia **TYPE OF ACTIVITY** Natural phenomena/gliding
FITNESS/EXPERTISE LEVEL High level of expertise and experience
required if gliding.
WHY NOW? The Morning Glories usually occur from September to
late October. **DESCRIPTION** Arise at dawn for the chance to watch a
meteorological wonder roll into northern Australia's Gulf of Carpenteria.
The Morning Glory is a tubular cloud, or series of clouds, up to 1000km
in length, that rolls across the sky in the early morning, pushing great
updrafts ahead of it. It's these updrafts that have made it one of the great
gliding and hang-gliding adventures. First soared in 1989, Morning Glories
have carried gliders for more than 700km and up to six hours. The northern
Queensland town of Burketown makes a good base for both viewing and
soaring the Morning Glories.

www.yearofadventures.com/october

Decisions, decisions. Scale the *jebels* (hills) of kaleidoscopic Wadi Rum or follow in the camel prints of Lawrence of Arabia? Why not both?

October

↙ GO: WADI RUM, JORDAN

week

↙ .03

www.yearofadventures.com/october

WHY NOW? BLAZING IN SUMMER, AND WITH COLD WINDS HOWLING DOWN FROM CENTRAL ASIA IN WINTER, NOW IS THE TIME TO DISCOVER THIS DESERT

Made famous by the presence of the Arab Revolt and TE Lawrence in the early 20th century, Wadi Rum offers some of the most extraordinary desert scenery you'll ever see. Its myriad moods and dramatic colours, dictated by the changing angle of the sun, make for a memorable scene, but it's a place to be experienced as much as it is to be seen. Blazing in summer, and with cold winds howling down from Central Asia in winter, now is the time to discover this desert.

Wadi Rum is a series of valleys about 2km wide, stretching north to south for about 130km. Among the valleys is a desert landscape of sand and rocks, punctuated by towering *jebels* (hills) that have eroded into soft sandstone over a period of up to 50 million years. These *jebels* offer some challenging rock climbing, equal to anything in Europe. While climbing is

↗ DO: **SANDBOARD AT SWAKOPMUND**

COUNTRY Namibia **TYPE OF ACTIVITY**
Sandboarding **FITNESS/EXPERTISE LEVEL**
Good fitness for climbing the dunes. **WHY
NOW?** It's one of the coolest times of the year
in the Central Namib Desert. **DESCRIPTION**
In the Central Namib Desert, Namibia's
most popular holiday resort aspires to be an
adventure centre (albeit dry) to rival Victoria
Falls. Among such offerings as quadbiking
and parachuting, sandboarding stands out
as the town's signature activity. Hire a board
and climb the high dunes around town,
laying down or, if you're proficient at skiing or
snowboarding, standing up to schuss down a
120m-high dune at speeds reaching
80km/h. Hire of a sandboard comes with
gloves, goggles, transport to the dunes and
enough sandboard polish to ensure a run as
slippery as marbles. Now all you have to do is
slog your way back to the top of the dunes.

If only someone could invent
a ski-lift for sandboarding…

still a nascent industry in Wadi Rum, and you'll need
to bring your own gear, the situation has improved
in recent years. There are at least six accredited
climbing guides, most of whom have been trained in
the UK. One of the more popular climbs for amateur
climbers is up Jebel Rum (1754m), Jordan's highest
peak. Minimal gear is needed and it's close to the
Rest House in Rum village, although a guide is still
required to find the best route and to help with the
climb. There are also a number of sites north of the
road to Diseh.

Excursions into the desert can be made by camel
or 4WD. If you have the time, travelling around Wadi
Rum by camel is highly recommended, enabling
you to experience the desert as the Bedouin people
have for centuries and to really appreciate the silent
gravitas of the desert. You can ride out and back from
Rum village, cross to the famed archaeological site
at Petra (about five nights), or follow in Lawrence of
Arabia's camel prints to Aqaba on the Red Sea coast
(three to six nights).

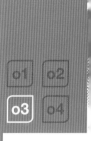

o1 o2 o3 o4

Slovenia's Karst region is a netherworld of caves and tunnels, including the nearly 6km long and 250m deep World Heritage-listed Škocjan Caves.

↗ DO: CAVE IN THE KARST REGION

COUNTRY Slovenia **TYPE OF ACTIVITY** Caving

FITNESS/EXPERTISE LEVEL From clunkers to spelunkers.

WHY NOW? Slip into the caves between the summer crowds and the winter chill.

DESCRIPTION For cavers, there are few sexier than 'karst' (limestone weathered into caves and fissures), which makes the eponymous Karst region in Slovenia a hot date for those who like the underworld. Thick layers of limestone deposits were laid down here millions of years ago. Earth movements then raised the limestone above sea level, where it was eroded by mildly acidic rainwater. Over hundreds of thousands of years, this slow, chemical erosion has produced limestone pavements, dry valleys, sinkholes, springs and, most notably, vast subterranean networks of caves and tunnels.

Foremost in the Karst region are the 5.8km long, 250m deep World Heritage–listed Škocjan Caves, carved out by the Reka River. The first section of the caves, called Paradise, is filled with beautiful stalactites, stalagmites and flow stones; the second part (called Calvary) was once the river bed. The Silent Cave ends at the Great Hall (Velika Dvorana), 120m wide and 30m high and a jungle of exotic dripstones and deposits.

The sound of the Reka River rushing through cascades and whirlpools below heralds your entry into the astonishing Müller Hall, with walls 100m high. To get over the Reka and into long, narrow Svetina Hall you must cross narrow Hanke Canal Bridge, 45m high and the highlight of the trip. Most visitors continue to Bowls Hall, remarkable for its rare bowl-like potholes; past Tominč Cave, where finds from a prehistoric settlement have been unearthed; and over a walkway near the Natural Bridge to a funicular, which carries you 90m up the rock face to near the reception area. Experienced spelunkers, however, can explore the 5km of caves and halls that extend to the northwest of Hanke Canal Bridge, ending at Dead Lake. www.park-skocjanske-jame.si

↗ DO: **BASE JUMP AT BRIDGE DAY**

COUNTRY USA **TYPE OF ACTIVITY** BASE jumping
FITNESS/EXPERTISE LEVEL Skydiving experience required.
WHY NOW? For the one day of the year you can throw yourself from New River Gorge Bridge.
DESCRIPTION Bridge Day might sound like a run-of-the-mill, small-town-America event in which the greatest danger is being trampled by baton-twirling marching girls, but wedged between the Eucharist service and the historic theatre production in Fayetteville's Bridge Day, there just happens to be a mighty BASE jumping event. Though BASE jumping is illegal here for 355 days of the year, on this one day, 450 BASE jumpers leap from the New River Gorge Bridge, opening their parachutes as they plummet 270m into the gorge – a drop of just eight seconds. BASE rookies can make their debuts here, but only if you come packed with an extensive skydiving history. If you prefer to maintain some contact with the bridge, you can also abseil from it. www.bridgeday.info

↗ DO: **PARAGLIDE AT ÖLÜDENIZ**

COUNTRY Turkey **TYPE OF ACTIVITY** Paragliding
FITNESS/EXPERTISE LEVEL Not required.
WHY NOW? To coincide with the International Air Games.
DESCRIPTION If you like the idea of plummeting off a cliff with another person strapped to your back, you won't find many better places than Turkey's resort town Ölüdeniz, set around a beautiful, sheltered lagoon. Many companies here offer tandem paragliding flights. The descent from Baba Dağ (Mt Baba), which is more than 1900m high, can take as long as 45 minutes, with amazing views over the lagoon, nearby Butterfly Valley and, on a clear day, out to the island of Rhodes. So popular is the sport in Ölüdeniz that it's now the venue for the paragliding International Air Games, held this week each October. www.babadag.com

You can't beat a paraglider's-eye view over Turkey's Ölüdeniz lagoon.

↗ DO: **VISIT AGDAM**

REGION Nagorno-Karabakh **TYPE OF ACTIVITY** Adventure travel
FITNESS/EXPERTISE LEVEL Not required.
WHY NOW? A comfortable time to be travelling through the discomforts of the south Caucasus.
DESCRIPTION The self-declared republic of Nagorno-Karabakh was racked by war between 1989 and 1994 as Azerbaijan and Armenia fought for its control. In 1994 Agdam, a city of 100,000 people, was captured, sacked and looted. Tall, shattered tower blocks now stand deserted, past a sprawling city centre of one- and two-storey buildings. Shredded playgrounds sprout shrubs, streets are cracking open with trees, and ponds fill bomb craters. Besides a few soldiers and scrap-metal hunters, Agdam is as dead as Pompeii. The Ministry of Foreign Affairs of Nagorno-Karabakh doesn't permit a visit to Agdam, though some people go anyway. Don't venture beyond the mosque at the town centre. You can climb one of the rickety minarets for a 360-degree view of the city. There are soldiers camped around the city so travel with a local guide.

24 Hours of Moab
www.grannygear.com
Mountain bike nonstop for 24 hours around the slickrock of Moab.

Vienna-Budapest Supermarathon
www.szupermarathon.hu
Five days to run, cycle or inline skate 352km between Vienna and Budapest.

Fitzroy Falls Fire Trail Marathon
www.fitzroyfallsmarathon.com
Marathon-length run around the sandstone escarpments south of Sydney; 5½-hour time limit.

Escape from the Rock Triathlon
www.envirosports.com
Triathlon that begins with a 2.4km swim to 'escape' the prison on Alcatraz.

week
.o3

www.yearofadventures.com/october

Moab's Slickrock Trail is a mountain biker's Holy Grail. If only you could stick to the saddle the way the rock sticks to your knobblies...

October

week

↙ .04

www.yearofadventures.com/october

↙ GO: MOAB, UNITED STATES

WHY NOW? GO IN OCTOBER AND YOU CAN CATCH THE MOAB HALLOWEEN BIKE FEST AS WELL

The Utah town of Moab would horrify its founding fathers and mothers. Established as a Mormon outpost, it has fallen to a cult of scabby, adrenaline-juiced mountain bikers who know only one kind of latter-day saint – those that can ride the Slickrock Trail without stacking.

Set at the heart of some of the United States' most striking desert, Moab's most famous feature is slickrock, the smooth sandstone named because horses found it so slippery. Beneath the knobbly tyres of a mountain bike it is, conversely, more like *stick*rock.

Foremost among the slickrock rides is the one that bears the name – the Slickrock Trail. A Holy Grail of mountain biking, Slickrock winds across the sandstone ridges directly above town, with glimpses of the Colorado River and Arches National Park as it circuits. Although around 100,000 cyclists follow its dashed lines every year, it's not a ride for the timid. It

↗ DO: SWIM WITH ORCAS IN TYSFJORD

COUNTRY Norway **TYPE OF ACTIVITY** Snorkelling/wildlife watching **FITNESS/ EXPERTISE LEVEL** Cold blood an asset. **WHY NOW?** Orcas generally arrive in the fjord in mid-October; come now before the Polar Night sets in. **DESCRIPTION** Mid-autumn signals the arrival of migrating herring and, behind them, hundreds of orcas into Norway's Tysfjord, around 250km north of the Arctic Circle. For three months the killer whales stay, chasing herring while rugged-up wildlife watchers chase them. You can remain in the trawler or Zodiac for a surface view, or seize the rare (if chilly) opportunity to snorkel among these sleek giants. You might also want to kayak in the few available daylight hours, hoping (or not) to find yourself among surfacing orcas. Sea eagles also have an appetite for Tysfjord herring, picking off the shoals as they're chased to the surface by the orcas. Lift your eyes from the fjord and you're also likely to be treated to the Northern Lights stellar spectacular. www.tysfjord-turistsenter.no/safari

Awe-inspiring encounters with orcas await north of the Arctic Circle in Norway's Tysfjord.

has climbs as steep as the pyramids and descents that'll cramp your braking hand. If you come away without 'bacon' – scabs – and you haven't pushed your bike at some point, you've arrived as an authentic mountain biker.

Cycling here, however, needn't be just about belting around the Slickrock Trail. Rides can be chosen as much for scenery as difficulties. Try the swirling sandstone at Bartlett Wash, or hit Canyonlands National Park for a few days of cross-country pedalling on the White Rim Trail above the Colorado and Green Rivers.

Get even closer to the rivers by indulging in Moab's next best thing to slickrock – river runs through water both flat and churning. Great numbers of companies run an overwhelming variety of trips on the Colorado and Green Rivers, and you can float like an inland cruise or you can be buffeted silly by rapids.

To round out your week, you might try jet boating, quadbiking or an extreme form of 4WDing in which you remove your vehicle's doors, put on tyres like doughnuts and head for tracks with names like Hell's Revenge. You'll never think of Utah in the same way again, especially if you come now when the Moab Halloween Bike Fest is on.

For more information, visit www.discovermoab .com and www.moabbikefest.com.

The pulsating heart of the matter – larger-than-life Gaza City will make your senses reel.

↗ DO VISIT GAZA CITY

01 02 03 **04**

REGION Palestinian Territories **TYPE OF ACTIVITY** Adventure travel
FITNESS/EXPERTISE LEVEL Not required.
WHY NOW? Come between Ramadan and the chill of winter.
DESCRIPTION The Gaza Strip is a narrow stretch of land, 40km in length and as little as 6km wide in places. Squeezed between the Mediterranean and the Negev Desert, it's parcelled up in razor wire and is infamous as the birthplace of the Intifada (the uprising against Israeli authorities in the Palestinian Territories and Jerusalem). The Strip's Palestinian inhabitants are centred in three main towns and eight refugee camps; Gaza (often called Gaza City) is the largest of the towns.

So, why should you want to visit Gaza City? True, there are no obvious tourist attractions such as ancient holy sites or beautiful landscapes, but there's a vibrancy in Gaza City rarely found in Israel. The place is teeming and chaotic and delivers an all-out sensory assault in the manner of a great Arab city such as Cairo. On the streets you'll be greeted with a profusion of 'salaams', offered tea, choke on car fumes, trip in potholes and get your shoes filled with sand. It's not an easy place to be and it's not set up to deal with visitors, but life in Gaza tends to make a searing impact on all those who make the effort to investigate.

Currently, the only entry/exit point is Erez, in the north of the Strip. Essentially, the only way to get there from Jerusalem is to take a special taxi from East Jerusalem with Al Zahra Taxi. Once at Erez, crossing into the Strip for non-Israeli or non-Arab passport holders is painless and only takes minutes. The only headache is the swarm of taxi drivers just beyond the Palestinian checkpoint who literally fight over the right to drive you into Gaza City, only 10km away.

You'll find a selection of hotels along and near the city's seafront.

↗ DO: BALLOON AT SERENGETI NATIONAL PARK

COUNTRY Tanzania **TYPE OF ACTIVITY** Hot-air ballooning
FITNESS/EXPERTISE LEVEL Not required.
WHY NOW? Witness the wildebeests' Serengeti return from the air.
DESCRIPTION A memorable way to observe wildlife in the Serengeti is from the air as you sail above the plains in a balloon. At the whim of the airstream and accompanied by bursts of flame, you drift over the park whose name translates as 'endless plains'. From the air you can spot otherwise invisible hyena dens, tracks crisscross the plains like some gigantic web, and groups of zebras, wildebeests, hartebeests and gazelles are visible for kilometres. The ride ends wherever the wind has blown you, and your champagne breakfast (complete with linen tablecloths) may be accompanied by whichever animals happen to be nearby. It's not a cheap morning out – US$449 at the time of writing – but it's the only way you'll ever look down on a giraffe. www.balloonsafaris.com

The ultimate low-impact travel ~ take only photos, leave only your shadow.

The postcard view of Kachoong – and after you've finished it there are 2000 more climbs to go.

Banff Mountain Film Festival
www.banffmountainfestivals.ca
See the year's finest collection of adventure films.

Grand Raid
www.grandraid-reunion.com
Run 130km, with climbs totalling more than 7000m, to traverse the island of Réunion.

Beast of the East
www.oarevents.com/event.asp?id=33&catID=1
Trek, mountain bike and white-water canoe through Virginia.

Karrimor International Mountain Marathon
www.kimm.org.uk
One of the forerunners to adventure racing, covering around 80km in two days.

week
.04

www.yearofadventures.com/october

↗ DO: CLIMB AT MT ARAPILES

COUNTRY Australia **TYPE OF ACTIVITY** Rock climbing
FITNESS/EXPERTISE LEVEL Routes cover all grades.
WHY NOW? Spring offers the best conditions, with climbers settling into the Pines for weeks. **DESCRIPTION** Mt Arapiles is an anomaly, a chunk of quartzite seemingly dropped by mistake on the ironed-flat Wimmera plain – something like Uluru (Ayres Rock) with a southern address. It's also among the best climbing sites in the world, boasting more than 2000 routes, which range from basic to advanced, and have colourful names such as Violent Crumble, Cruel Britannia and Checkmate. You can amble up glorified scrambles or you can destroy your fingers on something like Punks in the Gym (grade 31), which was once rated the most difficult climb in the world. Another classic route is Kachoong (21) – if you've seen just one photo of 'Araps' it's probably somebody hanging from the roof on this route. To do Araps correctly, you should set up home in the Pines camping ground – something akin to Yosemite's Camp 4 – at the base of the mountain.

↗ DO: HIKE THE HOERIKWAGGO TRAIL

COUNTRY South Africa **TYPE OF ACTIVITY** Hiking
FITNESS/EXPERTISE LEVEL Moderate fitness required.
WHY NOW? For pleasant walking conditions amid wild flowers on Table Mountain.
DESCRIPTION Discover one of the world's newest and most appealing hiking experiences as you walk between Cape Town and the tip of the Cape of Good Hope, crossing Table Mountain as you go. Three guided trail options are available. The three-day, luxury Table Mountain Trail, opened at the end of 2005, covers a section of the full trail and rather appropriately offers tablecloth service on Table Mountain. The six-day Tip to Top Trail, opening in December 2006, will begin at the Cape and conclude in the city, staying in luxury tents along the spine of the mountain. A year later, guided walks in the opposite direction – the Top to Tip Trail – will begin.
www.sanparks.org/parks/table_mountain/ht

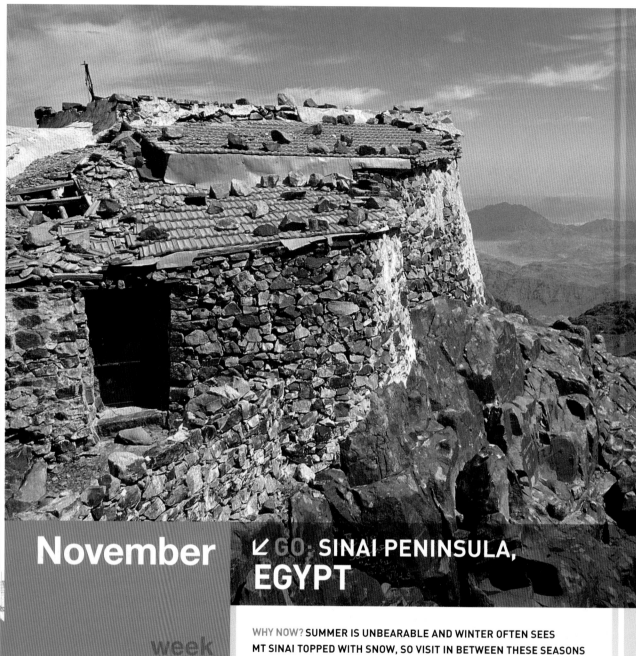

November

↙ GO: SINAI PENINSULA, EGYPT

week

↙ .01

www.yearofadventures.com/november

**WHY NOW? SUMMER IS UNBEARABLE AND WINTER OFTEN SEES
MT SINAI TOPPED WITH SNOW, SO VISIT IN BETWEEN THESE SEASONS**
Biblical and beautiful, Egypt's Sinai is a desert land conversely famous for
its water activities. Sat like a cork in the neck of the Red Sea, the Sinai's
southern coast between Tiran Island and Ras Mohammed National Park
features some of the world's most brilliant and amazing underwater
scenery. The crystal-clear water, the rare and lovely reefs and the
incredible variety of fish have made this a diving and snorkelling paradise,
attracting people from all over the globe to the sea Jacques Cousteau
once said gave him the 'happiest hours of my diving experience'.

The resort of Sharm el-Sheikh, the epicentre of the diving industry,
doesn't reflect the marine beauty, but it does have proximity to Ras
Mohammed National Park, which covers the southern tip of Sinai and
offers arguably the Red Sea's finest diving. There are 20 dive sites within
the park, including a selection of wrecks and Eel Garden and Shark

Resonant with Biblical history, the arid Sinai Peninsula gives no clues to the astounding marine diversity offshore.

↗ DO: FLY IN A MIG-25

COUNTRY Russia **TYPE OF ACTIVITY** Adventure travel **FITNESS/EXPERTISE LEVEL** Not required. **WHY NOW?** Most of your time will be spent on the ground, and Russia can be magical in autumn. **DESCRIPTION** Plane spotters and thrill seekers unite, for it's now possible to copilot a seriously quick and impressive piece of aircraft. The MiG-25 'Foxbat' is a fighter jet that can fly at more than twice the speed of sound (or around 3000km/h). One hour's drive southeast of Moscow, tourist flights take to the high skies from the formerly top-secret Zhukovsky Air Base, rocketing away to an altitude of around 25,000m – the outer limit of the atmosphere, from where you can see the curve of the earth. For your money (about US$14,000) you'll usually get your Russian visa, several nights at one of Moscow's premier hotels, transfers between airport, hotel and Zhukovsky Air Base, an English-speaking guide, flight instructions, training, a medical check and, finally, the 30-minute flight.

Reach stratospheric heights in the blink of an eye copiloting a MiG-25.

Observatory where you'll see – have a guess – eels and sharks.

Sinai's interior is as hard as its fringing corals. Row upon serried row of barren, jagged, red-brown mountains fill its southern end, surrounded by relentlessly dry, yet colourful, desert plains. The most famous of the mountains is 2285m Mt Sinai, reputed to be the place where Moses received the Ten Commandments, and now the peninsula's favourite hiking destination. Begin at St Katherine's Monastery and follow the camel trail or, if you're feeling penitent, the 3750 Steps of Repentance to the summit. It's customary to be here for sunrise, and if you're planning to spend the night on top, as many visitors do, come ready for a cold night.

Longer desert treks – up to a week or more – with a Bedouin guide can be arranged in the village of Al-Milga, 3.5km from St Katherine's. A guide is also required if you fancy the five-hour climb to the top of Gebel Katarina (2642m), Egypt's highest mountain.

o1 o2
o3 o4

An ancient meteor strike on Mexico's Yucatán Peninsula formed a honeycomb world of caverns and sinkholes.

↗ DO: CENOTE DIVE IN YUCATÁN

COUNTRY Mexico **TYPE OF ACTIVITY** Cavern diving

FITNESS/EXPERTISE LEVEL Open-water dive certification required.

WHY NOW? The cenotes are clearest between about November and March.

DESCRIPTION In a cataclysmic collision 65 million years ago, a huge meteor struck the area that is now Mexico's Yucatán Peninsula, leaving a 284km-wide crater on the land's surface. Millions of years later cracks formed just below the crater's limestone surface and rainwater began filling the cavities these fissures created. Eventually the surface layer around the underground chambers began to erode and crumble, revealing the intricate vascular system of underground rivers and *cenotes* (pools, sinkholes) that lay beneath.

The Yucatán is now pitted with around 3000 *cenotes*, the most famous of which is the Sacred Cenote at the Mayan site of Chichén Itzá. This is an awesome natural well, around 60m in diameter and 35m deep, but it lacks the one feature that draws thousands of adventurers to the Yucatán each year – you cannot dive in the Sacred Cenote.

Elsewhere on the peninsula, there are a number of *cenotes* that can be dived. Certified cave divers can delve to the caves' black depths but other divers will be limited to cavern diving, in which you're limited to staying within the area reached by sunlight. In most accessible caverns there are fixed lines to guide divers through the *cenote*.

Popular *cenote* dives include Ponderosa (also great for snorkelling), near Puerto Aventuras, with its rich aquatic life; and Cenote Azul, a 90m-deep natural pool on the shore of Laguna Bacalar.

Cenote Dos Ojos, near Tulum, is one of the most impressive caverns, with tremendous stalactites and stalagmites in an eerie wonderland. You can swim 500m through the *cenote* without leaving sunlight. This *cenote* also provides access to Nohoch Nah Chich, the largest underwater cave system in the world. Dos Ojos is part of the Hidden Worlds Cenote Park, which includes a couple of diving caverns and a range of snorkelling holes. www.hiddenworlds.com

↗ DO: **SNORKEL WITH MANATEES**

COUNTRY USA **TYPE OF ACTIVITY** Snorkelling/wildlife watching
FITNESS/EXPERTISE LEVEL Basic swimming skills required.
WHY NOW? Good manatee numbers and you'll beat the winter snowbirds
into town. **DESCRIPTION** With a walrus-like body that tapers to a beaver-
like tail, the shy and elusive manatee is slow, nearly blind and known
rather ingloriously as a sea cow, yet it's one of the state symbols of
Florida. Around 3000 manatees are thought to live in Florida waters, and
in the Crystal River in the state's north you can swim alongside them
to ponder how on earth these huge grey aquatic mammals were ever
mistaken for mermaids. Divers can pack away the tanks, as bubbles
scare manatees, making this a snorkelling-only adventure. Try to choose
a tour company that keeps the number of guests low – around six. Most
also have a 'Manatee awareness program' but go with an outfit that
incorporates this educational lecture into the tour itself and doesn't treat it
as an optional, extra-cost feature.

Reach out to a manatee (or is
that a mermaid in disguise?) in
Florida's Crystal River.

Come and see why New
Zealand's Milford Track is
considered a tramper's treat.

↗ DO: **TRAMP THE MILFORD TRACK**

COUNTRY New Zealand **TYPE OF ACTIVITY** Hiking
FITNESS/EXPERTISE LEVEL Moderate fitness required.
WHY NOW? The first weeks of the tramping season offer one of the best
chances to snare a permit. **DESCRIPTION** The famous Milford Track is a
four-day, 53.5km walk often described as one of the finest in the world.
So popular is the track that in the tramping season (late October to April)
permits are required and strict conditions are placed on all walkers:
the number of walkers starting the track each day is limited to 40;
accommodation is only in huts (camping isn't allowed); you must follow
a set four-day itinerary; and you can only walk in the one direction (Lake
Te Anau to Milford Sound). For your trouble you're treated to a wild (and
invariably wet) piece of New Zealand's World Heritage–listed Fiordland
National Park, showcased by Mackinnon Pass and the 580m-high
Sutherland Falls, one of the highest waterfalls in the world. www.doc
.govt.nz/Explore/002~Tracks-and-Walks/Great-Walks/Milford-Track

Himalayan 100 Mile Stage Race
www.himalayan.com
Run 160km over five days with views of
four of the world's five highest mountains.

Mt Everest Bike Rally
www.himalayan.com/b1.html
Five-day mountain-bike ride held in
conjunction with the Himalayan 100 Mile
Stage Race.

La Ruta de los Conquistadores
www.adventurerace.com
Three-day, 320km mountain-bike race
across harsh Costa Rican terrain; watch
out for the 1000m climb.

Molesworth Muster
www.bluedogevents.co.nz
An 80km mountain-bike ride along
otherwise closed roads beneath New
Zealand's Southern Alps.

week
.01

↗ DO: **CAMEL SAFARI IN DOUZ**

COUNTRY Tunisia **TYPE OF ACTIVITY** Camel safari
FITNESS/EXPERTISE LEVEL Not required.
WHY NOW? November is one of the few times that conditions permit
overnight treks. **DESCRIPTION** From the Tunisian town of Douz, camel
trekking ranges from one-hour rides to days-long desert adventures.
Overnight treks leave Douz in the afternoon, and involve about four hours
riding before pitching camp at sunset. Guides prepare an evening meal
of damper bread and stew, before you bed down beneath the stars for a
return the next morning. Longer expeditions can range as far as the oasis
town of Ksar Ghilane (seven to ten days). If you trek in November, you'll
not only have the best conditions, but the date harvest (which produces
some of the best dates in the world) will also have just finished, prices are
generally cheaper and you might be in Douz for the Sahara Festival, which
features camel racing and displays of traditional desert skills as well as
music, parades and poetry reading.

www.yearofadventures.com/november

Hong Kong's more than dim sum and downtown – get out and explore the 1000 sq km away from the tourist trail.

November

↙ GO: HONG KONG, CHINA

WHY NOW? TRAILWALKER IS ON; NOVEMBER ALSO BREWS UP THE TERRITORY'S BEST WINDSURFING CONDITIONS

Pack everything except your preconceptions and you might discover that über-urban Hong Kong is about more than downtown and dim sum. Almost seven million people call the territory home, but they're squeezed on to just 10% of the available land space, leaving around 1000 sq km of Hong Kong country open to exploration.

Walking trails in the territory are numerous, including four long-distance paths. The 50km Hong Kong Trail cuts through four country parks on Hong Kong Island. The 70km Lantau Trail follows mountain tops from Mui Wo, doubling back at Tai O along the coast to where it started. The 78km Wilson Trail is unusual in that it begins on Hong Kong Island but crosses the eastern harbour to New Kowloon and carries on into the New Territories.

Hong Kong's longest path is the 100km MacLehose Trail across the Kowloon Peninsula. It's on this trail that you can also experience the

↗ DO: LAND YACHT AT PENDINE SANDS

COUNTRY Wales **TYPE OF ACTIVITY** Land yachting **FITNESS/EXPERTISE LEVEL** Beginners to wind warriors. **WHY NOW?** November is among the windiest months in southern Wales. **DESCRIPTION** With speeds of up to 120km/h, land yachting is exhilarating and also quite easy to pick up. The giant sandy beach at Cefn Sidan, in Pembrey Country Park, is an ideal spot to try out these wheeled demons, but it's nearby Pendine Sands that's considered *the* place to sail. Conditions are best with a southerly or southwesterly filling your sails (the typical wind in southern Wales at this time of year is a westerly). The hard, flat 12-km beach at Pendine Sands was once a regular venue for land-speed records (most notably by Sir Malcolm Campbell). If you hear a loud bang as you're sailing, you probably haven't broken the speed of sound; unexploded munitions from a neighbouring testing ground are reputed to be found on the beach on occasions. To sail on Pendine you must join the Carmarthenshire Land Sailing Club (www.clsc.co.uk).

Propel yourself to high-speed freedom with the Welsh wind in your sails.

phenomenon of Trailwalker, usually held this week in November. Created in Hong Kong in 1981 as an endurance training programme for Gurkha soldiers (and subsequently spread to the UK, Australia and New Zealand), participants must cover the MacLehose on foot in 48 hours (the Gurkhas had to do it in half that time).

The MacLehose Trail passes another Hong Kong outdoor icon: Lion Rock, a natural king of this urban jungle. Rising above Kowloon, it's also a cornerstone of Hong Kong's climbing scene, offering two- and three-pitch routes on its east and west faces. More than a dozen other Hong Kong crags also see climbing action, with the finest (and often busiest) routes found on Tung Lung Chau. Boulderers also

have several playgrounds in which to perform their acrobatics.

Mountain-bike trails have been opened in 10 country parks, birdwatchers can tick off 450 species (head to Mai Po Marsh for the best twitching), and the fact that Hong Kong's only Olympic gold medal came in windsurfing testifies to that sport's popularity – November brews up the territory's best windsurting conditions. Hong Kong also has some surprisingly worthwhile diving spots, particularly in the far northeast.

For more information, visit www.discoverhongkong .com, www.oxfamtrailwalker.org.hk/eng and www .hongkongclimbing.com

You've never seen anything like the Everglades – 6070 sq km of labyrinthine waterways to paddle.

↗ DO: TAKE THE WILDERNESS WATERWAY

COUNTRY USA **TYPE OF ACTIVITY** Canoeing/kayaking

FITNESS/EXPERTISE LEVEL Moderate fitness required.

WHY NOW? For pleasantly mild conditions (23°C average) and the least number of mosquitoes.

DESCRIPTION Covering the southern tip of peninsular Florida, the Everglades form the third largest national park in the USA, at around 6070 sq km, and the world's first national park created not for its scenery but for its biological diversity. It's the country's largest subtropical wilderness; it's World Heritage–listed, an international biosphere and a wetland of international importance – quite simply, the Everglades are natural royalty.

Veined with waterways and estuaries, this watery maze is best explored by canoe or kayak. The chief paddling route is the Wilderness Waterway, a 159km journey through rivers and creeks (and, for a brief stint, in the Gulf of Mexico) along the Everglades' western edge, gliding by mangroves and sawgrass prairies.

The Wilderness Waterway begins in Everglades City in the park's north, winds through the Ten Thousand Islands (count them as you paddle past) and concludes at the Flamingo visitor centre at its very south. Allow about seven to nine days for the journey, and expect to see a few of the Glades' most famous inhabitants – alligators – possibly also more charming critters such as dolphins, manatees and roseate spoonbills.

Camp sites and camping platforms (known as chickees) are spread along the banks of the rivers and creeks, usually no more than 15km apart. Backcountry camping permits are required and can be obtained at the visitor centres in Everglades City or Flamingo. Canoes and kayaks can be rented in Everglades City. Be sure to travel with the necessary navigation charts – one turning can look very like another among the mangroves. The charts you'll need are numbers 11430, 11432 and 11433.

www.nps.gov/ever/visit/canoe-ww.htm

↗ DO: **HIKE THE ANNAPURNA CIRCUIT**

COUNTRY Nepal **TYPE OF ACTIVITY** Hiking
FITNESS/EXPERTISE LEVEL Good fitness and acclimatisation required.
WHY NOW? The best hiking season is October to December.
DESCRIPTION The Annapurna region is Nepal's most popular hiking area, and the 16-day circuit of the Annapurna massif is its showcase route. Such is the size of this massif, topped by one of the deadliest mountaineering summits in the Himalaya, that to walk around it means covering about 300km and climbing to one of the highest trekking points on earth, 5416m Thorung La. The route is lined with teashops and there are lodges in the villages, but be sure to acclimatise before attempting the crossing of Thorung La – trekkers have died from altitude sickness on this pass. If you prefer to see the massif from the inside, consider trekking into the Annapurna Sanctuary, the site of the Annapurna south-face base camp, encased by one of the planet's great mountain skylines.

↗ DO: **CLIMB PICO DE ORIZABA**

COUNTRY Mexico **TYPE OF ACTIVITY** Mountaineering
FITNESS/EXPERTISE LEVEL Good fitness and climbing skills required.
WHY NOW? Climb on the fringe of the mountain's busiest season.
DESCRIPTION Mexico's highest mountain (5611m) is also the third-tallest in North America – only Denali (Mt McKinley) in Alaska and Mt Logan in Canada are taller. Orizaba is a dormant volcano with a small crater and a three-month snow-cap, and unless you have navigation skills and some experience of snow- and ice-climbing techniques you shouldn't attempt this climb without a guide. The most common route up Orizaba is from the north, using the small town of Tlachichuca as a base. From Tlachichuca, take a taxi to Villa Hidalgo at 3400m, then walk 10km to the mountain hut at 4200m. The climb from here is moderately steep over snow that's usually hard – it's not technically difficult, but crampons are essential, as are ropes and ice axes for safety. Most climbers leave the hut at about 2am to reach the peak for sunrise, before mist and cloud envelop the summit.

↗ DO: **UNDERSEA WALK IN MAURITIUS**

COUNTRY Mauritius **TYPE OF ACTIVITY** Snuba
FITNESS/EXPERTISE LEVEL Not required.
WHY NOW? Get wet ahead of the approaching wet season.
DESCRIPTION The novel activity of undersea walking, or snuba, has caught on in a big way in Mauritius as it allows nondivers the chance to experience life below the waves. Participants don a weight belt and a diving helmet and stroll along the sea bed feeding the fish. Solar-powered pumps on the boat above feed oxygen to you during the 25-minute 'walk on the wet side', and divers are on hand in case there are any problems. In general, there's a minimum age requirement of seven years. The two prime spots for an underwater ramble are Grand Baie, in the north, and Belle Mare, on the east coast. www.captainemo-underseawalk.com

It's a long way to the top... but the magnetism of the Himalayas will put a spring in your step.

North America's third-highest peak, the dormant volcano Pico de Orizaba is a mecca for crampon-shod climbers.

Triple Challenge
www.triplechallenge.co.za
South African multisport event out of Pietermaritzburg; run, cycle and paddle almost 100km.

100km Pharaonic Race
www.egyptianmarathon.com.eg
Feel as old as the pyramids after running 100km through Egypt.

Kendal Mountain Film Festival
www.mountainfilm.co.uk
Visit the mountains from the comfort of a theatre chair in England's Lake District.

Highland Fling
www.wildhorizons.com.au
Mountain bike 100km through the Southern Highlands of New South Wales, Australia.

week
.02

The unspoiled escarpment of the Drakensberg Mountains is just one of KwaZulu Natal's outlets for the adventurous.

November

GO: KWAZULU NATAL, SOUTH AFRICA

week

↙ .03

www.yearofadventures.com/november

WHY NOW? AT THIS TIME OF YEAR THE 'BIG FIVE' ARE DRAWN TO THE DWINDLING WATERHOLES IN THE PROVINCE'S PARKS

KwaZulu Natal is South Africa's most populous province, yet it's the kind of place where you can be surfing one day, swimming with sharks the next, viewing white rhinos the following day and then hiking across the jagged Drakensberg before your week is out.

Durban is the province's major city, and you can get busy without even leaving the city. Durban has surf and culture to match anywhere in the world. Given the right swell, the city has a range of quality breaks: South Break and Addington are normally the best beginner spots. The more experienced might want to range along the KwaZulu Natal coast to Westbrook, Ballito Bay and Zinkwazi Beach in the north, and Greenpoint, Scottburgh, Happy Wanderers, St Michaels and the Spot (all right-handers) in the south. Each produces rideable 1m to 2.5m-plus grinders over rock and sand bottom.

↗ DO: SUQUTRA

COUNTRY Yemen **TYPE OF ACTIVITY** Adventure travel **FITNESS/EXPERTISE LEVEL** Not required. **WHY NOW?** Visit from mid-October to mid-May; outside this time, monsoons and high winds sometimes prevent flights into the island. **DESCRIPTION** Lying about 510km southeast of the Yemen mainland, the island of Suqutra has developed in near total isolation from the rest of the country. This accounts for its extraordinary fauna and flora – of Suqutra's 750 species of plant, 300 are endemic, while several hundred animal species are also endemic. One hotel on the island has designs on turning this natural wonderland into an Arabian adventure extravaganza, with plans to introduce mountain biking, hiking, diving, fishing, yachting and windsurfing. Bird and turtle watching is also planned, as well as ecotourism-related activities such as turtle-weighing. Caving is another activity planned – Suqutra is thought to boast one of the world's largest cave systems (18km have been mapped to date).

The near total isolation doesn't seem to have done the flora and fauna any harm – why not give it a try?

Deeper into the Indian Ocean, advanced divers who don't mind a shark or 200 will want to check out Protea Banks. At least 12 shark species frequent the banks. Look for grey reef, thresher, copper, sand, mako, tiger and even the occasional great white shark. For a more sedate and colourful diving experience, try the warm waters of Sodwana Bay.

One reason you'll want to come to KwaZulu Natal in November is to watch the wildlife at South Africa's oldest parks: Hluhluwe-Umfolozi and Greater St Lucia Wetlands. The former is the rhino capital of Africa, and also has KwaZulu Natal's only park with the full complement of 'big five' creatures, all drawn at this time of year to the dwindling waterholes. Greater St Lucia is one of Southern Africa's most important coastal wetlands, famed for its crocodiles and, in November, humpback whales, whale sharks and nesting turtles.

Set on the border with Lesotho, the Drakensberg is South Africa's most enticing mountain range and will satisfy any mountain walker with its sheer, sharp peaks. Walk for a few hours or a few days; the southern end of the range offers some of the country's most remote and rugged hiking.

Get a camel's-eye view of exotic Rajasthan, Land of the Maharajas, with the help of some friendly locals.

↗ DO: CAMEL SAFARI IN RAJASTHAN

COUNTRY India **TYPE OF ACTIVITY** Camel riding

FITNESS/EXPERTISE LEVEL Not required.

WHY NOW? The most comfortable time for a camel safari is from October to February.

DESCRIPTION It's debatable whether the Rajasthan city of Jaisalmer is more famous for its sandcastle-like fort or for its camel safaris. No place better evokes ancient desert splendour and exotic trade routes, making it one of the most evocative places to begin a desert safari.

A camel journey into the Thar Desert offers an evocative way to sample desert life, but don't expect a sea of dunes. The Thar Desert is mostly barren scrub, sprinkled with villages and ruins. You'll come across tiny fields of millet, and children herding flocks of sheep or goats, whose tinkling neck bells offer a nice change from the sound of your farting camels.

The camel's reins are fastened to its nose peg, so the animal is easily steered. Stirrups make the journey a lot more comfortable. At resting points, the camels are unsaddled and hobbled. They limp off to graze on shrubs while the drivers brew chai or prepare food. The whole crew rests in the shade of thorn trees. At night you'll camp out, huddling around a tiny fire beneath a ceiling of stars and listening to the camel drivers' songs.

Most safaris last three to four days and the traditional circuit takes in Amar Sagar, where there's a garden, dried-up step-wells and a Jain temple; Mool Sagar, a run-down oasis with a Shiva Temple; Bada Bagh, a fertile oasis with a huge old dam and sandstone sculpted royal *chhatris* (centopaths) with beautifully carved ceilings; as well as various abandoned villages along the way.

More and more travellers are opting for remote safaris. You're driven in a 4WD for around 30km and then head off on your camel, avoiding the major sights and other safari groups. www.jaisalmertourism.com

↗ DO: SAIL THE BRITISH VIRGIN ISLANDS

COUNTRY British Virgin Islands **TYPE OF ACTIVITY** Sailing
FITNESS/EXPERTISE LEVEL Sailing experience required if bareboat chartering. **WHY NOW?** It's the cusp of the high and dry season.
DESCRIPTION A felicitous combination of geography and geology positions the BVI as sailing's magic kingdom. You've got a year-round balmy climate, steady trade winds, little to worry about in the way of tides or currents, a protected thoroughfare in the 56km-long Sir Francis Drake Channel, and hundreds of anchorages, each within sight of one another. These factors make the BVI one of the easiest places to sail, which explains why more than a third of all visitors come to do just that. There are three basic options: a sailing school; a bareboat charter (bare of crew but fully equipped), with or without a skipper; or a more luxurious crewed charter, complete with captain, cook and crew. A typical week-long itinerary involves a sampling of the islands, while partially circumnavigating Tortola. To hire a crewed yacht, contact the British Virgin Islands Charter Yacht Society (www.bvicrewedyachts.com).

Sail away into the blue haven of the British Virgin islands.

From the heights of the Simien Mountains, Mother Africa is laid out at your feet.

↗ DO: HIKE IN THE SIMIEN MOUNTAINS

COUNTRY Ethiopia **TYPE OF ACTIVITY** Hiking
FITNESS/EXPERTISE LEVEL Moderate fitness required.
WHY NOW? Come early in the dry season (October to May) for green landscapes and wild flowers. **DESCRIPTION** Far from Africa's beaten mountain paths is a range unlike any other on the continent. The Simien Mountains are made up of several plateaus, separated by broad river valleys. A number of peaks rise above 4000m, including Ras Dashen (4543m), the fourth-highest mountain in Africa. At the range's northern edge is a 60km-long escarpment overlooking a land of rock pinnacles and mesas for some of the finest views in Africa. All treks begin and end in Debark, where the park headquarters are located. The most popular trekking routes are along the western side of the massif, taking in the most impressive sections of the escarpment. The most spectacular scenery is around the Geech Abyss, while the classic Simien trek continues past Geech to the summit of Ras Dashen; allow eight to 10 days for the return hike.

Southern Traverse
www.southerntraverse.com
Teams of four tramp, mountain bike, raft, abseil and kayak through New Zealand's South Island; expect to take around five days.

Real Ale Wobble
http://llanwrtyd-wells.powys.org.uk
Mountain bike up to 65km while quaffing half-pints of ale at various checkpoints. Stick around for the walkers' event a week later.

Cliff Young Australian Six-Day Race
http://sixdayrace.org.au
Run around a square in the Australian town of Colac and stop six days later; Yiannis Kouros covered 1036km in 2005.

↗ DO: RUN THE EVEREST MARATHON

COUNTRY Nepal **TYPE OF ACTIVITY** Running
FITNESS/EXPERTISE LEVEL Good fitness and acclimatisation required.
WHY NOW? To race in the world's highest marathon. **DESCRIPTION** Discover the painful feeling of running a marathon at heights usually limited to mountaineers and hardy trekkers. With its starting line at Gorak Shep (5160m), in the shadow of Mt Everest, it takes 17 days of trekking just to get here. Then, with the temperature somewhere around -20°C, you face the prospect of running 42km back to Namche Bazaar, dodging yak trains and crossing rickety bridges only to clock a personal worst time – most runners take twice as long to complete the Everest Marathon as they do a normal marathon. To gain entry into this most difficult of races, you must have experience of major cross-country, mountain running or adventure events; road marathon experience is not sufficient.
www.everestmarathon.org.uk

week
.03

www.yearofadventures.com/november

185

The thunderous roar and smoky spray of Victoria Falls is just the start of what the Zambesi has to offer.

November

week

.04

www.yearofadventures.com/november

⤿ GO: **VICTORIA FALLS, ZAMBIA/ZIMBABWE**

WHY NOW? THE ZAMBESI RIVER RAPIDS ARE RUNNING AT THEIR BEST

Victoria Falls' thick, thundering curtain of water is so utterly overpowering it's regarded as one of the seven natural wonders of the world. Over this 1.7km-wide precipice, an average of 550,000 cu metres of water plummets 100m into the narrow Batoka Gorge every minute. In full flood, the spray – 'the smoke that thunders' – can be seen from 80km away.

Victoria Falls doubles as Africa's adventure capital, offering a staggering array of activities – some travellers have so much fun bungy jumping and/or rafting they forget to visit the falls! The headline act here are water activities, headed by some of the world's best water-water rafting. The Zambesi River below the falls is said to have the highest concentration of grade-five rapids of any watercourse on earth, and right now they are running at their best. Wild, low-water runs, taking in the winding 22km from rapids four to 18 (or 23) in Zimbabwe, or rapids one to 18 (or 23)

↗ DO: MUCK DIVE ON SAMARAI ISLAND

COUNTRY Papua New Guinea **TYPE OF ACTIVITY** Muck diving **FITNESS/EXPERTISE LEVEL** Not required. **WHY NOW?** Diving is best from October to March, when winds are lightest. **DESCRIPTION** Muck diving sounds like the ocean equivalent of bog snorkelling, but it's more akin to underwater macrophotography. Put simply, it's diving in silty water, enjoying the ocean's obscure smaller inhabitants, such as nudibranches. PNG is the muck-diving world capital and Samarai Island is the epicentre. Anyone who can swim can witness the extravagant coral, fantastic tropical fish and the detritus of history side by side beneath the Samarai piers – Samarai was once the second-largest town in PNG but in 1942 Australian forces destroyed almost every building in anticipation of a Japanese invasion that never came. The easiest place to enter is just north of the Samarai Island Trading Company wharf. To reach Samarai Island, take the *Kavieng Queen* from the Milne Bay Province capital, Alotau; the daily crossing takes 1 ½ hours.

There's nothing yucky about muck diving in PNG: it's a journey into history with an underwater garden thrown in.

in Zambia, operate from roughly 15 August to late December. All operators walk around rapid nine, which is affectionately nicknamed Commercial Suicide.

If you want all the thrills of rafting without the raft, consider riverboarding, in which you surf the Zambezi with nothing between your body and the swirling maelstrom except a piece of foam.

Kayakers might be enticed here by images of kayaks tossed around in the Boiling Pot below the falls, but most canoeing and kayaking tours operate above the falls, paddling the wide river, exploring its mid-stream islands and shooting its mini-rapids.

Dry off with a quick leap from the Victoria Falls Bridge – at one time this 111m plunge was the world's highest bungy jump. If you have a few days left in your week, take your pick from horse, elephant and walking safaris, abseiling, high-wiring, microlighting, jet boating, a helicopter ride or drown your nerves with a spot of booze cruising. If it all sounds like an adventuring equivalent of a fast-food joint, you can even opt for an activity 'combo'...would you like a bungy jump with that?

o1 o2
o3 **o4**

Take a slow boat to Timbuktu and back again at least once in your life.

↗ DO: TIMBUKTU BY BOAT

COUNTRY Mali **TYPE OF ACTIVITY** Adventure travel
FITNESS/EXPERTISE LEVEL Not required.
WHY NOW? The river's at its highest from August to mid-December.
DESCRIPTION The name Timbuktu has the very ring of adventure: remote, desert-licked and exotic. And it can still be an adventure to get here if you come on one of the large passenger boats that ply the Niger River between Koulikoro (60km northeast of Bamako) and Gao, via Korioumé (18km from Timbuktu).

Passenger boats run from August to mid-December, when the river is high, and you should expect a floating mass of jostling humanity for the five days of sailing between Koulikoro and Korioumé. Luxe and first class consist of two-berth cabins; second is a four-berth cabin; third is either an eight-berth or 12-berth cabin (although you can sleep and hang out on the upper deck); and fourth class is in the packed and basic lower deck (which even the most hardened travellers rate as the pits). Whatever class you're in, it'll be sweltering and the toilets will be flooded.

For a less gritty river experience, you can travel to Timbuktu by more traditional motorised canoes called pinasse. From the city of Mopti you can board a large, laden cargo pinasse, but this can be slow. A more serene, comfortable and quicker option is to get a group together and hire a tourist pinasse, journeying along the pale luminous swell of the Niger, banked by sand dunes, passing boats with rice-bag sails, makeshift villages, waving people and wading fishermen. You sleep on the river bank or in the boat – nights are magical, silent and star-lit, but also cold, so pack a blanket or sleeping bag. It will take you about three days to reach Korioumé (18km from Timbuktu), from where you catch a shared taxi to Timbuktu.

01 02
03 04

↗ DO: HILL-TRIBE TREK IN NORTHERN THAILAND

COUNTRY Thailand **TYPE OF ACTIVITY** Hiking
FITNESS/EXPERTISE LEVEL Good fitness required.
WHY NOW? The best time to trek is November to February, when the weather is refreshing, there's little or no rain and wild flowers are in bloom. **DESCRIPTION** Thousands of visitors trek into the hills of northern Thailand each year, though many people feel awkward walking through hill-tribe villages and playing the role of voyeur. In general, the trekking business has become more conscious of the need to tread carefully in hill-tribe villages, and most companies limit the number of visits to a particular area and are careful not to overlap areas used by other companies. Chiang Mai and Chiang Rai are the main centres for hill-tribe trekking, while many people now also do short treks on their own, staying in villages along the way. It's not necessary to bring a lot of food or gear, just money for food that can be bought en route. The Tourism Authority of Thailand, however, discourages trekking on your own because of safety risks.

Tread lightly on a trek into Thailand's enticing hill-tribe region.

↗ DO: SKYJUMP IN AUCKLAND

COUNTRY New Zealand **TYPE OF ACTIVITY** Cable-controlled BASE jumping
FITNESS/EXPERTISE LEVEL Not required.
WHY NOW? Spring...a wonderful time to spring from a tall building.
DESCRIPTION Think bungee jumping, but with a very urban, very Auckland twist. New Zealand's largest city also presents one of the country's largest adrenaline rushes: Skyjump, a 192m, cable-controlled BASE jump from the tallest building in the southern hemisphere. Storeys above the gaming tables, restaurants and bars that fill the tower, you're fitted into a harness and a Superman-coloured suit and clipped to a cable. As you leap, a drum feeds out the cable, with descent speeds limited to around 60km/h by a fan descender. It's 20 seconds of superhero flight that almost impales jumpers on the city below. Instead, the descender – the sort used by Hollywood movie makers to film falling stunts (think *Entrapment* or *Titanic*) – slows the fall at the end, delivering you to earth on your feet. www.skyjump.co.nz

Move over Spiderman I'm coming down! (From the southern hemisphere's highest building, no less.)

Lake Taupo Cycle Challenge
www.cyclechallenge.org.nz
Ride 160km or 320km around the New Zealand volcanic caldera, Lake Taupo.

Sani Stagger Endurance Race
www.sanistagger.com
A knee-crunching marathon as you descend, then ascend, 1300m along the only road to cross South Africa's Drakensberg mountains.

Tuatara Peninsula Race
www.bloodygoodevents.co.nz/Tuatara
Two-day, 85km run, ride and kayak race on the Banks Pensinsula, out of Christchurch.

week .04

www.yearofadventuroo.com/november

↗ DO: CRUISE THE SUNDERBANS TIGER RESERVE

COUNTRY India **TYPE OF ACTIVITY** Wildlife watching
FITNESS/EXPERTISE LEVEL Not required.
WHY NOW? Tiger sightings are most likely between October and March.
DESCRIPTION Home to one of the largest tiger populations on the planet, the lush 2585-sq-km Sunderbans Tiger Reserve seemingly floats atop the waters of the world's largest delta in West Bengal. The Royal Bengal tigers (estimated to number 274 in 2004) not only wander the impenetrable depths of the mangrove forests, but also swim the delta's innumerable channels. Although they're known to have an appetite for humans, tigers are typically shy and sightings are the exception, not the rule. Visiting independently is difficult, with seemingly never-ending permits, fees and tricky transportation connections. The West Bengal tourist department in Kolkata organises weekly boat cruises through the present high season. www.wbtourism.com

December

↙ GO: MÉRIDA, VENEZUELA

WHY NOW? IN DECEMBER, THE NORTHERN ANDES ARE ENTERING THE DRY SEASON

Every continent should have a place that devotes itself to bringing adventure and adrenalin to the masses. South America has Mérida, set among the northern Andes, in the western corner of Venezuela, and now entering its dry season. It's surrounded by beautiful mountains, including the country's highest mountain, 5007m Pico Bolívar, just 12km away. It's home to the famous teleférico, the world's highest and longest cable-car system, running 12.5km from the bottom station of Barinitas (1577m) in Mérida to the top at Pico Espejo (4765m), covering the ascent in four stages. Even if you take the journey straight through you'll be on the teleférico for around 1½ hours.

The list of adventure sports and outdoor activities on offer in Mérida is longer than the menus in its restaurants – hiking, mountaineering, bird-watching, paragliding, horse riding, rafting and mountain biking might just

The world drops away beneath your feet as you ascend the Pico Espejo by teleférico.

↗ DO: VISIT THE ALASKA CHILKAT BALD EAGLE PRESERVE

COUNTRY USA **TYPE OF ACTIVITY** Wildlife watching **FITNESS/EXPERTISE LEVEL** Not required. **WHY NOW?** To witness one of the planet's greatest gatherings of eagles. **DESCRIPTION** Each year from October to February, more than 4000 bald eagles congregate along Alaska's Chilkat, Klehini and Tsirku Rivers to feed on spawning salmon. They come because an upwelling of warm water prevents the river from freezing, thus encouraging a late salmon run. It's a remarkable sight – hundreds of birds sitting in the bare trees lining the river, often six or more birds to a branch. The eagles can be seen from the Haines Hwy, where turnouts allow motorists to park and watch. The best view is between Mile 18 and Mile 22, where you'll find telescopes, interpretive displays and paved walkways along the river. The state park office in the town of Haines can provide a list of state-authorized guides who conduct preserve tours. www.dnr .state.ak.us/parks/units/eagleprv.htm

Can't let those bears get there first... 4000 bald eagles flock to Alaska's rivers to feast on spawning salmon each year.

be the specials board. Mountains form the city's staple diet, and the most popular high-mountain trekking area is the Parque Nacional Sierra Nevada, east of Mérida, which has all of Venezuela's highest peaks, including Pico Bolívar, Pico Humboldt (4942m) and Pico Bonpland (4883m). Guided ascents are offered by most of Mérida's tour operators – Bolívar, particularly, is a mountaineering feat. The Parque Nacional Sierra La Culata, to Mérida's north, also offers some amazing hiking territory, and is particularly noted for its desert-like highland landscapes.

Tandem paragliding is another Mérida condiment, usually launching from Las González, an hour's drive from the city. From here you glide for 20 to 30 minutes down 850 vertical metres. Rafting is organised on several rivers on the southern slopes of the Andes, while canyoning is among the adventuring desserts.

If you'd rather look at animals than be one, Mérida is a centre for trips into Los Llanos, an immense plain savanna south of the Andes that is Venezuela's great repository of wildlife, particularly birds. It's also excellent ground to get close – not too close, mind – to piranhas, anacondas, caimans and capybaras.

o1 o2 o3 o4

Time to reflect – the jagged massif of the Cuernos del Paine is mirrored in the waters of Lago Pehoé at sunrise.

↗ DO: HIKE AT TORRES DEL PAINE

COUNTRY Chile **TYPE OF ACTIVITY** Hike

FITNESS/EXPERTISE LEVEL Good fitness required.

WHY NOW? The shoulder summer season of December is one of the best trekking times.

DESCRIPTION Soaring more than 2000m above the Patagonian steppe, the Torres del Paine (Towers of Paine) are spectacular granite pillars that dominate the landscape of what is arguably South America's finest national park, Parque Nacional Torres del Paine. For hikers, this 181-sq-km park is an unequalled destination, with a well-developed trail network and *refugios* and camping grounds at strategic spots.

For most trekkers the question is whether to circuit or to 'W'. Circuiting takes around eight days, while the popular W trek, named for the route's in-and-out shape, takes around five. Most hikers start both routes from Laguna Amarga – the W climbs to the spectacular Torres del Paine Lookout, immediately below the towers. With their mighty columns ringed by shelf glaciers and meltwater-streaked rocks, this is one of Patagonia's classic scenes. The W goes on via Los Cuernos and Lago Pehoé to Lago Grey, where the unstable, 200m-thick snout of Glaciar Grey continually sends blocks of ice – some as big as a house – plunging into the freezing waters. Patagonia's notoriously strong winds drive the icebergs across the lake to strand on the shore.

Walking the complete Torres del Paine circuit takes in the W plus the more remote back side of the massif. There are eight *refugios* for trekkers in the park, and the availability of hired camping equipment at all *refugios* and at Campamento Los Perros has made it theoretically possible to trek the circuit or the W without carrying a tent. For hikers on the circuit, however, this means covering the most difficult and remote stretch between Campamento Los Perros and Refugio Grey, including the crossing of the circuit's highest pass, in a long day. Some hikers find this is beyond them.

01 02
03 04

↗ DO: CAVE TUBE AT WAITOMO

COUNTRY New Zealand **TYPE OF ACTIVITY** Cave tubing
FITNESS/EXPERTISE LEVEL Rookies to full-blown spelunkers.
WHY NOW? Come early in summer to beat the high season.
DESCRIPTION The name Waitomo, which comes from *wai* (water) and
tomo (hole or shaft), is appropriate: dotted throughout the countryside
around this North Island town are numerous shafts dropping abruptly into
at least 300 underground caves and streams. Tourism here began with
sedate cave visits but in typical Kiwi fashion the list of things to do has
become ever more daring. Cave tubing – floating through glow-worm-lit
caves on inner tubes – has become Waitomo's signature activity, but even
this simple activity now has more flavours than an ice-cream store. You
can abseil up to 100m into caves; you can make belayed rock climbs out;
and you can swim, leap and whoosh through the dark on flying foxes.
www.waitomocaves.com

↗ DO: CYCLE THE MEKONG DELTA

COUNTRY Vietnam **TYPE OF ACTIVITY** Cycle tour
FITNESS/EXPERTISE LEVEL Moderate fitness required.
WHY NOW? The rains have moved on and the temperature is bearable.
DESCRIPTION You want flat? You've got it on the sprawling delta of one of
the world's great rivers. The Mekong River begins on the Tibetan Plateau
and travels 4500km, and through six countries, to the pancake-flat rice
bowl of southern Vietnam. Here, you might well ride over more bridges
than in any other part of the world. Water will be the dominant theme of
your ride – as well as the massive Mekong there are countless tributaries,
canals and streams along the way. A good tour (of about four days) begins
in Ho Chi Minh City, joining the Mekong at My Thuan and pedalling on to
Chau Doc on the Cambodian border. The traffic is pretty busy between Ho
Chi Minh City and Cantho but the wide roads make the traffic bearable.

↗ DO: PLYMOUTH–BANJUL RALLY

COUNTRIES England, France, Morocco, Mauritania, Senegal, Gambia
TYPE OF ACTIVITY Motoring rally
FITNESS/EXPERTISE LEVEL Not required.
WHY NOW? Cars leave from Plymouth through December.
DESCRIPTION Like the look of the Paris–Dakar Rally but haven't the
necessary money or the speed? Perhaps the Plymouth–Banjul Rally is the
event for you. To take part in this annual, noncompetitive rally, your vehicle
must have cost less than £100 (Ladas are a favourite) and you must have
spent no more than £15 on preparing the car. Then all you have to do is
nurse the thing across six countries and 6000km into the Gambian capital
of Banjul, where your car will be auctioned in aid of local charities. There's
no fixed departure date and it'll probably take you around three weeks –
you can take even longer if you want to look around a bit as you drive.
www.plymouth-dakar.co.uk

Lower yourself into a subterranean wonderland at Waitomo.

Cycling down the Mekong doesn't have to be done at break-neck speed.

Kepler Challenge
www.keplerchallenge.co.nz
Run 60km through the Fiordland
mountains along New Zealand's Kepler
Track.

Goat Alpine Adventure Run
www.thegoat.co.nz
Get your horns around a 21km run on
to the ski fields of periodically eruptive
Mt Ruapehu.

Baja Traversia
www.exploreca.com
Three- to five-day multisport race that
includes canyoning and a desert car rally.

Eddie Aikau Big Wave International
www.quiksilver.com/eddiewouldgo
The 24 invited surfers wait up to three
months for a 6m swell on Oahu's
Waimea Bay.

week

.01

www.yearofadventures.com/december

193

Emperor penguins are serious adventurers when it comes to breeding, trekking miles through some of the harshest conditions imaginable.

December

↙ GO:
ANTARCTICA

week

↙ .02

www.yearofadventures.com/december

WHY NOW? DECEMBER OFFERS UP TO 20 HOURS OF DAYLIGHT AND THE CHANCE TO SEE HATCHING PENGUINS

The earth's most isolated continent, Antarctica must be earned, through either a long, often uncomfortable voyage or an expensive flight. Weather and ice – not clocks or calendars – set the schedule, and itineraries are subject to the continent's changing moods. What you'll find, however, is a spectacular wilderness of snow, ice and rock, teeming with wildlife.

Unless you're planning your own expedition, you'll visit Antarctica as part of a group tour, most likely on a ship. The most popular Antarctica trip involves an exploration of the Antarctic Peninsula, one of the continent's richest breeding grounds for seabirds, seals and penguins. Trips leave from Ushuaia, on South America's Tierra del Fuego, and you'll most likely make your first landing at one of the South Shetland Islands, a 540km chain of islands at the northern end of the Antarctic Peninsula with spectacular scenery and abundant wildlife.

↗ DO: **BOULDER AT FONTAINEBLEAU**

COUNTRY France **TYPE OF ACTIVITY** Bouldering **FITNESS/EXPERTISE LEVEL** Beginners to pros, but bring strong fingers. **WHY NOW?** The sandstone is at its best in the French winter. **DESCRIPTION** Look past the elegance and splendour of Fontainebleau, the former royal residence 67km southeast of Paris, and you'll find its antithesis, the gritty world of bouldering, at play in the Forêt de Fontainebleau. To boulderers (who climb without ropes near to the ground) this is the enchanted forest, a place where they can't see the trees for the rocks. 'Font' is prized for its diverse routes and its collection of circuits, in which problems are linked together into a single route. The circuits might feature up to 75 problems, and one stretches out for around 10km. Each circuit at Font is colour-coded according to its difficulty, with yellow the easiest and black the most tendon-tearing.

Get a grip on adventure in France by rope-free bouldering in the Forêt de Fontainebleau.

On the Antarctic Peninsula your schedule will depend on the expedition leader's judgment, though most tours ultimately visit the same landing sites because they offer easy access to wildlife, a station or a museum. Likely landings include the former British base-turned-museum at Port Lockroy; Neko Harbor, where the glacier across from the landing site often calves with a thunderous roar; and the US Palmor research station.

You'll almost certainly call in at Paradise Harbor, described in tour brochures as 'the most aptly named place in the world'. That may be overstating it a little but with its majestic icebergs and reflections of the surrounding mountains, Paradise Harbor is undeniably beautiful. It's a favorite place for 'Zodiac cruising' around the ice that's calved from the glacier at the head of the bay.

The Antarctic tour season is short – about four months, with each month offering its own highlights. Coming in December, at the height of the austral summer, you'll find penguins hatching eggs and feeding chicks, and you'll have up to 20 hours of sunlight every day.

Real-life rollercoaster as daredevil train sufers roar down the Devil's Nose.

↗ DO: TRAIN SURF EL NARIZ DEL DIABLO

COUNTRY Ecuador **TYPE OF ACTIVITY** Train surf

FITNESS/EXPERTISE LEVEL Not required.

WHY NOW? The more the merrier atop the train, so come now as the Ecuadorian high season begins.

DESCRIPTION As the railway runs south from the city of Riobamba it makes a hair-raising descent from Alausí to Sibambe, down a death-defying stretch of track called El Nariz del Diablo (the Devil's Nose). Built more than a century ago – and the only surviving section of the once spectacular Ferrocarril Transandino (Trans-Andean Railway), which ran from Guayaquil to Quito – a series of switchbacks was carved into the rock (and many lives were lost in the process) that would allow the train, by advancing and reversing, to ascend nearly 1000m to Alausí, at 2607m. The completion and first ascent of the Nariz del Diablo in 1902 was the most incredible feat of railway engineering the world had seen.

The steep descent after Alausí is still accomplished by a series of switchbacks down the steep mountainside. Occasional rickety-looking bridges cross steep ravines, and the great game for daredevil passengers is to ride on the train's flat roof, with nothing but empty space between them and the valleys far below. The local machos even stand up on the roof, especially when going through tunnels, where there is barely enough clearance for the sombrero jammed jauntily on their heads. In truth, the greatest hazard is probably the train's emission of steam, soot and cinders during the ride, so don't wear your tuxedo.

The train leaves Alausí daily at 9.30am, and tickets go on sale at 8am. It usually arrives at Alausí from Riobamba and the roof is already often full with riders from Riobamba or tour groups who pile on while their guide stands in line to buy tickets. The trip takes around two hours to go through El Nariz del Diablo.

↗ DO: RAFT THE SOURCE OF THE NILE

COUNTRY Uganda **TYPE OF ACTIVITY** White-water rafting
FITNESS/EXPERTISE LEVEL Not required.

WHY NOW? Rafting is good year-round, with water levels constant, but December is one of the drier months in Jinja.

DESCRIPTION The source of the Nile out of Lake Victoria is one of the world's most spectacular white-water rafting destinations, and a place where you come to tackle the 'big four' – the source's four grade-five rapids – not the 'big five' usually sought in Africa. There are three companies offering rafting trips out of the town of Jinja (about 1½ hours by bus from the Ugandan capital, Kampala), and the growing list of white-water accoutrements is turning Jinja into one of Africa's burgeoning adventure destinations. The brave-hearted can try riverboarding, in which you take on the Nile armed only with a boogie board, or take instruction in white-water kayaking. Or you can just drop in from the 44m-high Nile High Bungy at the Jinja Nile Resort.

↗ DO: ZORB IN ROTORUA

COUNTRY New Zealand **TYPE OF ACTIVITY** Zorbing
FITNESS/EXPERTISE LEVEL Not required.

WHY NOW? Decent weather and Rotorua's holiday crowds are a week or two from arriving.

DESCRIPTION Zorbing is simple in theory: wriggle inside a large plastic ball and roll down a hill at speeds of up to 50 km/h. A cushion of air protects you from the hard bumps, while the centrifugal force pins your body to the ball in the manner of a gravity-defying show ride. It's dizzying and disorienting, but it wouldn't be a New Zealand adventure if there wasn't a way to spice up the activity even further. In this case, the evil sister is Hyrdo-Zorbing, where a bucket of water is poured into the Zorb, drenching you as you scream your way downhill. Cold water or warm water, it's your choice. The creators of Zorb claim nobody has ever thrown up inside the ball. Wanna be the first? www.zorb.co.nz

↗ DO: LEMUR TRACK IN PARC NATIONAL D'ANDASIBE-MANTADIA

COUNTRY Madagascar **TYPE OF ACTIVITY** Wildlife watching
FITNESS/EXPERTISE LEVEL Not required.

WHY NOW? The park fills up during Madagascar's high tourist season between July and September, though now is actually a better time to visit.

DESCRIPTION Parc National d'Andasibe-Mantadia consists of beautiful primary forest studded with lakes, and is the home of the rare indri, Madagascar's largest lemur. The wondrous indri has been described as looking like a four-year-old child in a panda suit, and is famous for its eerie wailing cry, which sounds like something between a fire siren and the song of an operatic tenor – it's an amazing creature to behold. There are about 60 family groups of two or five indris in the park; their cry, which can be heard up to 3km away, is used to define a particular group's territory. Indris are active on and off throughout the day, beginning about an hour after daybreak, which is usually the best time to try to see them. www.parcs-madagascar.com/mantadia (in French)

Lake Victoria disgorges turbulently into the Upper Nile, creating a white-water rafter's playground.

Turn your life upside down and round and round (and your insides possibly out) in a Zorb.

Canmore Ice Climbing Festival
www.canmoreiceclimbingfestival.com
Four days of crampon and ice-axe worship in Alberta.

Oman Adventure
www.authentiqueaventure.com
Five-day adventure race through Oman.

Action Asia Challenge Hong Kong
www.actionasia.com/aae/index.jsp
Single-day adventure race involving river-rock scrambling, ocean swimming and orienteering.

week
.02

www.yearofadventures.com/december

Make a dive for the 2000 islands of Micronesia strewn across the turquoise waters of the North Pacific.

December

↙ GO:
MICRONESIA

week
↙ .03

www.yearofadventures.com/december

WHY NOW? DECEMBER TO FEBRUARY IS MANTA RAY SEASON IN MILL CHANNEL

In contrast to the vast North Pacific seas they span, the total land area of the 2000 Micronesian islands is so small that many world maps don't even bother to dot them in. But they are on every diver's map.

Micronesia's clear, 27°C waters teem with coral gardens and tropical fish. Around Palau, three ocean currents converge to bring in some of the most varied and dazzling marine life in the world. In Chuuk, the lagoon bed holds an entire Japanese fleet, frozen in time where it sank in February 1944. Complete with sake cups and skeletons, jeeps and tanks tied on board and fighter planes still waiting in the holds, the wrecks have been declared an underwater museum.

Thanks to Bikini Atoll's ominous nuclear history – the USA conducted 23 nuclear tests here in 1946 – the atoll has become one of Micronesia's premier dive sites, with divers massing to see the wrecks created by

↗ DO: ELEPHANT TREK IN MONDULKIRI PROVINCE

COUNTRY Cambodia **TYPE OF ACTIVITY** Elephant trekking **FITNESS/EXPERTISE LEVEL** Not required. **WHY NOW?** The ideal time to visit Cambodia is December and January, when humidity levels are low, there's little rainfall and a cooling breeze whips across the land. **DESCRIPTION** Nestled against the eastern border, Mondulkiri is Cambodia's most sparsely populated province, with just two people per square kilometre. This has helped make it a great spot for elephant trekking. The villages of Phulung and Putang, near the provincial capital, Sen Monorom, are the most popular places to arrange a trek. Most of the guesthouses around Sen Monorom, as well as the tourist office, can arrange day treks, and it's also possible to negotiate a longer trek with an overnight stay in a Pnong village. Two guesthouses – Long Vibol and Pech Kiri – organise overnight elephant treks in which you sleep on wooden platforms or camp. It can get uncomfortable riding an elephant after a couple of hours, so carry a pillow to ease the strain.

Riding high on the back of a behemoth will give you a whole new perspective on Cambodia.

the testing. One highlight is the USS *Saratoga*, the world's only diveable aircraft carrier, which still holds planes and racks of bombs. Another memorable dive is the *Nagato*, the Japanese battleship from the deck of which Admiral Yamamoto ordered his warplanes to attack Pearl Harbor. Bikini is a great spot for diving with sharks – grey reef sharks abound, and spotting a silvertip on the wrecks is not uncommon.

Yap also has good diving, including virgin reefs with excellent coral, vertical walls, sea caves, channel drifts, schools of grey sharks and barracuda, sea turtles and a couple of shipwrecks. Its most novel attraction, however, is manta rays. From December to February divers go to Manta Ridge in Mill Channel, where a school of manta rays cruise about. These gentle creatures, which can have a wingspan up to 3.6m, swim through the channel as divers cling to a ledge about 9m below the surface. The manta rays often come close enough to brush divers with their wingtips.

The main air gateways into Micronesia are Honolulu and Guam, but there are also direct flights from Asia to Palau and from Australia to Nauru and Guam. www.visit fcm.org

At nearly 6000m, the symmetrical cone of Ecuador's Volcán Cotopaxi lures mountaineers in search of a summit out of the ordinary.

↗ DO: CLIMB COTOPAXI

COUNTRY Ecuador **TYPE OF ACTIVITY** Mountaineering
FITNESS/EXPERTISE LEVEL Mountaineering experience essential.
WHY NOW? December to February (and June to August) offer the best climbing conditions.
DESCRIPTION Volcán Cotopaxi (5897m), rising prominently 55km south of Quito, is Ecuador's second-highest peak, a symmetrical cone that forms the centrepiece of the country's oldest national park and its most popular outside of the Galápagos Islands. It's also the most popular high climb in Ecuador, no doubt due to a combination of its proximity, ease of access from Quito and its classic form.

The ascent is technically easy by mountaineering standards, but the route is crevassed and climbers are killed almost every year. Glacier travel skills are essential and so is adequate acclimatisation. If you don't have such skills, hire a guide, preferably a member of Aseguim, the Ecuadorian professional guides association.

The ascent is generally commenced from a climbers' *refugio* on the mountain's northern slopes soon after midnight, aiming to reach the summit in the early daylight hours, before cloud envelops the peak, and to descend before the snow softens. It normally takes five to seven hours to reach the summit and perhaps three hours to descend. Route details vary due to changes in the glacier. The view from the summit includes Chimborazo (6310m), Ecuador's highest peak and, owing to a bulge around the equator, the world's furthest point from the centre of the earth.

To get to the climbers *refugio* from Quito, take a bus south down the Panamericana and ask to be dropped off at the park entrance turn-off, just north of Lasso. There are usually vehicles waiting at the turn-off that will take you up to the *refugio* car park at 4500m. It's a 30-minute to one-hour walk from the car park up to the *refugio*, at 4800m.

↗ DO: **CLIMB THE SYDNEY HARBOUR BRIDGE**

COUNTRY Australia **TYPE OF ACTIVITY** Bridge climbing
FITNESS/EXPERTISE LEVEL Not required.
WHY NOW? See Sydney Harbour in the purity of dawn.
DESCRIPTION Nominated by BBC viewers in 2003 as one of '50 things to do before you die', climbing to the top of the great metal coat-hanger that spans Sydney Harbour was once the domain of bridge painters. Now everyone can do it, with daily 3½-hour tours guiding visitors through the metalwork to the bridge's apex, 134m above the water of Sydney Harbour. You can climb during the day, at twilight or at night, and a few days a year – including this week – you can also climb at dawn to see the Harbour City as it wakes. Such is the climb's popularity, bridge climbing has spread to the Auckland Harbour Bridge and Brisbane's Story Bridge. www.bridgeclimb.com

↗ DO: **CANOPY TOURS AT SANTA ELENA**

COUNTRY Costa Rica **TYPE OF ACTIVITY** Zip line (flying fox) **FITNESS/ EXPERTISE LEVEL** Not required. **WHY NOW?** Zip through the rainforest at about the driest time of year. **DESCRIPTION** In green and clean Costa Rica, the term 'canopy tour' might sound like a sedate peek into the foliage of a cloud forest but that would be a lie. Think instead of being strapped into a harness, hooked on to a cable-and-pulley system and sailing through the rainforest at high speeds á la *George of the Jungle*. Operators sell this as a great way to see nature, though the only way you're going to see a quetzal on one of these things is if you run smack dab into the poor bird. But what the heck; they really are a lot of fun. The zip-line craze began in the northwestern town of Santa Elena and there are now around 80 zip lines throughout Costa Rica, generating an estimated US$120 million annually. You'll still find many of them in Santa Elena and the neighbouring Quaker settlement of Monteverde. www.monteverdeinfo.com; www.monteverdecostarica.info

↗ DO: **WATCH JIGOKUDANI'S SNOW MONKEYS**

COUNTRY Japan **TYPE OF ACTIVITY** Wildlife watching
FITNESS/EXPERTISE LEVEL Not required.
WHY NOW? To watch the monkeys bask in the hot springs as you stand chilled outside.
DESCRIPTION In Japan *onsens* (natural hot springs), are a way of outdoors life, so much so that even the country's native monkeys have claimed a few *onsens* all of their own. Although the name Jigokudani means Hell Valley, Japanese macaques, more commonly known as snow monkeys, have turned these hot springs near Tokyo into a private winter paradise for primates. If you're prepared to fight through the snowfalls to get into Jigokudani, inside Jōshinetsu Kōgen National Park, you can watch the macaques descend from the forest each morning to recline in the hot pools through the day. The snow monkeys only come here in winter – in summer they're too smart to want to soak in hot water; they leave that to Jigokudani's human visitors.

It's one way to avoid bumper-to-bumper traffic ... climbers scale the Sydney Harbour Bridge.

Let fly on a zip-line through the canopy of the Costa Rican jungle.

Tai Po Mountain Marathon
www.seyonasia.com/koth/tp.html
Run 32km through the Hong Kong mountains, climbing more than 2000m.

Morgan's Run
www.ontrackclub.co.za
Bi-annual, 400km adventure race along the Eastern Cape coast in South Africa.

Sabie Experience
www.sabiexperience.co.za
Four-day, 248km bike race around Sabie, South Africa's mountain-bike heartland.

Sheep Mountain 150
www.sheepmountain.com
Very brisk 240km Alaskan dog-sled race; winner takes around 24 hours.

week

.o3

Is that sleigh bells I hear? Look out for this pair when you're enjoying Lapland's winter wonderland.

December

week

↙ **.04**

www.yearofadventures.com/december

↖ GO LAPLAND,
SCANDINAVIA

WHY NOW? **VISIT NOW FOR FESTIVITIES AND FUN IN SANTA'S BACKYARD**

Santa was here, though right now he may be too busy to bother with visitors, so you'll need to find other Scandinavian distractions. Even with Lapland cloaked in the Polar Night, such distractions aren't difficult to find.

Begin in the Finnish city of Rovaniemi, the self-styled home of Santa Claus. Here, you'll find the Santa Claus Tourist Centre, the Santapark amusement park, Santa Claus Village straddling the Arctic Circle, an airport classified as Santa's official airport by the International Aviation Association, and a school for Santa assistants. When you've had your fill of the fat man in the red suit (is five minutes enough?), you'll discover that Rovaniemi is also a convenient base for dog or reindeer sledding, skiing, ice-fishing or snowmobile safaris.

Hop across the border to Sweden and the world's northernmost ski field, Riksgränsen, where you'll find testing downhills and options

↗ DO: TRAVEL ON AN AFRICAN TRUCK

CONTINENT Africa **TYPE OF ACTIVITY** Adventure travel **FITNESS/EXPERTISE LEVEL** Not required. **WHY NOW?** It's been a good year, now really put your life on the line. **DESCRIPTION** In many out-of-the-way places in Africa, trucks are the only reliable form of transport. They primarily carry goods, but drivers don't mind supplementing income by throwing aboard a few passengers. For this reason, most of the time you'll travel on top of the truck's load – if you're feeling less adventurous you may be able to squeeze in the cab for about twice the price. Lifts on trucks are usually arranged the night before departure at the 'truck park' – a compound or dust patch that you'll find in almost every African town of any size. Just ask around for a truck that's heading the way you want to go; for regular runs there's more or less a fixed price.

Travelling by truck in Africa is a guaranteed heart starter.

such as heli-skiing. For a Nordic outing, you could sample Sweden's most famous hiking trail on skins. Kungsleden (King's Trail) stretches 450km from Abisko in the north to Hemavan in the south.

Eighteen kilometres from Sweden's northernmost town, and 200km above the Arctic Circle, you'll also find the Ice Hotel, reconstructed annually from tonnes of ice taken from the local river. If you can wriggle out from beneath your reindeer-skin blankets (the average December temperature is around -13°C), you'll find an activity menu long enough to fill an entire week: take a snowmobile for a night out at a wilderness camp; venture to a moose wintering pasture; go mushing on a dog-sled tour; or simply discover your inner Scandinavian by hitting the hot tub.

If you'd like some adventure but can't resist the Christmas moment, you're probably ripe for a reindeer safari. Norway's Øvre Pasvik National Park offers the most remote safari choice. Tucked hard against the border with Finland and Russia, it's the last corner of the country where wolves, wolverines, lynx and brown bears still roam. Or you can return to where you began, in Rovaniemi, for a reindeer sleigh ride between Santapark and Santa Claus Village. Ho, ho, ho.

For more information, visit www.rovaniemi.fi.

o1 o2
o3 **o4**

The Franklin River wilderness is pure back-to-nature bliss, blending the adrenaline of white-water with the majesty of untamed bush.

↗ DO RAFT THE FRANKLIN RIVER

o1 o2
o3 o4

COUNTRY Australia **TYPE OF ACTIVITY** White-water rafting

FITNESS/EXPERTISE LEVEL Extensive white-water experience required if rafting independently.

WHY NOW? The rafting season is December to March – December offers reliable rainfall and good river levels.

DESCRIPTION After an ardent and successful campaign to prevent it being dammed in the early 1980s, Tasmania's Franklin River is almost a byword for Australian environmentalism. Today, this wild river is also a rafting hotspot, offering a 100km-plus expedition-style adventure through Tasmania's pristine Southwest World Heritage region. Experienced rafters (or kayakers) can tackle it independently if they're fully equipped and prepared. For the inexperienced (about 90% of all Franklin rafters), tour companies offer rafting packages.

The trip down the Franklin starts below the Lyell Hwy, on the Collingwood River, and ends at Sir John Falls, on the Gordon River, taking around eight days. Rafters are usually met at Sir John Falls by a yacht, which takes them into the tourist town of Strahan. The greatest paddling rush – literally – comes in the Great Ravine, a 5km-long gorge bubbling with invitingly named rapids such as the Cauldron, Thunderush and the Churn. Expect to take at least a day to push, paddle and portage your way through the Great Ravine.

Water levels on the Franklin rise and fall like the stockmarket, and will have a major impact on the style of your trip. High-water will do much of your paddling work but can make the Great Ravine treacherous, while low-water can turn parts of your journey into a bushwalk, especially along the Collingwood River.

Visual highlights include the deep, still Irenabyss, and iconic Rock Island Bend (a photo of which fronted conservation campaigns in the 1980s) with its adjacent, mossy waterfall, the unfortunately named Pigs Trough.

Detailed notes about rafting the Franklin are available on the Tasmanian Parks & Wildlife Service website (www.parks.tas.gov.au).

↗ DO: **CLIMB AT POTRERO CHICO**

COUNTRY Mexico **TYPE OF ACTIVITY** Rock climbing
FITNESS/EXPERTISE LEVEL Low and high grades.
WHY NOW? Potrero Chico is a winter climbing wonderland.
DESCRIPTION With its limestone walls and sharp fins, the Potrero Chico
canyon, around 1 ½ hours north of the city of Monterrey, has more than
600 marked climbing routes, both sport and traditional. It's considered
among the best places in the world to learn the gymnastic artistry of rock
climbing, but it's also a winter favourite for experienced climbers, offering
everything from simple single-pitch sport routes to Mexico's most difficult
climb, the 30m Sick Dimension (rated at 5.14b). It also contains one of
the world's longest sport routes, the 24-pitch Time Wave Zero, a climb
of around 700m. You can camp near the canyon at Rancho Cerro Gordo.
Come for a few days and you may end up staying for the season.

Dizzying winter climbing
possibilities are on offer at
Mexico's Portrero Chico.

Follow up your morning swim in
the Mediterranean with a day on
the pistes at Lebanon's highest
ski resort.

↗ DO: **SKI AT THE CEDARS**

COUNTRY Lebanon **TYPE OF ACTIVITY** Skiing
FITNESS/EXPERTISE LEVEL Ski bunnies to Arctic hares.
WHY NOW? Feel festive by skiing on the nearest snow to Bethlehem.
DESCRIPTION Lebanon likes to boast that it's the only country in which
you can ski in the morning and swim in the Mediterranean in the
afternoon. It's an appealing mix in which to wind down from a busy year.
Lebanon's highest and oldest ski field, the Cedars, is located less than
30km from the Mediterranean coast and people have been skiing here
since the 1920s. It's less developed than other Lebanese ski resorts, but
it's the second-most popular, particularly for those who actually ski (rather
than pose). And with runs that begin above 3000m, the season usually
starts in mid-December, ahead of other resorts in the country. There are
also numerous off-piste opportunities at the Cedars if you're feeling more
adventurous.

Murray Marathon
www.redcross.org.au/vic/
murraymarathon.htm
Paddle 400km in five days along
Australia's longest river.

Sydney to Hobart Yacht Race
http://rolexsydneyhobart.com
Sail out of Sydney Harbour and through
the Tasman Sea into Hobart's Derwent
River.

Marathon des Dunes
www.marathondunes.com
Three-day stage-race marathon (14km a
day) through the Algerian Sahara, 650km
south of Algiers.

week
.04

↗ DO: **ROBINSON CRUSOE ISLAND**

COUNTRY Chile **TYPE OF ACTIVITY** Adventure travel
FITNESS/EXPERTISE LEVEL Not required.
WHY NOW? If you're feeling more Scrooge than Santa.
DESCRIPTION Wanting to spend this Christmas alone but with a tale
to tell on your return? How about the island, 670km from the South
American coast, named for its very solitude? In 1704 Alexander Selkirk
was put ashore on the island (at his own request) after a dispute with his
ship's captain. He lived here for four years, becoming the role model for
Daniel Defoe's fictional *Robinson Crusoe*. Today, Robinson Crusoe Island
is entirely national park (but for a small town of 500 people), receives less
than 100 tourists a month, and is singularly serene. It's also developing a
reputation as the best place to scuba dive in Chile. To reach the island, you
can fly from Santiago de Chile or you can brave the seas for a couple of
days by joining a naval supply ship or freighter out of Valparaíso.

www.yearofadventures.com/december

205

Marvel at the design planning of a crop circle – a UFO work of art?

THE MISSING WEEK

07 HEAVENLY OBJECTS

From the earth, seven objects in our solar system are visible to the naked eye – the sun, moon, Mercury, Venus, Mars, Jupiter and Saturn – and it is these that formed the origin of our seven-day week.

For the moment – and perhaps just for the moment – this space septet is inaccessible as travel destinations, so until we can get to them, make an adventure of seeing the places where they might have come to us.

Anybody wanting to mingle with aliens should begin at Roswell, New Mexico, oddly famous as both the United States' largest producer of wool and its UFO capital. Roswell has built a major industry around the alleged crash of a UFO here in July 1947. In a press release, the government identified the object as a crashed disk. A day later it claimed the disk was really just a weather balloon,

confiscated all the previous press releases, cordoned off the area as they collected all the debris, and posted armed guards to escort curious locals from the site of the 'weather-balloon' crash.

A local mortician fielded calls from the mortuary office at the government airfield inquiring after small, hermetically-sealed coffins for preventing tissue contamination and degeneration after several days of exposure to the elements. To this day, eyewitness accounts, rumor, and misinformation continue to swirl, fueling all manner of speculation over what really happened in the desert that day. The local convention and visitors bureau even suggest that Roswell's special blend of climate and culture attracted touring space aliens who wanted a closer look!

Come for the UFO Festival at the start of July for alien-costume competitions and lectures about UFOs, or visit the International UFO Museum & Research Center at any time to see original photographs and witness statements about the 1947 crash and supposed cover-up. The library claims to have the most comprehensive UFO-related materials in the world.

Trundle north into Colorado's San Luis Valley and you can put what you've learned in Roswell into practice as you try to spy spacecraft from the UFO Watchtower in Hooper. This humble dome with a small second-storey viewing deck was created after farmers in the area allegedly reported strange sightings. You can even camp here, if you're game for a night of UFO spotting.

Also in the USA – a theme is developing here – you can brush antennae with Nevada's top-secret Area 51. Set on Hwy 93, dubbed the 'Extraterrestrial Hwy,' Area

51 is part of Nellis Air Force Base and a supposed holding area for captured UFOs. Apart from the air of mystery, there are two items of interest here to travellers: the black mailbox (now white) that's a popular spot for sky-watching; and the Little A'Le'Inn, in the town of Rachel, which accommodates earthlings and aliens alike, and sells extraterrestrial souvenirs.

Cross the border to Alberta, Canada, and you'll find the town of St Paul, with its flying-saucer landing pad (still awaiting its first customer). Residents built the 12m-high circular landing pad in 1967 as part of a centennial project and as a stunt to try to generate tourism to the remote region. It worked: UFO enthusiasts have been visiting ever since.

Across the Atlantic you can indulge your intergalactic interest by taking a crop-circle tour. Circle-central is the Wiltshire town of Avebury, coincidentally noted for its stone circles, prompting the wide belief that the two are related. These close encounters of the barley kind typically appear from around mid-April until the end of August. Several companies offer tours to crop-circle sites, while you can hang out with 'croppies' at their chosen social headquarters, the Barge Inn at the town of Honeystreet. Here, you need look no further than the mural on the pub's ceiling to witness a crop circle.

If you happen to be buzzing through the neighbourhood you might also want to check out Bonnybridge (Scotland), Britain's official UFO capital, where there has been discussion of an alien theme park; the Maipo River region in Chile, declared a UFO tourism zone by its mayor; and the roadhouse town of Wycliffe Well, dubbing itself the UFO centre of Australia.

Index
Activities

Index
Places

A YEAR OF ↗ ADVENTURES

A GUIDE TO WHAT, WHERE AND WHEN TO DO IT

August 2006

PUBLISHED BY
Lonely Planet Publications Pty Ltd
ABN 36 005 607 983
90 Maribyrnong St, Footscray,
Victoria, 3011, Australia

www.lonelyplanet.com

Printed through Colorcraft Ltd, Hong Kong. Printed in China
Cover image Philip & Karen Smith, Getty Images

Many of the images in this book are available for licensing
from Lonely Planet Images (LPI). www.lonelyplanetimages.com

ISBN 1741048389

LONELY PLANET OFFICES
AUSTRALIA Locked Bag 1, Footscray, Victoria, 3011
Phone 03 8379 8000 Fax 03 8379 8111
Email talk2us@lonelyplanet.com.au

USA 150 Linden St, Oakland, CA 94607
Phone 510 893 8555 Toll free 800 275 8555 Fax 510 893 8572
Email info@lonelyplanet.com

UK 72-82 Rosebery Ave London EC1R 4RW
Phone 020 7841 9000 Fax 020 7841 9001
Email go@lonelyplanet.co.uk

↗ COORDINATING AUTHOR ANDREW BAIN
A reformed sportswriter, Andrew prefers adventure to avarice and can
usually be found walking or cycling when he should be working. He's
trekked, cycled and paddled in various parts of five continents, and is the
author of the book Headwinds, the story of his 20,000km cycle journey
around Australia, as well as Lonely Planet's Walking in Australia. He
confesses to naming his daughter for the Khmer word for 'mountain', and
once hallucinated that he was Reinhold Messner.

↗ THANKS FROM THE AUTHOR
Foremost thanks to all the LP authors, without whose work this project
would have been as tricky as the Hillary Step. I'm grateful to Chris Rennie
for lending his surfing knowledge, and to a swag of expert others for
enduring my questioning about morning glories, land yachting, maneless
lions and the likes. For willingly diving through a sea of files for me
(and for unravelling the mystery of the lunar year), I doff my hat to Ben
Handicott (and, in his absence, Marg Toohey). Thanks to Carroll for finding
a spot in her shed where I could work and, finally, to Janette and my own
little adventures, Kiri and Cooper, for anything and everything.

PUBLISHER Roz Hopkins
PUBLISHING MANAGER Chris Rennie
COMMISSIONING EDITOR Ben Handicott
PUBLISHING PLANNING MANAGER Jo Vraca
IMAGE RESEARCHER Mel McVeigh
CREATIVE DIRECTOR Jane Pennells
DESIGNER Mark Adams
DESIGN TEAM Brendan Dempsey and Daniel New
LAYOUT Jim Hsu
EDITORIAL AND PRODUCTION MANAGER Jenny Bilos
EDITORS Simon Williamson and Margedd Heliosz
PROJECT MANAGER Annelies Mertens
PRE-PRESS PRODUCTION Ryan Evans
PRINT PRODUCTION MANAGER Graham Imeson

↗ WITH MANY THANKS TO
Francesca Coles, Vanessa Battersby, Jennifer Garrett, Steve Caddy,
Rebecca Dandens, Fiona Siseman and Lyahna Spencer.

↗VISIT WWW.YEAROFADVENTURES.COM

FOR MORE INFORMATION, LINKS TO EVENTS AND SPECIAL
OFFERS TO GET YOUR ADVENTURES UNDER WAY.